HESIOD'S COSMOS

Hesiod's Cosmos offers a comprehensive interpretation of both the *Theogony* and the *Works and Days* and demonstrates how the two Hesiodic poems must be read together as two halves of an integrated whole embracing both the divine and the human cosmos. After first offering a survey of the structure of both poems, Professor Clay reveals their mutually illuminating unity by offering detailed analyses of their respective proems, their teachings on the origins of the human race, and the two versions of the Prometheus myth. She then examines the role of human beings in the *Theogony* and the role of the gods in the *Works and Days*, as well as the position of the hybrid figures of monsters and heroes within the Hesiodic cosmos and in relation to the Hesiodic *Catalogue of Women*.

JENNY STRAUSS CLAY is Professor of Classics at the University of Virginia. She has held Fellowships and research grants from the Center for Hellenic Studies, the National Endowment for the Humanities, the DAAD, the American Academy in Rome, and the American School of Classical Studies in Athens. She has also lectured extensively throughout the United States and Europe. Her research interests focus mainly on archaic Greek poetry, on which she has written extensively, including two books: *The Wrath of Athena: Gods and Men in Homer's Odyssey* (Princeton 1983) and *The Politics of Olympus: Form and Meaning in the Major Homeric Hymns* (Princeton 1989). In addition, she has published over forty articles on Greek and Roman poetry.

HESIOD'S COSMOS

JENNY STRAUSS CLAY
University of Virginia

CAMBRIDGE
UNIVERSITY PRESS

CAMBRIDGE UNIVERSITY PRESS
Cambridge, New York, Melbourne, Madrid, Cape Town, Singapore, São Paulo, Delhi

Cambridge University Press
The Edinburgh Building, Cambridge CB2 8RU, UK

Published in the United States of America by Cambridge University Press, New York

www.cambridge.org
Information on this title: www.cambridge.org/9780521117685

First published 2003
Third printing 2006
This digitally printed version 2009

A catalogue record for this publication is available from the British Library

Library of Congress Cataloguing in Publication data
Clay, Jenny Strauss
Hesiod's cosmos / Jenny Strauss Clay.
p.   cm.
Includes bibliographical references (p. 183) and index.
ISBN 0 521 82392 7
1. Hesiod. Theogony.   2. Hesiod. Works and Days.   3. Hesiod – Knowledge – Cosmology.
4. Religious poetry, Greek – History and criticism.   5. Didactic poetry, Greek – History and
criticism.   6. Cosmology, Ancient, in literature.   7. Mythology, Greek, in literature.
8. Human beings in literature.   9. Gods, Greek, in literature.   10. Monsters in
literature.   I. Title.
PA4009.T5C48   2003
881'.01 – dc21   2003046175

ISBN 978-0-521-82392-0 hardback
ISBN 978-0-521-11768-5 paperback

To my students

Contents

Preface

This study of the *Theogony* and the *Works and Days* is intended primarily as a contribution to scholarly debate on Hesiod. At the same time, I have tried to make it accessible to students and those interested readers who may be less familiar with the Hesiodic poems. To that end, I have translated quotations from Hesiod and avoided scholarly polemics and academic jargon. I simply find it impossible to use words like conceptualize, thematize, or problematize. I hope my colleagues will forgive such queasiness. Chapters 1 and 2, insofar as they provide an overview of the poems' contents, can serve as a general introduction to Hesiod's work. Sections of Chapter 3 (on the Muses), Chapter 6 (on Hecate), and Chapter 7 (on the monsters) are in part revised versions of earlier articles (Clay [1984], [1988], [1993a], and [1993b]). Some readers may prefer to ignore the notes where I have acknowledged the work of my predecessors, including both agreements and disagreements. I have also tried to make these more explicit than has become customary by including specific quotations that I have found especially apt or telling.

At a cocktail party, someone once asked me what I was working on. After explaining the general outline of the book, I suddenly realized that I could already compose the book reviews. "Her analysis, while at times interesting, is flawed by a fundamental shortcoming: she attributes to Hesiod a conscious subtlety and coherence of thought that is altogether out of keeping with what we know about the farmer from Ascra." Some recent scholarship, however, suggests that the time may be ripe for a reconsideration of Hesiod's work as a whole. καὶ τοῦτο μὲν δὴ ἕξει ὅπη ἂν ἡ φήμη ἀγάγῃ.

All translations from the Greek are my own unless otherwise specified. The text of Hesiod used throughout is that of the Oxford editions of M. L. West (*Theogony* [1966], *Works and Days* [1978]). My divergences from those texts are indicated in the notes. Articles reprinted in E. Heitsch's *Wege der Forschung* Hesiod volume are cited from that volume's pagination.

Acknowledgments

This study has had a lengthy gestation period, longer than that of an elephant. Many contributed to this book, some in ways they do not know or would not recognize (they are blameless as far as the results are concerned). It began as a series of lectures at Marcel Detienne's seminar at the Ecole des Hautes Etudes. A year at the American School of Classical Studies in Athens as Whitehead Professor allowed me to pursue my research; while there, I learned about the steep, sweaty road to virtue when Merle Langdon dragged me up to the site of Ascra; a visit to Hecate's temple at Lagina was included in John Camp's tour of Ionia. I am also grateful to the National Endowment for the Humanities, the Onassis Foundation, and the University of Virginia for their financial support. Bits and pieces of this project were presented at the Universities of Athens, Berkeley, Berlin, Cambridge, Chicago, Crete, North Carolina, Siena, Stanford, and Urbino. On each of those occasions, the many comments and suggestions of my auditors improved the final product. The faculty of the Classics Department at the University of Virginia, above all, its Chair, John Miller, created a collegial atmosphere conducive to work. Diskin Clay faithfully read several drafts. Paul Barolsky and Roger Stein pretended to be general readers, but were indeed much more. The latter, whose patience I constantly tried, managed nevertheless to provide steady encouragement. My thanks go first and foremost to my students in the seminars I taught over the years and to whom this book is dedicated. Among them, I must make special mention of Daniel Mendelsohn, Chris Nappa, and Steve Smith for their friendship and to Grace Ledbetter, David Mankin, Jo-Anna Rios, and Kate Stoddard, who contributed countless insights as they all developed their own approaches to Hesiod. Finally, thanks to Susan P. Moore, copy-editor for Cambridge University Press, for her tactful and meticulous attention to my manuscript. Errors that remain are mine alone.

The translation of *Works and Days*, 293–94 in Chapter 2, n. 45 has been reproduced from A. N. Athanassakis, *Hesiod Theogony, Works and Days, Shield* (Baltimore 1983) (Copyright 1983 The Johns Hopkins University Press). I am grateful to the publisher for permission to quote.

Abbreviations

A&A	*Antike und Abendland*
AAHG	*Anzeiger für die Altertumswissenschaft*
AAN	*Atti della Accademia di Scienze morali e politiche della Società nazionale di Napoli Scienze, Lettere ed Arti di Napoli*
AJPh	*American Journal of Philology*
CA	*Classical Antiquity*
CJ	*Classical Journal*
CPh	*Classical Philology*
CW	*Classical World*
DK	*Die Fragmente der Vorsokratiker*, 5th edn., eds. H. Diels and W. Kranz. Berlin 1934
EC	*Etudes classiques*
GGA	*Göttingische Gelehrte Anzeigen*
GR	*Greece and Rome*
GRBS	*Greek, Roman and Byzantine Studies*
Heitsch	Heitsch, E., ed. *Hesiod*. Darmstadt, 1966
HSCPh	*Harvard Studies in Classical Philology*
JHS	*Journal of Hellenic Studies*
LSJ	Liddell, H. G. and Scott, R., et al., *A Greek–English Lexicon*, 10th edn. Oxford 1996
MD	*Materiali e discussioni per l'analisi dei testi classici*
Métier	*Le Métier du mythe: Lectures d'Hésiode*, eds. F. Blaise, P. Judet de la Combe, and P. Rousseau. Lille, 1996
MH	*Museum Helveticum*
M–W	*Fragmenta Hesiodea*, eds. R. Merkelbach and M. L. West. Oxford, 1967
PCPhS	*Proceedings of the Cambridge Philological Society*
PMG	*Poetae Melici Graeci*, ed. D. L. Page. Oxford 1962
PMGF	*Poetarum Melicorum Graecorum Fragmenta*, vol. 1, ed. M. Davies. Oxford 1991

PP	*Parola del passato*
QUCC	*Quaderni Urbinati di Cultura Classica*
RE	*Paulys Realencyclopädie der classischen Altertumswissenschaft,* eds. G. Wissowa et al. Stuttgart 1894–
REG	*Revue des études grecques*
RhM	*Rheinisches Museum*
RHR	*Revue de l'histoire des religions*
RMM	*Revue de métaphysique et de morale*
RPh	*Revue de philologie*
SO	*Symbolae Osloenses*
SIFC	*Studi Italiani di Filologia Classica*
SMSR	*Studi e materiali di storia delle religioni*
TAPhA	*Transactions and Proceedings of the American Philological Association*
WJA	*Würzburger Jahrbücher für die Altertumswissenschaft*
YClS	*Yale Classical Studies*

Introduction

The present study constitutes a complement to my earlier work on Homer and the Homeric Hymns. My approach and focus here is similar: an examination of what I call early Greek theology. I mean by that term the speculation inherent in those works concerning relations between gods and men and, since those relations have changed in the course of time, their evolution to the world's present state. Unlike other ancient societies, the theology of the ancient Greeks was developed neither by priests nor holy men, but by the poets. These, in turn, did not expound dogma or religious doctrine, but recounted myths about the gods as well as stories of the famous deeds of the heroes of old. Heroic epic describes the actions of those semi-divine mortals who belong to an era prior to ours when a greater intimacy with the gods obtained. The narratives of the Homeric Hymns trace the evolution of the Olympian pantheon after Zeus becomes king of the gods. By recounting the origins of the cosmos up to the accession of Zeus in the *Theogony* and by explaining the age of iron in which we live in the *Work and Days*, the Hesiodic poems both frame and fill out the mythic history of both gods and mortals. Thus, they form part of a larger whole constituted by early Greek hexameter *epos*. Despite significant differences in style, especially between narrative and non-narrative genres, archaic *epos* presents a coherent picture of the way men view their gods and their relationship to them, which, in turn, constitutes a fundamental component of their understanding of the cosmos and their place within it.

The two Hesiodic compositions, both only about a thousand lines long, thus embrace both the beginning and end of the process of cosmic evolution. The *Theogony* offers an account of the genesis of the cosmos and the gods and culminates in Zeus's final and permanent ordering of that cosmos; in the *Works and Days*, Hesiod advises his wayward brother Perses how best to live in the world as it is constituted under Zeus's rule. These two compositions are clearly interrelated and in a sense complementary, the one offering a divine and the other a human perspective on the universe. Taken together, the *Theogony* and the *Works and Days* offer perhaps the earliest sustained and systematic reflections in the Greek sphere on the perennial and fundamental issues which haunt us still: what is the relationship between human beings and those powerful beings called gods? Is the world in which we find ourselves friendly, hostile, or indifferent to human life? And how should human beings live in the world as it is constituted? Hesiod's views on these questions were tremendously influential throughout antiquity; yet overshadowed by his great contemporary Homer, Hesiod has inevitably suffered by comparison. He may not move us as much as the great heroic figures of the *Iliad*, nor charm us with his Odyssean tales; but because he offers a more systematic exposition of his thought and describes a post-heroic world, Hesiod may be closer to our concerns. Moreover, the range of his vision – from Chaos to nail-clippings – has no parallel in ancient literature. This study, then, sets out to explore the complementarities of the *Theogony* and the *Works and Days* and thereby to come to terms with Hesiod's understanding of the divine and human order.

In dealing with Hesiod, we must, I suppose, confront some old prejudices that impede our appreciation of his accomplishments. First, the sense that he is a bit of a bore, with the welter of names in the *Theogony* relieved occasionally by digressions whose significance is obscure and by narratives containing only sparse characterizations. Likewise, the *Works and Days* presents an apparent jumble of myths, fables, proverbs, advice, as well as fairly incoherent precepts on farming and sailing. Although recent scholarship has begun to change this picture, the image of the rustic farmer from the backwoods of Boeotia whom the Muses inspired to sing, but who nevertheless retained his gruff rural wisdom, still lurks in the minds of many critics.[1] Even when they acknowledge Hesiod to be eloquent on occasion or even profound, they still believe that his mind, concerned with immediate effects, can focus on only one thing at a time. To ignore such prejudices and attempt to demonstrate a coherent plan that unites the poems into a consistent vision that is both thoughtful and subtle may meet with skepticism. We will nevertheless attempt to recover the reputation the Hesiodic poems long enjoyed in antiquity. As I will try to show, Hesiod's cosmic vision offers the first systematic presentation of the nature of the divine and human cosmos, of Being and Becoming. Thus, Janus-like, he synthesizes earlier

---

[1] My choice of Gustave Moreau's rather startling image of Hesiod for the cover illustration is intended to unsettle those old prejudices.

traditions and at the same time prepares the way for the Pre-Socratics, especially Parmenides, Empedocles, and Heraclitus.[2] The questions that preoccupied them were already adumbrated by Hesiod; one could in fact argue that Hesiod was the first to set the terms of the debate. The same can be said of the Greek tragedians, who, for all their differences, wrestle with the same fundamental issue of man's relation to the gods, often within the framework constructed by Hesiod. Understood in this way, Hesiod can be restored to the standing he had for later Greeks as a crucial figure in Greek thought.

It is impossible, I suppose, to sidestep completely the vexed question of the traditionality and individualism of Hesiod, in other words, *das Hesiodische bei Hesiod*. (A concomitant question, Hesiod's relation to Homer and the epic tradition will be addressed in the Conclusion.) To what extent can we discern Hesiod's debt to inherited material from his original contribution? Or is the issue based on a false dichotomy? Most commonly, Hesiod, in contrast to Homer, has been regarded as the first individual voice in Greek literature, a poet who gives us details of his personal biography and whose poetry is conditioned by his personal circumstances.[3] The recent eclipse of the biographical approach has, however, opened new lines of inquiry. Some recent scholars interpret Hesiod as a crystallization of a didactic poetic tradition and his personal voice as a generic construct within that tradition.[4] The truth probably lies somewhere between these opposing positions, but for our purposes it does not matter much. Suffice it to say that the voice we hear is constructed within the text for its own ends.[5] I will continue to call that voice Hesiod, the name he assigns to himself.[6]

---

[2] I intend to deal with the question of Hesiod's relation to the Pre-Socratics in a future study. The issue has of course been much dealt with but is usually predicated upon Hesiod's "primitive" or pre-philosophic mentality.

[3] See, for instance, Fränkel (1962) 104–6; and Arrighetti (1975). For a recent restatement of the biographical approach, see Stein (1990) 6–54, who links the presence of Hesiod's personal voice with the introduction of writing.

[4] Cf. Nagy (1990) 47–82; and Lamberton (1988) 1–37.

[5] Cf. Griffith (1983).

[6] Nagy (1990) 47 (see also Nagy [1979] 296–97) views the name as a generic and traditional one, which should be etymologized as "he who emits the voice," rather than the name of an individual. One would expect an explanation for other names beginning with 'Hσι- like Hesione, Hesioneus, and Hesidoros. Meier-Brügger (1990) reviews the various suggestions and offers: "he who takes pleasure in the journey." For many scholars (see most recently Arrighetti [1998] 313), Hesiod's self-naming still constitutes the first assertion of the authorial "I," whereas for Nagy and his followers the name signifies a performer who presents a certain type of traditional poetry. While it is surely true that any singer who performs the Hesiodic poems before an audience assumes the persona of Hesiod and that "Hesiod" may have created the persona adopted in his poems, it is nevertheless unnecessary to deny all historicity to the composer of these works.

Even in the absence of similar compositions from the archaic period, it would be rash to maintain that the *Theogony* and the *Works and Days* are creations *ex nihilo*. Comparative research into Near Eastern and Indo-European mythological and cosmogonic traditions has shown striking parallels to Hesiodic materials concerning the evolution of the gods and of mankind.[7] These materials likewise show signs of undergoing certain kinds of modification within the Greek sphere. Most important, perhaps, is the divorce of cosmogony from the ritual role it plays in New Year's festivals throughout the Near East.[8] The insertion of the heroes in the metallic myth of the races also seems to be a Greek innovation. Closer to Hesiod, and maybe even contemporaneous with him, Homer offers glimpses of both parallel and perhaps competing cosmological traditions. In the case of the *Theogony*, then, it is quite safe to say that much, perhaps even most, of Hesiod's material is traditional, especially his recounting of the myth of the succession in heaven and his genealogies of the familiar gods of cult. And since both Homer and Hesiod allude to alternative theogonic traditions, there is even good reason to presuppose the existence of a developed genre of theogonic poetry.[9]

We cannot then with certainty claim the Hesiodic invention of any specific divinity or genealogy; even his personifications of abstractions, like Strife and Peace, for which there are precedents in Homer, may not be his innovations. One could in fact argue that Hesiod's achievement resides in his incorporation of previous theogonic traditions into his poem, which thus became canonical and thereby precipitated the disappearance of earlier or alternative versions. This impulse to completeness and universality may indeed be the most characteristic feature of the *Theogony*, which synthesized various local traditions and theogonies into a Panhellenic *epos*.[10]

Even if we are prepared to assign much of Hesiod's material to earlier traditions, we may nevertheless – with all due caution – be able to discern his hand in the systematic arrangement and disposition of that material. In analyzing the *Theogony*, I will draw special attention to certain moments in the poem, which I call nodal points, where it becomes possible to detect Hesiod's crucial decisions about the structuring of his composition.

---

[7] For Near-Eastern parallels, see the compendium of West (1997) 276–333 and the introductions to his editions of the poems.

[8] Naddaf (1986) argues that the deritualization of cosmogony forms the crucial element in the movement from cyclical to linear time.

[9] Cf. *Hymn to Hermes* 426–33, where Hermes enchants Apollo with his singing of a theogony, which likewise recounts the birth of the gods in order and their acquisition of their allotted shares.

[10] Cf. Nagy (1990) 37–47; and Clay (1989) 9–10.

In the absence of other similar contemporary compositions, it is far more difficult to assess Hesiod's individual contribution in relation to the *Works and Days*, a composition that many regard as far more "personal" than the *Theogony*. Some elements of the poem's dramatic occasion and even certain facets of Hesiod's self-representation may, however, be traditional features of a pre-existent didactic genre. West's catalogue of "Wisdom Literature" documents the widespread dissemination of such moralizing and didactic compositions throughout the Near East and beyond;[11] however, none of West's examples, it should be noted, depicts a relationship exactly parallel to that of Hesiod and his brother. Closer to Hesiod are some of the longer Homeric speeches, which, like Hesiod's exhortations to Perses, have a paraenetic purpose and frequently deploy similar rhetorical tropes such as myth, allegory, fable, and *gnomai*.[12] Moreover, it seems perfectly plausible to posit a tradition of calendar poetry, such as we find in Hesiod's "almanac" of the farmer's year, and in the catalogue of the Days; and there may even have existed versified collections of proverbs and sayings for which, despite formal differences, the *Theognidea* offers the closest Greek parallel. Again, the peculiarly Hesiodic character of the composition may lie not so much in the materials themselves as in Hesiod's structuring and manipulation of traditional material and in the specificity of the situation presented, whether fictive or not, between the speaker and his addressee.

The massive differences between the *Theogony* and the *Works and Days*, both in their structure and their content, should be clear from these preliminary remarks. Scholars have, of course taken cognizance of these differences and have generally adopted an evolutionary or diachronic model to explain them, thereby emphasizing the development of Hesiod's poetry from the more "traditional" *Theogony* to the more "individualistic" *Works and Days*. Such a scheme fits into a larger interpretive pattern, long dominant in the study of early Greek poetry and still influential, detailing the "discovery of the mind" or the "rise of the individual" during the archaic period. In the case of Hesiod, it is argued that one can trace a personal progression of his world-view between the earlier and the later poem. Thus, for example, Hesiod's purportedly hostile attitude to the kings in the *Works and Days*, after his positive celebration of them in the *Theogony*, is explained by his personal experiences at their hands.[13] In a sophisticated variant of this

---

[11] West (1978) 3–25; and West (1997) 306–31 for further Near-Eastern parallels.

[12] See Martin (1984) 29–48. Arrighetti (1998) 376–78 argues for the untraditional character of the *Erga*.

[13] Even more amusing are the comments of Meyer (1910) 483, n. 25, who traces the changes in Hesiod's views toward women to his marital experiences: "In seiner Jugend, als er in Not war, hat ihn offenbar seine Ehehälfte arg geplagt . . . ; im Alter, als sie sich nicht mehr putzte und er ein wohlhabender Bauer geworden war, scheint seine Ehe ganz behaglich geworden zu sein . . ."

approach, a recent critic has argued that one of Hesiod's most important innovations arises from his insistence on the temporal progress between the two poems to which he draws attention by his allusions to, and "corrections" of, the *Theogony* in the later composition.[14] The *Works and Days* does indeed refer to the *Theogony* and thus reveals itself as composed after the *Theogony*, but this does not automatically entail the conclusion that an older Hesiod is correcting his earlier views or repudiating his youthful errors. In fact, in the *Works and Days*, Hesiod appears to allude proudly to the *Theogony* as the work with which he won a poetic contest (656–59) – hardly a sign of rejection.

Another, and I believe ultimately more convincing, model of the relationship between the two poems can be posited with equal probability: a synchronic view that sees the two poems as generically divergent, but fundamentally complementary and interdependent. It has often been suggested that the *Iliad* is to the *Theogony* as the *Odyssey* is to the *Works and Days*, with their differences being those of genre. To simplify the equation, the two Hesiodic compositions can be understood synchronically as two halves of an organic whole, a diptych, as it were, in which each component illuminates the other. We would then be dealing neither with simple allusions nor with corrections of earlier doctrines, nor even with an attempt to construct a temporal progression between the two compositions. Rather, we would be able to discover a denser, more complex, and finally more interesting relationship, one that would genuinely deserve the frequently used, but rarely accurately applied, label of intertextuality.[15] One could well imagine that from the beginning Hesiod conceived of the poems as a diptych, and as he composed, he continually revised and reworked the one in the light of the other.[16] Thus, when the *Works and Days* alludes to the *Theogony*, it emphasizes both the differences and interconnections between the two poems and simultaneously brings to the surface their divergent but complementary perspectives that must be integrated into a larger whole.

A perfect example and indeed a paradigm of such an intertextual approach can be found in the "correction" of the doctrine of Eris, so prominently positioned at the very beginning of the *Works and Days*:

---

[14] Most (1993) 76: "Hesiod seems to be not only the first, but also one of the most striking examples of the attempt to establish an unequivocal and necessary temporal succession among the texts divulgated under his name, as an expression of the temporal succession of what he thereby implicitly declares to be his own personal development." For Most, this textualization of personal temporality presupposes Hesiod's use of writing.

[15] The term seems to have been coined by Kristeva (1969). See also Genette, *Palimpsestes* (1982) 8.

[16] Cf. Masaracchia (1961) 220: "Le *Opere* realizzano un disegno che già era chiaro al poeta quando scriveva la *Teogonia*."

οὐκ ἄρα μοῦνον ἔην Ἐρίδων γένος, ἀλλ' ἐπὶ γαῖαν
εἰσὶ δύω.

So it turns out that there was not just one race of Strife, but
on earth,
There are two. (11–12)

In the context of the *Theogony*, Eris, the daughter of Night, precipitated generational conflict and violence among the gods that culminated in the Titanomachy. Thereafter, Zeus invented a means of neutralizing the noxious influence of Eris and her grim offspring on the gods by instituting the great oath of Styx, a device that precludes the outbreak of dangerous conflicts among the gods in the future:

ὁππότ' ἔρις καὶ νεῖκος ἐν ἀθανάτοισιν ὄρηται,
καί ῥ' ὅστις ψεύδηται Ὀλύμπια δώματ' ἐχόντων,
Ζεὺς δέ τε, Ἶριν ἔπεμψε θεῶν μέγαν ὅρκον ἐνεῖκαι.

Whenever strife and quarreling arise among the immortals,
And someone of those who possess Olympian homes lies,
Zeus sends Iris to bring the great oath of gods. (782–84)

Iris then fetches the water of Styx on which the gods pronounce their great oath, here defined as a "great bane to the gods" (792). Whoever forswears himself falls into a state Hesiod calls an "evil coma" and an illness (*nousos*); in addition, he is exiled for nine years and deprived of all contact with the other gods; but in the tenth year, he is allowed to rejoin the divine company. Through this mechanism, quarrels and deceits are regulated in the world of the gods; neither strife nor conflict can henceforth threaten the stability of the Olympian order. In Zeus's regime, Strife can possess only negative qualities.[17] Where she once wielded her pernicious influence among the gods in heaven, now her power is confined below where she offers no further threat to Zeus's order.

The beneficial Eris of the *Works and Days*, on the other hand, who inhabits the earth and inspires human beings to compete with each other, only has influence over mankind – for what need would the gods "who live easy" have for such competition, conditioned as it is by the scarcity of resources available to men? There is thus no contradiction between the two poems.[18] What was said about Eris in the *Theogony* was not wrong,

---

[17] Prior to Zeus, Eris, like Eros, plays a more ambiguous role in promoting divine succession.

[18] Stein (1990) 28 speaks of Hesiod correcting his errors. But cf. Wilamowitz (1928) 43: "Im Himmel hat eine solche Eris nichts zu schaffen, sondern betätigt sich nur unter den Menschen." Bravo (1985) 711 denies that the passage in the *Works and Days* alludes in any way to the *Theogony* because "dans

but it was incomplete. A full understanding of Eris must embrace both the divine and the human perspectives.

Given its prominent position, the passage on the two Erides puts us on notice from the beginning that the two poems must be interpreted together as complementary parts of a larger whole. The splitting of Eris thus points to the unity of Hesiod's *œuvre*.

When, to give another example, Hesiod presents a second version of the Prometheus story in the *Works and Days*, he does not correct or repudiate his earlier account; rather, he expects us to be aware of both versions and to take cognizance of both their similarities and differences, as well as their divergent contexts and functions within the two poems. To point out only one facet of that difference: the Prometheus story occupies a central position in the *Theogony*, but in the *Works and Days* it comes shortly after the poem's opening; the myth's placement has much to do with the argument of the respective compositions. Conversely, Dike (Justice) is a central concern of the *Works and Days* and prominent from the outset, but she comes into being as a daughter of Zeus only toward the end of the *Theogony* (902).[19] And, finally, the *Works and Days*, through its allusion to Hesiod's account of his initiation by the Muses (658–59), links the two compositions and invites us to reflect on the function of the Muses in each. These numerous points of contact and contrast between the two poems are mutually and reciprocally illuminating if we acknowledge the intertextuality of the two compositions.

The *Theogony* recounts the genesis of the gods and the other eternal forces that regulate the cosmos; it culminates in the establishment of Zeus's order, henceforth permanent and unchanging, an order that encompasses both the brightness of Olympus above and murky Tartarus below. The *Works and Days* explores the character of human life as it has evolved and as it is now lived on earth under Zeus's dominion: mortals are inevitably earthbound, ephemeral, subject to the seasons of the year, the transience of the days, and the vicissitudes of human existence. To grasp the whole, in other words, the cosmos of Hesiod, we must explore the relations between the two poems, their differences as well as the similarities and the complementarities that link them together.

---

la *Théogonie*, en dehors du bref passage en question, la Rivalité ne jouait aucun rôle [!]". Homeric epic is surely aware of the good Eris: one thinks of the Funeral Games of book 23, as well as the *eris* of Nausicaa and her companions in doing the laundry (*Od.* 6.92) and Odysseus' challenge (ἔρις ἔργοιο) to the suitor Eurymachus (*Od.* 18.366–75).

[19] See the provocative remarks in the Discussion following Verdenius (1962) 166–67.

The present study focuses on the texts of the two Hesiodic poems that have come down to us. There are many worthwhile questions it does not pursue: for instance, what Hesiod may tell us about his historical and cultural milieu or the relation of the poems to oral composition and/or writing. These questions I feel should be raised only after, not before, an analysis of the texts, since premature answers may prejudice our sense of what Hesiod can or cannot say. I believe, however, that my substantive arguments do not preclude acceptance – or rejection – by both oral traditionalists and textualists. Historians, whether material, cultural, or focusing on ancient religion or *mentalités*, may likewise find my readings compatible with their concerns. To be sure, structuralist analysis has influenced my approach, in large part because the Greeks at least (I cannot speak for the rest of mankind) seem to construct their views of the world in terms of binary oppositions, especially the one that concerns me most, gods and mortals. But in focusing on underlying patterns, structuralism tends to downplay linear and narrative movement, whose importance is self-evident in the *Theogony*, but, as I will try to show, equally relevant to an understanding of the *Works and Days*. Concentrating on the poems themselves, I also do not deal with the rich field of Hesiod's *Vor*- and *Nachleben* nor with psychoanalytic and deconstructive approaches that attempt to formulate sub- or unconscious meanings. That leaves, of course, conscious meanings and the specter of authorial intention.

I have been called an unabashed intentionalist, but consider myself a bashful one. There is no reason to believe that texts and their composers do not intend to communicate something, and I am unconvinced by arguments that declare such communication impossible. Despite the practical and theoretical obstacles in the way, retrieving that intention remains a worthwhile undertaking. At the very least, it can moderate the tendency to read ourselves into every text. Furthermore, I am convinced that meaning inheres in form. Hence my analysis of the Hesiodic poems focuses on what has recently been re-christened intratextuality, that is "how parts relate to parts, wholes, and holes"[20] as well as bumps, unexpected swerves, leaps, and apparent contradictions. In the history of Hesiodic criticism, many such discontinuities and inconsistencies have been regarded as interpolations and textual disturbances or attributed to Hesiod's carelessness, lack of precision, clumsy revisions, or even to his inherent inability to see the

---

[20] Sharrock (2000) 5. Authorial intention pops up in note 19, p. 10. If, as Sharrock claims, all (but surely not all) reading inevitably discerns parts and wholes and hunts for unity, it does not follow that it invents them.

forest for the trees. Such problematic passages, I suggest, should rather attract our renewed scrutiny; they may lead to fresh perspectives and invite us to reformulate what we thought we had understood. My debt to previous scholarship, from the ancient scholiasts to recent feminist readings, should be evident on every page. Unapologetically, I have promiscuously borrowed, incorporated, and synthesized whatever I have found useful, persuasive, or even provocatively exasperating. My primary aim throughout has been to take Hesiod seriously as a thinker and poet and to show what rich insights we may find if we do.

In the present study, the first two chapters offer a general overview of the two poems and thus an orientation for readers not intimately acquainted with the Hesiodic *œuvre*. But, at the same time, I attempt to go beyond mere summarizing to expose the organizing principles of the two works while tracing their dynamic progress from beginning to end – the way, in fact, we first encounter them. Such a general orientation is all the more necessary since scholarship has so often concentrated on a few famous passages: the proem to the *Theogony*, the Prometheus narratives, and the myth of the human races. I too give those passages sustained attention subsequently, after their positioning within the overall framework has been established.

The genealogical armature of the *Theogony* more or less dictates its structure, as generation follows generation. Yet the arrangement of the narrative sections, especially the repeated interruptions of the genealogical process through the succession myth, as well as other apparent digressions reveal their significance only within the context of the whole. The seemingly diffuse organization of the *Works and Days* renders a linear analysis all the more crucial. Only then does the progressive narrowing of its spatial focus emerge: from the larger community as a political entity to the farm, the *oikos*, and family, and finally to the human body in all its imperfection. Temporally too, we move from the recurring cycle of the year, with its well-defined and predictable seasons and months, to the individual days with their obscure and ominous significance.

How the proems of the *Theogony* and the *Works and Days* convey the divine and human perspectives on the cosmos is the subject of Chapter 3. Their generic differences – the fact that the former resembles a hymn, while the latter partakes of the features of prayer – indicate their divergent frameworks. The fourth chapter examines the differing accounts of the origins of mankind, the one explicit in the myth of the races, the second implicit within the theogonic framework, as well as their implications for their respective poems. Subsequently, I focus on Hesiod's two versions of the Prometheus story. While superficially similar, their narrative strategies reveal diverse perspectives on the relations between gods and men. An examination of the role of human beings in the *Theogony* and that of the gods in the *Works and Days* (Chapter 6) further illuminates these intricate interrelationships. To complete the study of the complex fabric that makes up Hesiod's cosmos, in the final chapter I take up the question of two species of hybrid beings: the monsters, who embody strange mixtures of divine and animal characteristics; and the heroes, those hybrid offspring of gods and men, who belong to an epoch that precedes our own. In this context, I offer some discussion of the fragmentary *Catalogue of Women*, attributed to Hesiod in antiquity. The heroes, in turn, raise the question of Hesiod's relation to heroic epic, which I touch upon in the Conclusion.

Hesiod's cosmos embraces both the divine and the human, the eternal and the evanescent; and just as the divine and the human are interdependent and defined in complementary relationship to one another, so the *Theogony* and the *Works and Days* mirror the divine and human perspective on that totality to form Hesiod's *cosmos epeon*.

CHAPTER I

Orientations: the Theogony

> Whence each of the gods came into being, or whether they always
> existed, and what their functions were, the Greeks did not know until
> recently – yesterday, so to speak. Hesiod and Homer . . . were the ones
> who made a theogony for the Greeks and gave the gods their names
> and distinguished their honors and skills and indicated their forms.
>
> (Herodotus 2.53.1–2)

Herodotus' statement is of course not literally true; yet neither is it completely false, for it contains a deeper truth. Homer did not invent the gods,
but the images of the gods contained in his poetry were the ones that
continued to dominate the Greek imagination. Homer reveals the gods in
their interactions with men, or rather, with those grand human beings of
the past, the heroes, with whom the gods consorted more intimately and
more openly than they did subsequently. From Homer we can learn much
about the functioning of the Olympian pantheon, the prerogatives and
honors (*timai*), and characteristic modes of action of each individual god
under the supreme authority of Zeus, who is both king and father of them
all.

   Homer alludes in passing to various stories about the earlier history of
the gods before the stabilization of the Olympian order, and his narrative
presupposes a familiarity on the part of his audience with such tales, but he
has no interest in being either exhaustive or systematic. Thus, for example,
Homer seems to know of a cosmogonic model in which Okeanos and Tethys
were the primordial parents when he calls the former the θεῶν γένεσις (*Iliad*
14.201); and he mentions the Titans confined to Tartarus (*Iliad* 8.479–81;
cf. 5.898, 14.274, 279, and 15.225), as well as other earlier conflicts among
the gods (*Iliad* 1.396–406; 15.18–24). Moreover, the relations between Zeus,
Thetis, and Achilles, which underpin the plot of the *Iliad*, presuppose a
version of the succession myth.[1] But for a systematic exposition of the

---

[1] Cf. Slatkin (1991); also Muellner (1996).

origins of the gods, we must turn to Hesiod, whose *Theogony* provides an account of their genesis and genealogy.

The *Theogony* constitutes an attempt to understand the cosmos as the product of a genealogical evolution and a process of individuation that finally leads to the formation of a stable cosmos and ultimately achieves its *telos* under the tutelage of Zeus. The organization of such a theogony would seem to be completely inevitable and utterly predictable insofar as it starts from the first beginnings (πρώτιστα) and progresses chronologically until the divine cosmos is complete. Yet even within this apparently predictable scheme, there is room for some flexibility, and certain choices must be made. It is in the disposition of his material that we can perhaps most clearly detect Hesiod's originality or thought. That material falls into two major categories: the genealogies proper and the story of the succession among the gods, which in a sense forms the narrative armature of the poem. As West well puts it: "If the succession Myth is the backbone of the *Theogony*, the genealogies are its flesh and blood".[2] In addition, Hesiod incorporates a number of apparent digressions, containing material related neither to the succession story nor to the genealogies proper, which have no predictable place in the overall chronological scheme. In positioning these diverse elements, Hesiod makes choices, perhaps most obviously when he departs from a strictly chronological framework – as he frequently does – but also when he chooses the exact point at which to insert the episodes of the succession story within the genealogies. Even – and this feature has not received the attention it deserves – the genealogies themselves are not exempt from manipulation. Hesiod may anticipate or postpone a genealogical line, dislocating it from its expected position, or he may interrupt it with the insertion of non-genealogical material.[3] Commentators frequently disregard the Hesiodic organization of the genealogies and in their discussions bridge over Hesiod's disruptions.[4] These nodal points, as we may call them, have, as we shall see, important bearings on Hesiod's argument and hence his understanding of the cosmos.

[2] West (1966) 31. Muellner (1996) 56 explains the relation between the narratives and the genealogies as follows: "these [narrative] digressions occur only when the procreative processes that generate the world are disturbed or interrupted, and they explain how those processes are restored."

[3] West's (1966) 37–39 rather mechanical attempt to outline the principles of Hesiod's arrangements is not very helpful. Note that H. Schwabl (1970) 442–43 disputes West's claim that the genealogies are ordered matrilinearly. The only deviation from the patrilinear pattern Schwabl finds is, interestingly enough, Hecate.

[4] Philippson (1936), for example, follows the offspring of the line of Chaos to its end before picking up the line of Gaia. She likewise pursues the line of Gaia and Pontos by jumping over to Nereus and his descendants. This is of course perfectly logical, but raises the question as to why Hesiod does not do so.

There have, of course, been many attempts to outline the "architecture" of the *Theogony*, and many of them have much to recommend them.[5] I myself have previously suggested that the birth of Zeus, flanked by the Prometheus story and the "Hymn to Hecate," forms the centerpiece of the poem.[6] But it must be recognized that the very notion of an architectonic form tends to substitute a static model for a linear and dynamic one – and genealogy is by its nature dynamic – and to underplay and even overlook the many decisions Hesiod had to make as he composed his poem. It is in observing and assessing these organizational choices that we can watch Hesiod thinking.

Unlike the biblical Genesis, Hesiod's model for the coming into being of the cosmos is not that of purposeful creation by a designing Creator, but follows instead the procreative pattern of a human family. As D. Clay has succinctly put it, Hesiod's cosmogony constitutes a "teleology without purpose" and "without design".[7] In addition, the divine family in Hesiod, the ἀθανάτων ἱερὸν γένος, includes a cast of characters that we would never group together into a family unit since it includes members of very different species: the gods both present and past, but then also natural phenomena like the sun, moon, and stars as well as various monsters; finally a host of abstractions such as Death, Strife, Peace, Festivity, and Justice.[8] What would seem to unite this diverse group into a uniform species in Hesiod's mind is their immortality. Now, parents unite to reproduce sexually (or asexually in some species) offspring who resemble them and who may even bring out latent features of their begetters; the offspring in turn tend to intermarry and produce increasingly complex interrelationships and families that share certain common characteristics. Yet unlike human families, the race of the gods is immortal; the parents do not die. As a result, divine generation simultaneously becomes a process of increasing proliferation and differentiation that eventually reveals the familiar contours of the cosmos; nevertheless, the first entities abide. To trace Hesiod's genealogies means to understand the unfolding of his cosmic hierarchies and the principles that determine them; here too we can observe Hesiod making choices and thinking. The following analytic summary of the *Theogony* is not meant to be exhaustive, but offers an outline that draws attention to the organization

---

[5] Schwabl (1970) 447–50 offers a useful outline. Hamilton (1989) 4–14 gives a recent summary of scholarly views. Hamilton's own interpretation involves a rather artificial distinction between genealogies, and narrative and non-narrative digressions and the poem's chronological framework. See also Thalmann (1984) 38–45, who emphasizes the role of ring composition.

[6] Clay (1984) 30.   [7] Clay (1992) 138–39.

[8] West (1966) 31–33 offers the following categories: gods of cult, gods of mythology, neither of the preceding, individual members of divine guilds, elements of the visible world, and abstractions.

and certain salient features of Hesiod's cosmogony and its representation in his poem, his *cosmos epeon*.[9]

After a lengthy proem celebrating the Muses and recounting Hesiod's meeting with them on Mount Helicon (to be discussed later), the *Theogony* proper begins from what came into being (γένετο) first of all (πρώτιστα), which Hesiod calls *Chaos* (116). This is apparently not, as we might think, a jumble of undifferentiated matter, but rather its negation, a featureless void.[10] A neuter noun in Greek, Chaos has no epithets and apparently no features that can be described. Next, but unrelated to Chaos, comes Gaia (116–18), the Earth, who is defined as possessing solidity ("broad-breasted") and location ("sure seat of the gods") – qualities Chaos would seem to lack. Moreover, the features of Gaia help make comprehensible what Hesiod means by his Chaos; for Gaia's first act is to bring forth Uranus, her counterpart, "so that he might enclose her on all sides so as to be forever the sure seat of the blessed gods" (ἵνα μιν περὶ πάντα ἐέργοι, | ὄφρ᾽ εἴη μακάρεσσι θεοῖς ἕδος ἀσφαλὲς αἰεί, 127–28).[11] Noticeable also is the fact that negation (Chaos) – absence of qualities – precedes the positive, Earth, and that the negative in some sense receives its definition from its opposite number – as will become even clearer in the sequel. This movement from undefined to increasing definition is characteristic of Hesiod's cosmogony. In addition, Hesiod describes Gaia proleptically as the "seat of all the gods who inhabit Olympus," gods who have not yet been born. From the beginning, then, Hesiod alludes to the final disposition of the cosmos, a disposition that is somehow immanent from the outset.

Whether misty Tartara, mentioned in the next line, should be considered the third principle or merely a part of Earth has been debated since antiquity.[12] The text is ambiguous and complicated by the fact that Hesiod later describes Tartarus as a separate realm beneath the earth (729–819) and also as a living entity with whom Gaia will mate to produce the monstrous

---

[9] I have found most useful for my purposes, Philippson (1936); Bonnafé (1985); and Muellner (1996) 52–93. Cf. also S. Benardete (2000).

[10] Cf. Mondi (1989); and Bussanich (1983). For the various interpretations of Chaos that have been put forth, see Podbielski (1986) 254–56.

[11] With Solmsen (1970) I prefer ἐέργοι ("enclose") to the variant καλύπτοι ("hide," "cover") (cf. West [1966]; Arrighetti [1998]; Marg [1970]), since it more clearly brings out the notion of boundedness that is an essential quality of Gaia and her line as opposed to the unbounded character of Chaos. Only after being delimited by Sky can Earth produce the mountains and sea that define her contours (129–31).

[12] Cf. the Scholia (Di Gregorio [1975]) at lines 115, 119, and 120 and West (1966) on line 119. West counts Tartarus as one of the first principles, although he views its insertion here as a Hesiodic afterthought. Cf. the provocative remarks of Miller (1977); and the response of Ballabriga (1986) 282–90. See also Muellner (1996) 57. Marg (1970) 108 and Schwabl (1970) 447 posit only three "Urwesen."

Typhoeus (820–22). There is, then, a progression from the neuter plural to a masculine singular in the evolution of this entity. I myself believe that the plural *Tartara* first represents the interior of earth – for earth possesses not only a substantial surface but also an inner dimension. It is within this inner space that Earth will later hide Cronus and Zeus. In the subsequent phases of cosmic evolution, it will develop into the more clearly defined nether regions where the Titans will again be imprisoned beneath the earth. Ultimately, it will become sufficiently differentiated and separated from the Earth to emerge in a final manifestation as the personified Tartarus, a male with whom Earth can unite to produce Typhoeus. Finally, to complete the first phase of genesis, Eros, "most beautiful among the immortal gods," who overpowers both gods and men, represents the universal principle of generation, the force that causes generation and the proliferation that activates the cosmic process, but curiously does not himself generate anything (120–22).

Hesiod now returns to Chaos, who produces by scissiparity Darkness (Erebus) and black Night, both of whom may be considered aspects of their parent; these two then unite sexually to bring forth their opposites, Brightness (Aither) and Day (123–25). Here again, the negative precedes the positive, and sexual reproduction appears to have a more positive and "progressive" character than parthenogenesis. The genesis of Night and Day may also be considered the beginning of time, which can now be measured by their alternation. After tracing Chaos' lineage for three generations, Hesiod picks up with Gaia, whose line remains completely separate from that of Chaos – intercourse between these two fundamentally opposed cosmic entities seems impossible. At any rate, by parthenogenesis, Earth produces Uranus, the Heaven, to cover or enclose her in all directions, as if she somehow required such delimitation in order to possess the localization and solidity that characterize her. Indeed, only afterwards do the features and contours of Earth come into being: the Mountains, along with their inhabitants, the Nymphs, and the barren salt Sea, all generated "without desirable love." Through these three asexual productions, Earth defines herself in opposition to Chaos as having form and substance.

Mating now with Uranus, Gaia gives birth first to the sweet water that encircles the earth, Okeanos,[13] and then to the eleven other Titans, of whom Cronus is the youngest. Two monstrous sets of triplets follow: the Cyclopes and the Hundred-handers, both of whom diverge from what is

---

[13] Note that Okeanos and Tethys, Homer's primal parents, are first and last – except for Cronus – in the list. Bonnafé (1984) 185–86 draws attention to Hesiod's downgrading of Okeanos as merely one member of the generation of the Titans from Homer's primal parent.

evidently an already established theomorphic standard of appearance. (For Hesiod, human beings are anthropomorphic because they resemble the gods.) Hesiod notes that the former have only one eye, while the latter have a hundred hands and fifty heads (126–53).

Genealogy now gives way to narrative as Hesiod relates how Uranus refused to allow his offspring to be born, "but kept all of them hidden and did not allow them to come up into the light" (157) – apparently by blocking the birth canal through continuous sexual intercourse. To relieve the painful pressure within, Gaia concocts a plot to remove the offending member and exhorts her children to avenge their father's outrageous conduct. In the *Theogony*'s first speech, Gaia justifies her actions in moral terms based on the doctrine of vengeance. Once set in motion, however, the cycle of revenge, fueled by mutual hatred of parent and child, can only repeat itself. The name Uranus collectively assigns to his children, Titans, which is doubly etymologized as "those who stretched their hands against their father" and "those who would pay the penalty for their actions," embraces the vicious and apparently endless circle of crime and punishment.

After her youngest son, Cronus, alone agrees to undertake the task, Gaia stations him strategically so that he can, as Hesiod puts it, "harvest the genitals of his father" (180–81) with the adamantine sickle Gaia has given him.[14] Uranus now approaches, desiring intercourse and "bringing on night" (176). This enigmatic expression points to the fact that Uranus' actions turn back the clock, so to speak, by reinstating the primal darkness prior to the birth of Day and hence the genesis of time. This brutal narrative, which culminates in the castration of Uranus, constitutes the first act of the succession myth (154–210); at the same time, it forms a critical component of the cosmogonic process, which has been blocked and denied its natural generative proliferation. Only with the separation of Heaven and Earth and the emergence of their children from the womb of mother Earth can the next generation of gods truly be said to come into existence.

A pattern begins to emerge here that will become more evident and more elaborate in each subsequent episode of the succession myth: the generative principle, identified with the female, promotes change, as Gaia does here when she instigates the plot against Uranus and encourages her youngest son Cronus to depose his father. This continual impetus for change constitutes a radically destabilizing force in the cosmos. Gaia will always be on the side of birth and of the younger against the older generation. Moreover, once set in

[14] Hesiod seems to be punning on λόχος, "ambush" and the root λοχ-, "relating to child-birth." Cf. O'Bryhim (1997). Muellner (1996) 64 also sees a word play in μήδεα and ἥμησε. Note also that the sickle is the first manufactured object.

motion, there seems to be no inherent reason for this cosmogonic process to stop. Left to itself, procreation would continue, infinitely multiplying and proliferating without brakes. Countering this force for constant change, however, is the male principle, first embodied in Uranus, that attempts to discourage birth and unlimited fertility and to block generational change and the instability it entails. In fact, the history of the gods as a whole can be viewed as an account of the various attempts on the part of the supreme male god to control and block the female procreative drive in order to bring about a stable cosmic regime. Thus Uranus tries to keep his children from being born while Cronus swallows them at birth. Both attempts are of course foiled by the guiles of Gaia. Only Zeus succeeds by pre-emptively swallowing Metis, Guile personified, and thereby incorporating the female principle within himself. The opposition of violence (*bie*) and guile (*metis*) as vehicles promoting succession are already visible in the first instantiation of the repeated pattern.[15] But while *bie* appears to be the prerogative of the male, and *metis* belongs to the female sphere, males like Cronus and Prometheus, who share the epithet *ankulometis*, "with crooked *metis*," also make use of cunning with limited success. For each act of trickery (Cronus' swallowing of his children, Prometheus' attempt to deceive Zeus) provokes a counter-deception. The chain of violence and deception only comes to an end with Zeus's complete absorption of *metis*/Metis.

But this is to get ahead of ourselves. In addition to releasing the Titans imprisoned in Gaia's womb (but not the Cyclopes or the Hundred-Handers),[16] the castration of Uranus gives rise to an odd brood: first the Erinyes, then the Giants and the Melian Nymphs, whose place in the cosmos is as yet undefined, and finally Aphrodite, born from Uranus' semen and incubated by the barren salt Sea.[17] In making her one of the by-products of Uranus' mutilation, Hesiod reinterprets Aphrodite's epithet "Uranian," and sets her far earlier in the cosmic scheme than her traditional Homeric filiation as "daughter of Zeus"; at the same time, the primordial Eros joins her entourage and becomes her subordinate. Paradoxically, Uranus' male sexuality, which perversely denied its natural issue, here gives rise to a female divinity, who embodies the attraction between the sexes. Nevertheless, she

---

[15] Cf. Detienne and Vernant (1974), esp. 61–124.

[16] Cf. Schmidt (1988a) 55 solves an old aporia by arguing, convincingly, I feel, that the Cyclopes and Hundred-Handers remained imprisoned under Cronus and were liberated by Zeus only in the course of the Titanomachy (501–6, 617–86). Only Zeus had the brains to exploit their power and finally gave them a job and a place in his scheme as jail-keepers of the Titans in Tartarus (734–35). Schmidt is now followed by Arrighetti (1998) 328–29.

[17] On ἐθρέφθη (line 192) and the uniqueness of Aphrodite's genesis, see Bonnafé (1985) 136, n. 14. Also Moussy (1969) 66.

does not belong to the first principles, but is fully personified as she joins the "tribe of the gods" after her birth (202).

In one of those organizational choices which I have called nodal points, Hesiod only now returns to complete the primal line of Chaos (cf. 123–25) by cataloguing the offspring of Night and her daughter Strife, Eris (211–32).[18] The significance of this postponement and the rationale for its insertion here is not difficult to grasp. The dark forces personified in Night's brood have so to speak just been unleashed upon the universe in the course of the preceding narrative. Uranus' excessive sexuality, the mutual hatred of father and children, the brutal violence and sexual outrage inflicted by Uranus on Gaia, her suffering, deception, and plotting for revenge, Cronus' willingness to wreak violence upon his father, the consequences of Uranus' castration, and the promise of further violence – all the events enacted in the narrative – now emerge as eternal destructive forces, personifications whose influence on the cosmos must henceforth be reckoned with.[19]

We can now detect more clearly the operation of two cosmic forces, Eros, which brings things together, and Eris, who forces them apart.[20] It bears emphasizing, however, that they do not simply correspond to the male and female principles, yet both are necessary for the coming-to-be of the cosmos. The story of Uranus and Gaia and its aftermath demonstrates the complexity of their interaction. His *eros* inevitably arouses her *eris* that leads to separation. Indeed, the by-products of that separation, Aphrodite and the Furies, ensure that the process of joining and separating will continue. As the primal Eros already subsumes Eris, so Eris herself is sister to Philotes. The two forces, inseparable and intertwined, make cosmogony possible, but they also continually destabilize the process. The subordination of Eros to Aphrodite, which is necessary for the establishment of a stable cosmos, is the first step in the taming of the generative principle. The accommodation of Eros from primal principle into the realm of the gods will be repeated

---

[18] The Homeric Eris is a sister of Ares (*Iliad* 4.440). For the children of Night, see Ramnoux (1986); and Arrighetti (1993).

[19] Schwabl (1970) 446 recognizes that Hesiod's arrangement here is intentional in that he places "die finsteren Leidmächte nach der Uranosentmannung und ihren Folgen." See also Schmidt (1985) 84–85. The names of some of the personifications included in the family of Night have appeared in the preceding narrative: Apate, "Deception" and Philotes (224), cf. ἐξαπάτας (205) and φιλότητα (206); Neikea, "Quarrels" (229), cf. νεικείων (208). The naming of the Muses in the proem likewise follows, and derives from, the preceding narrative description of their activities. Muellner (1996) 66 emphasizes that Night's offspring are "important creatures for the next episode of the myth." However, they are already operational in what precedes. The action precedes the abstraction.

[20] Cf. Bonnafé (1985) and Rudhardt (1986). In this context, I need hardly remind the reader of Empedocles' Neikos and Philia.

in Hesiod's treatment of Tartarus and Chaos. Divisive Eris too – despite Achilles' wish that she disappear from the cosmos (*Iliad* 18.107) – will also find a place in the final order.

Having brought the line of Night to a close, Hesiod continues with the line of Pontos, the Sea, which represents a highly varied tribe, embracing both negative and positive characteristics and which must ultimately be integrated into the cosmogonic mainstream. In what appears to be a unique instance of male parthenogenesis,[21] Pontos generates Nereus, a single male offering a positive counterweight to the preceding host of largely female negative forces, one whose gentleness, truthfulness, and justice counterbalance, but do not cancel out, the existence of the violent, deceptive, and brutal brood of Night and her daughter Eris. In the first exogamous union linking the lines of the Pontids and the Ouranids, Nereus, son of the salt Sea, will, in union with a daughter of Okeanos, the fresh water, generate the Nereids whose lovely and musical names embody the benign nature of their father (lines 240–63).[22]

The lengthy genealogical catalogue that follows extends for over 200 lines until the birth of Zeus and his siblings leads into the second act of the succession myth. First, in an incestuous union that harks back to the earliest phases of cosmogony, Pontos mates with his mother Gaia, the Earth herself, with all her luxuriant, if sometimes irresponsible, fecundity. Of their four offspring, two form forward-looking exogamous marriages:[23] Thaumas ("Mr. Wonderful") and an Oceanid produce Iris and other windy phenomena, while Eurybie will later become the consort of the Titan Kreios (375). The two remaining children, Phorkys and Keto, join in an incestuous union, thus concentrating the elemental characteristics of their parents, to produce the monsters.[24] Both barren and fertile, Pontos and his family embrace unexpected combinations of opposing qualities, traits that re-emerge in their monstrous progeny.

The descendants of Phorkys and Keto, who will be examined in detail in a later chapter, constitute an endogamous tribe of monstrous beings. Promiscuous combinations of features and qualities that are subsequently

---

[21] Most commentators assume that Pontos mates with Gaia to produce Nereus, but Bonnafé (1985) 148 recognizes his unparalleled parthenogenic birth from the male. See also Deichgräber (1965) 190. The case of the neuter Chaos is slightly different.

[22] Note that the last of the Nereids (262) is named Nemertes, ἣ πατρὸς ἔχει νόον ἀθανάτοιο. Cf. line 235 and Bonnafé (1985) 17; also Bonnafé (1984) 194; and Deichgräber (1965) 194.

[23] While mother/son alliances of necessity dominate the first generation, and sister/brother unions are common in the second, exogamy increasingly becomes the norm. Cf. Bonnafé (1985) 48. The most striking exception is Zeus himself with his pseudo-parthenogenesis of Athena and his various marriages to his sister Olympians.

[24] I examine the monster catalogue in greater detail in Chapter 7. Cf. Clay (1993).

distinguished and kept apart in the course of the cosmogonic process characterize these hybrid creatures. The monsters reveal the emerging categories of the evolving cosmos precisely through their violations of its norms. Hesiod limits and encloses the contagion of their chaotic promiscuity by confining the monster clan to endogamous unions and thus cutting it off from the theogonic mainstream.

In the proem, Hesiod had described the song the Muses sing to entertain Zeus on Olympus; they begin from Gaia and Uranus, then:

οὓς Γαῖα καὶ Οὐρανὸς εὐρὺς ἔτικτεν,
οἵ τ' ἐκ τῶν ἐγένοντο, θεοὶ δωτῆρες ἐάων.

> those whom Earth and Sky brought forth,
> And those who were generated from them, the gods,
> givers of good things.   (45–46)

For his own program, however, Hesiod insisted that the Muses enlarge the scope of their song to include not only the descendants of dusky Night, but also those "whom salty Pontos nurtured" (οὓς θ' ἁλμυρὸς ἔτρεφε Πόντος, 107). The θεοὶ δωτῆρες ἐάων ("gods, givers of good things"), who distribute and choose wealth and honors and as Olympians are ultimately responsible for the disposition of our cosmos (111–13), are the descendants of Uranus and Gaia, the Ouraniones, as Hesiod calls them.[25] The Pontids, on the other hand, descendants of Gaia and Pontos, can be considered a clan at a somewhat tangential angle to the line of cosmic progress, anti-gods who, if left to themselves, would generate a cosmos antithetical to the one over which Zeus reigns.[26] Of course, this does not happen: through intermarriage, the Pontids are rapidly integrated into the Ouranid clan. Nevertheless, with the incestuous, interbred, and ultimately sterile tribe of monsters, Hesiod gives us a glimpse of what such an anti-cosmos might be.

After the primordial principles (Gaia, Uranus, etc.), the cosmos takes on its recognizable configuration in the generation of the Titans; but only in the following generation, that of the Olympians, does it acquire its permanent organization under the rule of Zeus. Having moved forward several generations in his account of the monsters, Hesiod now (337ff.) backtracks to elaborate on the offspring of the Titans, who had been enumerated some two hundred lines earlier (133–38). Two endogamous unions produce the Rivers and the Oceanids and the Sun, Moon, and Dawn. These are followed by further couplings that bring together the lines of the Pontids

---

[25] *Theogony* 461, 919, 929.
[26] Schwabl (1970) 450 characterizes the Pontid line as having, on the one hand, a close relation to the elemental (cosmic) spheres and, on the other, possessing a certain "Unheimlichkeit."

and the Ouranids; the remaining daughter of Pontos, Eurybie, joins with a Titan and in the following generation their offspring produce the winds and stars. At this point, the features of the natural world as we know it are more or less complete.

Before the birth of the Olympians and the next act of the succession myth, Hesiod recounts proleptically the tales of two mighty goddesses: Styx, who prefigures the policy that will lead to Zeus's triumph; and Hecate, who will play a crucial role as mediator in the new order established by Zeus. Styx is introduced as the most prominent (προφερεστάτη ἐστὶν ἀπασέων, 361) of the daughters of Okeanos and Tethys, who at least in the Homeric cosmogonic tradition played the role of primordial couple. In *Iliad* 14.201, Hera falsely claims to be en route to visit "Okeanos, *genesis* of the gods, and mother Tethys" (Ὠκεανόν τε, θεῶν γένεσιν, καὶ μητέρα Τηθύν). Later in the same book (line 246), Sleep calls Okeanos "the *genesis* for all things" (ὅς περ γένεσις πάντεσσι).[27] The prominence Hesiod assigns to Styx suggests that he was well aware of this alternative tradition. Styx's venerable ancestry could indeed make her a potential threat to Zeus; the powerful offspring Hesiod attributes to her, Might, Victory, Zeal and Force, would indicate as much. At any rate, under the regime of Cronus, she was apparently left without honors (ἄτιμος, 395), and she is the first to accept both Zeus's offer to join his side and his assurance of honors and prerogatives to those divinities who had none under the old dispensation. Zeus's policy of co-opting older gods and assimilating them into his regime prefigures his triumph in the Titanomachy. Styx's dedication of her powerful children to Zeus thus becomes an emblem for Zeus's political acumen at the same time that it suggests how the failure to integrate the power of female fertility might lead to further instability and even disaster. Later, Zeus adds to her prerogatives by making her the great oath of the gods (775–806), in a sense the oath of allegiance to uphold his own regime.

Hecate resembles Styx in being a powerful female divinity who is like-wise integrated into Zeus's order and given an important function within it. We will examine that role later, in Chapter 4. But in the present context, it is significant that the elaborate description of Hecate (411–52) comes just before the center of Hesiod's poem, and it is followed immediately by the account of the birth of Zeus and the other Olympians. Hesiod thus gives the impression that Hecate is the last-born of the gods who belong to the generation preceding the Olympians – a false impression, as it turns out, since, as we shall see, the genealogy of the sons of the Titan Iapetos is

---

[27] On Homer's cosmography and its relation to Hesiod, see D. Clay (1992) 131–37.

postponed until after the deposition and binding of Cronus. Thus, while neither episode occurs in its strictly chronological position, Hecate and Prometheus are arranged so as to frame the pivotal event of the *Theogony*: the birth of Zeus. Both episodes are proleptic: in the Prometheus story, Hephaestus and Athena, who mold and adorn the first woman, have not yet been born; and Zeus's concession of *timai* to Hecate presumably cannot occur until after the defeat of the Titans and the final *dasmos* (885). Moreover, both episodes adumbrate the final ordering of the cosmos under Zeus's sovereignty, especially, as we shall see, in relation to the human species. Thus theology rather than strict chronology determines the placement of the Hecate episode.

By manipulating her position within his poem, Hesiod brings out Hecate's unique position as inheritor of the three cosmic realms, Pontos, Gaia, and Uranus, a goddess who sums up in her person all of the cosmogonic processes that have preceded her. The epithet *mounogenes*, twice applied to the goddess (426, 448), offers an indication of Hecate's uniqueness and her special status. The situation of *mounogenes* Hecate resembles that of an *epikleros*, who as sole daughter does not herself possess the right of inheritance but can convey it via marriage.[28] Hecate's unusually powerful status would doubtless have made her a good match for Zeus. But, on second thought, perhaps not. The marriages of Zeus have been studied,[29] but it might be equally important to study the marital unions that do not occur. Here too the parallel to the story of Styx is revealing; Zeus does not marry her, but in a sense he co-opts or adopts her powerful children, children who could in fact become a threat to his sovereignty if not kept within his control. There is, to be sure, no marriage between Zeus and Hecate, even though her genealogical heritage and her possession of multiple honors under the old regime might thereby endow the supreme ruler with a certain legitimacy.[30] But the goddess also embodies a potential danger: the threat of powerful legitimate children who could succeed their father. Perhaps it is more expedient for Hecate to remain a virgin. As he has done with Styx, Zeus will endow Hecate with a crucial role in his new regime that will be appropriate to her high status, but will also neutralize the potential threat that her female power may pose. Zeus will make her *kourotrophos*,

[28] Cf. Arthur (1982) 68. At *W & D* 376 Hesiod calls an only son who is to be the sole heir to the paternal estate *mounogenes*.

[29] See Bonnafé (1985) 92–102; Ramnoux (1987); and C. Miralles (1993) 17–44. Note that Hecate's aunt, Leto, is absorbed into Zeus's regime by becoming his wife and mother of Artemis and Apollo. Hesiod repeatedly emphasizes Leto's gentleness, i.e. her non-threatening character (406–8).

[30] One thinks of Penelope's suitors or Oedipus' marriage to Jocasta.

the guardian of human offspring, an appropriate compensation for her childlessness.[31]

In the first act, as I have called it, of the succession myth, the attempted suppression of the next generation by Uranus, the plot to overthrow him, the birth of his children, and Cronus' succession to the kingship in heaven[32] all seem to take place almost simultaneously. In the meantime, however, the cosmos has evolved and become more highly articulated; as a result, the second reenactment of the myth exhibits a far greater degree of complexity and elaboration. In the more evolved cosmos, the birth of Cronus' children, his attempt to repress their birth by swallowing them, the plot devised by Rheia and Gaia to deceive Cronus, their hiding of Zeus in a cave and his growth, and Cronus' regurgitation of the swallowed children constitute only the first phase in the drama of succession (453–500).[33] Both the Titanomachy and the Typhonomachy must intervene before Zeus can finally take his place as sovereign god.

The next section, while largely narrative, incorporates several lengthy digressions whose placement within the overall structure of the *Theogony* constitute significant nodal points. Moreover, Hesiod embroiders upon, and twice interrupts, the narrative sequence. First, Hesiod emphatically disrupts the temporal framework of the succession story with the genealogy of the Iapetids and the Prometheus myth. That digression, in turn, is flanked by two parallel episodes: the release of the Cyclopes, who provide Zeus with the thunderbolts, "trusting in which, he rules over mortals and immortals" (506), and the release of the Hundred-Handers, who guarantee his victory over the Titans.[34] I will examine the meaning of Hesiod's narrative arrangement in this section of his poem in connection with the Prometheus story (Chapter 5).

After the defeat of the Titans, Hesiod again digresses from his narrative with a lengthy description of the geography of Tartarus that opens up a whole new dimension of the cosmos. Just as the mutilation of Uranus was followed by the birth of the Children of Night, so here the defeat of the Titans brings to light the previously obscure and undifferentiated features of Tartarus. The two passages are also linked by the reappearance of some of Night's offspring who inhabit these shadowy realms. More precisely, these

---

[31] As protector of the young, Hecate is later assimilated to Artemis. Griffith (1983) 54 downplays the potential threat in Hecate's femaleness. But cf. Arthur (1982) 69–70.

[32] In fact, one could say that Uranus was never really king of the gods, because in a sense, there was not even a kingdom for him to rule.

[33] Muellner (1996) 52–93 shows how each of the episodes of the succession story recapitulates and elaborates on the previous ones.

[34] For the traditional problems of the Titanomachy and the roles of Zeus and the Hundred-Handers in the battle, see Blaise and Rousseau (1996); Saïd (1977) 183–99.

nocturnal beings are now given a clearer definition and function as well as a precise location in the cosmic economy.[35]

The Hundred-Handers, imprisoned under the reign of both Uranus and Cronus as threats to their regimes, return to the world of darkness, but Zeus's political acumen assigns them a function that exploits their overwhelming physical force. As guardians of the imprisoned Titans, they both serve Zeus's order and are removed as potential menaces to its realization. Even the primordial Chaos who, as one of the first principles, abides eternally, is accommodated in the final dispensation.[36] Nevertheless, Zeus cannot be fully invested in the kingship of heaven until his defeat of the monstrous Typhoeus, the last of Earth's children conceived in union with Tartarus, now sufficiently articulated that he can act as a begetter.[37]

Never a favorite of critics, the Typhonomachy cannot, as frequently claimed, merely stand as a doublet of the war with the Titans.[38] Both episodes are necessary, and not only, as some defenders have claimed, because in the second battle Zeus defeats his opponent single-handedly.[39] Both these conflicts are cosmic in their scope and touch all parts of the cosmos; one could even say that they are battles *for* the control of the cosmos itself, and their outcome determines its fate. The progressive evolution of the cosmos requires that Zeus first take on and defeat the previous generation of gods, the Titans sprung from Uranus. In addition, the nether realms of the cosmos must come under his sovereignty. The defeated Typhoeus is hurled back into the infernal Tartarus from which he was begotten – yet another strange inversion and permutation of the primordial act of Uranus, who refused to allow his children to emerge from Gaia's womb, and of

---

[35] Cf. D. Clay (1992) 136: "the successive threats to the world order and Zeus posed by the Titans and Typhoeus have the effect of revealing the order of the world in its hidden complexities." In lines 746–66, as Stokes (1962) 23 notes, "the order of the vignettes [of Night and her offspring] is the order in which the births of the deities concerned are described in the genealogical part of the Theogony." Fränkel (1962) 114 notes that the offspring of Night are first explained genealogically and then spatially in the Tartarus passage. For the many difficulties in the description of the geography of the underworld, see Ballabriga (1986) 257–75; and D. Clay (1992)143–52.

[36] Cf. Mondi (1989) 15: "as a result of the subsequent genesis of other parts of the universe Hesiod's cosmogonic χάος was relegated to a subterranean location, where it abides to the present day."

[37] The oddness of the phrase διὰ χρυσῆν Ἀφροδίτην (822) in this particular context underlines the oddness of the union of these primordial beings at this late stage of cosmogony. Typhoeus is literally a throwback to an earlier era.

[38] For a summary of earlier scholarship, see Blaise (1992) 350–54, who points out that even the defenders of the authenticity of the passage damn it with faint praise. For example, West (1966) 381–82, who rejects the arguments against the passage, nevertheless finds that the "difficulties and awkwardnesses in the section [are] just what one would expect of a poet like Hesiod writing on a theme like the Typhonomachy." For defenses of the episode against its critics, see Blaise (1992) 355–69; Saïd (1977) 199–210; and Stokes (1962) 4 and 33–36. Worms (1953) argues that the passage is old, but not Hesiod's.

[39] Bonnafé (1984) 212–16 shows how Zeus is the focus of the battle with Typhoeus, which is simultaneously the defeat of Gaia. See also Blaise (1992) 366–67.

Cronus, who ingested his offspring. Perhaps the reminiscence of those ancient crimes explains Zeus's grief as he disposes of his last opponent (868).[40]
The Earth herself groans as Typhoeus is flogged by Zeus's bolts. Engulfed
by the ensuing cosmic conflagration, she dissolves like molten tin or iron,
momentarily losing the solidity that characterized her from the beginning:
Typhoeus' defeat is also hers.[41] If her campaign for generation began from
the manufacture of an adamant sickle (161–62), her final capitulation is
signaled by one of the rare similes in the *Theogony* drawn from metal-
working. Her days of devising instruments of succession are over. As her
last offspring, Typhoeus is *acosmia* incarnate, with his puppy-dog yelps, his
bullish bellows, and his fire-breathing eyes, an embodiment of the total disorder that threatens to dismantle the articulated cosmos through universal
conflagration.[42] To render his rule permanent, Zeus must here fight fire
with fire and ultimately put an end to Earth's fecundity; he must neutralize
her strategy of always siding with the younger against the older generation
in order to promote change at the expense of cosmic stability.

Some have found the behavior of Gaia, as Hesiod describes it, paradoxical
if not incomprehensible:[43] she first helps Rheia and Zeus to depose Cronus,
then even advises Zeus to release the Hundred-Handers before his battle
with the Titans:

> ἀλλά σφεας Κρονίδης τε καὶ ἀθάνατοι θεοὶ ἄλλοι
> οὓς τέκεν ἠΰκομος 'Ρείη Κρόνου ἐν φιλότητι
> Γαίης φραδμοσύνῃσιν ἀνήγαγον ἐς φάος αὖτις·
> αὐτὴ γάρ σφιν ἅπαντα διηνεκέως κατέλεξε,
> σὺν κείνοις νίκην τε καὶ ἀγλαὸν εὖχος ἀρέσθαι.

---

[40] ἀκαχών (868), which elsewhere is transitive, is surely curious. For the motif of hurling into Tartarus, see Harrell (1991).

[41] Cf. Ballabriga (1990) 22, who sees a connection between the simile of the smelting crucible and the volcanic activity elsewhere associated with Typhoeus.

[42] Blaise (1992) 362 calls him a "perfect anti-Zeus."

[43] Cf. Solmsen (1949) 53, n. 172, who finds it a reason to reject the Typhoeus episode: "Gaia who is normally on the side of Zeus would in this episode be opposed to him. It is unlikely that she should give the gods friendly advice and help Zeus to supremacy (v. 882) if he had just crushed her son." Stokes (1962) 4, however, seems to be on the right track when he says: "There seems to be no reason why Earth should not again bring forth a son, present him with the necessary weapons and cunning advice, and so ensure the overthrow of Zeus." Blaise (1992) 356–59 interprets the action of Gaia as an attack against Zeus's absolute power and the "sterile immobility" of his regime. In addition, she sees the union of Earth with Tartarus as a means of integrating the latter into the cosmos. But that integration has already taken place via the preceding description. Insightfully, Robert (1905) in Heitsch 170–73 bases his defense of the Typhoeus episode on the role of Gaia, whom he calls "die eigentliche Führerin der Handlung. . . . Sie ist nicht nur die alles gebärende Mutter, sondern auch die Diplomatin, die alles weiß, alles ersinnt, alles in die Wege leitet" (171). "Können nicht eben von dieser Seite dem Zeus . . . Gefahren drohen, wenn Gaia, die Allmutter, weiter gebärt?" (172). Cf. also Bonnafé (1984) 209–12.

But the son of Cronus and the rest of the immortal gods,
Whom fair-haired Rheia bore in union with Cronus,
Brought them [the Hundred-Handers] back into the light **on the advice of Gaia;**
For she told them everything in detail,
How with them they would achieve victory and accomplish their
   splendid boast.   (624–28)

But shortly thereafter, when her help has proved critical to the Olympian victory, she appears to change sides, now opposing Zeus by giving birth to the monstrous Typhoeus, "who would have ruled over gods and men".[44] But her role as kingmaker among the gods and orchestrator of succession is perfectly consistent, and an understanding of her motivation is crucial to the *Theogony*. Cronus was not only his father's successor, but also and simultaneously the youngest son of Gaia. In the later more highly articulated epoch, however, these two roles are differentiated and split: Zeus must not only prevail against his father and his father's generation, but he must also overthrow the youngest – and in this case, last – offspring of Earth.[45] Only after the victory over both the Titans and Typhoeus does Gaia finally align herself with Zeus's cause, first, by advising the gods to elect Zeus their king and then by helping him anticipate the threat of a successor. Hesiod's description of her role, first in relation to Cronus, and then in relation to Zeus, can usefully be compared. In the first case, Cronus swallows the children as they emerge from Rheia's womb:

τὰ φρονέων, ἵνα μή τις ἀγαυῶν Οὐρανιώνων
ἄλλος ἐν ἀθανάτοισιν ἔχοι βασιληίδα τιμήν.
πεύθετο γὰρ Γαίης τε καὶ Οὐρανοῦ ἀστερόεντος
οὕνεκά οἱ πέπρωτο ἑῷ ὑπὸ παιδὶ δαμῆναι.

Thinking that no one else of the awesome family of Uranus
Should have the royal privilege among the immortals.
For he [Cronus] had learned from Earth and starry Heaven
That it was destined for him to be overcome by his son.
                                                                      (461–64)

When on the other hand, Metis, Zeus's first wife, is on the point of giving birth to Athena, Zeus:

. . .τότ᾿ ἔπειτα δόλῳ φρένας ἐξαπατήσας
αἱμυλίοισι λόγοισιν ἑὴν ἐσκάτθετο νηδύν,
Γαίης **φραδμοσύνῃσι** καὶ Οὐρανοῦ ἀστερόεντος·

---

[44] Thalmann (1984) 44 elides Gaia's role in giving birth to Typhoeus and hence does not confront the ambiguities of her relations to Zeus.
[45] Typhoeus (821), Cronus (137), and Zeus (478) are all called ὁπλότατοι.

τὼς γάρ οἱ φρασάτην, ἵνα μὴ βασιληίδα τιμὴν
ἄλλος ἔχοι Διὸς ἀντὶ θεῶν αἰειγενετάων.
ἐκ γὰρ τῆς εἵμαρτο περίφρονα τέκνα γενέσθαι.

Then when he had deceived her mind by a trick
With seductive words, he put her in his belly,
On the advice of Earth and starry Sky;
For thus they advised him, so that no one of the
   eternally-born gods
Would possess the royal privilege of Zeus.
For from her [Metis] it was destined that children of
   outstanding intelligence would be born.   (888–94)

Despite the obvious similarities in these passages, Hesiod's language indicates a subtle but important difference; Cronus learned – how, we know not – of his destined overthrow from Gaia. But only in the second case does Gaia take an active role, when she warns and advises Zeus how to evade the threat of succession and thus to stabilize the cosmos under his eternal rule. Zeus's preemptive strike succeeds where Cronus' had failed. In swallowing the pregnant Metis, Zeus reiterates the first two episodes of the succession myth, but with a difference; in giving birth to Athena, he appropriates the female function of procreation;[46] and he permanently incorporates into himself the feminine principle of guile (*metis*) that had hitherto been the instrument of generational change.[47]

Elected by the gods to the kingship of heaven, Zeus immediately undertakes to "divide their honors well" (885). While Hesiod often alludes to this final distribution, he never gives a systematic account of the division of prerogatives and spheres of influence within the Olympian pantheon.[48] To be sure, his audience was well aware of the distribution of roles and functions among the gods. Hesiod's omission, however, may also be motivated by the fact that such accounts are accommodated in a different genre of poetry, the hexameter hymn, of which the collection known as the Homeric Hymns is the best representative. Those compositions have as their focus the birth and acquisition of honors by the Olympian gods, precisely those stories that are excluded from the *Theogony*.[49] Thus

---

[46] The monstrous aspect of Zeus's pregnancy should not be ignored. Zeus's pseudo-parthenogenesis is also reminiscent of Pontos' anomalous bringing forth of Nereus and thus constitutes a throwback to one of the earliest phases of cosmic evolution.

[47] For the workings of *metis*, see Detienne and Vernant (1974).

[48] Fränkel (1962) 107 remarks disappointedly: "es gibt in der Theogonie keine dürrere und lebenslosere Partie als die wo Hesiod in aller Kürze das homerische Göttersystem referiert (912–42)."

[49] See Clay (1989) 268–70.

Hesiod's theogonic poetry reveals a cognizance of that genre of hymnic verse, and the Hymns likewise show familiarity with the theogonic tradition. When Hesiod assigns new or non-traditional functions to a divinity, he provides details. It is thus perhaps no accident that he elaborates on the prerogatives of Hecate in what critics have called a "hymn" to that goddess.

While excluding a detailed account of the functioning of the Olympians, Hesiod does, however, describe how Zeus's marital policies continue the integration of the old gods into the Olympian order, a policy that had previously proved critical to his victory over the Titans.[50] Some of his children complete the Olympian pantheon as we know it from, for instance, the Homeric poems. With the closing of the cycle of succession, however, no one of his sons can offer a serious threat to Zeus's supremacy.[51] The oldest daughter of Cronus, Hestia, like Hecate, remains a virgin. Leto's gentleness disarms her mighty son, Apollo; Demeter has only one daughter; and the possible threat posed by Ares, the only legitimate son of Hera and Zeus, is resolved through his marriage to Aphrodite (933–37). Hera's other son, Hephaestus, is both illegitimate and defective. Between these two males, Athena, whose allegiance is to her father alone and who combines in herself both war and art, is born.

The offspring of Zeus's earlier marriages constitute allegorical emblems of his regime, offering counterweights to the darker primal powers, especially the offspring of Eris and Night, who, as eternal entities, do not disappear in the new order, but henceforth at least are counterbalanced by their opposite numbers; thus, for example, the pleasant daughters of Themis, the Horai, Eunomia (Good Order), Justice, and Peace, form counterweights to Dusnomia (Disorder), Strife, and Battles. Most telling in this context is the birth of a new set of Moirai. While the grim triplets sprung from primordial Night manifest themselves only as spirits of inexorable vengeance for the crimes of both gods and men (220–23), their later namesakes dispense good and evil but only to human beings at their birth.[52] Similarly significant in characterizing the harmony and order of the new dispensation is Zeus's marriage with the Titaness Mnemosyne (Memory), perhaps the only

---

[50] Cf. Bonnafé (1985) 87–102, Ramnoux (1987), and Miralles (1993), who stress Zeus's co-option of the feminine through his marriages.

[51] One such potential intra-Olympian rivalry is dealt with in the Homeric *Hymn to Apollo*. There, Hera plays the role of jealous wife. Hesiod, however, has Zeus's marriage to Leto precede his union with Hera. See Clay (1989) 17–94; and Miralles (1993) 33–39. It is worth noting that the first five marriages of Zeus produce only females. The *Hymn to Demeter* represents the potential threat of Demeter – like Hera, Zeus's sister-wife – to Olympian stability.

[52] See West (1966) 229.

"love-match" in the whole *Theogony*,[53] a union that produces the lovely and lovable Muses from which the poem began. Their presence here also fulfills their command to Hesiod to celebrate them both at the beginning and at the end of his composition (34).

We cannot hope here to resolve the question of where the *Theogony* ended, a question on which it seems no two scholars can agree. I think it is safe to say that the poem concluded with a catalogue of at least some off-spring of unions of gods and human beings; these heroic genealogies were continued and expanded in the *Catalogue of Women*, universally ascribed to Hesiod in antiquity.[54] Yet unless the sands of Egypt should suddenly become more generous in producing additional papyrus fragments, the details of this composition, of which only tatters survive, may permanently elude us. Nevertheless, the heroes, generated by the unions of gods and men, are already mentioned earlier in the *Theogony* and form its necessary continuation. With Gaia subdued, Metis incorporated, and thus the removal of the threat of succession, the stabilization of the cosmos appears complete. Yet even Zeus cannot simply abolish the principle of proliferation embodied in the procreative drive. He must discover an outlet for it, preferably one that does not unleash a new threat to his eternal rule. Zeus's solution to this crucial conundrum is the generation of the heroes. Through their intercourse with mortals, the gods are able to deflect the more troublesome aspects of generation away from the gods themselves. In a later chapter, I will examine the genesis of the heroic race and its demise within the context of Hesiod's cosmogonic scheme.

---

[53] Only here (915) does Hesiod employ a form of the verb ἔραμαι, cognate with *eros*, to describe a divine union. Note the adjectives, "lovely" and "desirable" (8, 65, 67, 70), to describe the Muses and their song, as well as the name Erato (78) of one of them.

[54] For an overview, see West (1985).

CHAPTER 2

Orientations: the Works and Days

The preceding pages have offered a rough sketch of the *Theogony*'s contents, highlighting those points where Hesiod makes significant organizational choices in the arrangement of his genealogies and in the placement of his digressions, choices that underline certain fundamental conceptions concerning the articulation of the cosmos. But the *Theogony*'s armature remains essentially and necessarily tied to a genealogical framework as it traces the development and evolution of the divine cosmos from its origins to its present state. The organization of the *Works and Days*, however, possesses no such intrinsic necessity or obvious structure. As West remarks:

> To anyone who expects an orderly and systematic progression of ideas, it is liable to appear a bewildering text. The same themes recur several times in different places, connections between neighbouring sections are often difficult to grasp, trains of thought are interrupted by seemingly irrelevant remarks, the didactic intention is here and there suspended in favour of pure description; and taken as a whole, the variety of contents is so great that it is hardly possible to describe the subject of the poem in a single phrase.[1]

In the opinion of others, Hesiod's mode of composition involves a fairly fluid association of ideas whereby each section leads to the next, but the poem inevitably lacks an overall coherence or argument.

Any study of the poem must first confront a fundamental problem: the unity and coherence of the *Works and Days* as it has come down to us. For the poem contains not only suspect lines but even whole sections, which at least some scholars have found unworthy of the enlightened spirit of Hesiod. By way of example, I need only mention the so-called "Days" and the religious prohibitions that precede them. Others, conversely, consider Hesiod's thought process "primitive" so that coherence of

---

[1] West (1978) 41. Cf. Sinclair (1932) x: "It [the *Works and Days*] is admittedly a curious mixture, full of digressions and disjointed lines." Evelyn-White (1936) xix, however, sums up the poem quite well when he says: "its real aim is to show men how best to live in a difficult world."

structure and argument cannot be expected or discovered. In fact, generations of scholars have denied the composition any genuine unity. Unlike the *Theogony*, it seems at first glance to be composed in blocks or chunks which are strung together in no particular order, a relic of an archaic mode of thought which could not discern the forest of the whole from the trees of the parts. To speak, then, of the architecture of the *Works and Days* might seem to some an oxymoron.[2] Perhaps the word "design" would better serve our purpose, since "architecture" suggests a static edifice, while "design" implies a dynamic progression along with patterns as well as shifting perspectives and chromatic tonalities that emerge in the course of the composition.

If, in the *Theogony*, Hesiod proposed to sing of the "holy race of the immortals," here he declares his intention "to declare to Perses things as they are" (ἐγὼ δέ κε Πέρσῃ ἐτήτυμα μυθησαίμην, 10). With these words Hesiod indicates something about the contents of the poem that will follow. While it will embrace real things or "reality," its form will resemble a *muthos*, a speech, or even at moments a story. μυθέομαι, "to make a *muthos*," is clearly a marked term .[3] In the course of the *Works and Days*, Hesiod will in fact lay claim to the right to speak both to his wayward brother and, more surprisingly, to the kings. He will alternatively threaten and cajole, promise and instruct, command and exhort. Moreover, he deploys a grand array of rhetorical tropes and strategies: fables, allegories, myths, and proverbs. Hesiod's μυθησαίμην goes well beyond a bare account; it implies a rhetoric and an argument that, even as it seeks to persuade, simultaneously reveals and hides "things as they are." Perhaps the best approach to revealing Hesiod's design would demonstrate that the building blocks that make up the *Works and Days* cannot in fact be rearranged without destroying his argument, an argument which only emerges by moving through the poem from beginning to end. Here, I will examine some of those building blocks

---

[2] Schwabl (1970) 469 in fact speaks of the "architectonic structure" of the *Works and Days*, but views it largely in numerical terms. Thalmann (1984) 56 finds that "the basic principle of composition is the juxtaposition of discrete sections. The important connections between these parts are to be found . . . in recurrences of important ideas that are often stressed by verbal echoes." Similarly, according to Verdenius (1962) 111–59, Hesiod structures his composition largely through the association of ideas: "Hesiod hat kein festes Schema vor Augen, sondern er lässt sich durch den Strom der Gedanken mitführen" (p. 127). Heath (1985) offers a simple tripartite structure. Some other attempts: Kerschensteiner (1944); and Blusch (1970). For earlier literature, see the summary in Fuss (1910) 1–22.

[3] μυθέομαι is a secondary formation from *muthos*. Martin (1989) has argued that in Homer *muthos* as opposed to *epos* denotes not just speech, but authoritative speech. However, the distinction Martin tries to establish is problematic. Cf. Clark (2001); Murad (1998). Also Mueller (1954). The phrase, ἐτήτυμα μυθήσασθαι, occurs at *H. Demeter* 44, where neither gods nor men were willing to tell Demeter what had *really* happened to her daughter Persephone.

in summary fashion and attempt to outline the linear progress and inner dynamic of Hesiod's argument.

After the short proem invoking both the Muses and Zeus, Hesiod abruptly turns from them to announce his intention to tell Perses "things as they are." With equal abruptness, he launches into the task he has set himself with an apparent "correction" of his own *Theogony*'s teaching about Eris (Strife), thus both linking and distinguishing this work from his earlier one. On earth, at least, there are not one but two Erides, of which one is destructive, while the other inspires men to work and compete with their fellows. In yet another abrupt transition, Hesiod proceeds to address directly the Perses mentioned earlier, whom we only now learn to be the speaker's brother. While outlining a complex scenario embracing himself, his brother, and the kings, Hesiod then applies his doctrine of the two kinds of Strife to the particular situation of Perses, who is exhorted to embrace the good Eris rather than the bad one to which he has become habituated.

The poem as a whole purports to record a speech addressed primarily to Perses and, to a lesser extent, the kings.[4] Yet neither the kings nor Perses ever speak or reply. Hesiod silences both the kings and Perses; both parties are *nepioi* and are never given the opportunity to respond.[5] After Hesiod, the silent presence of the addressee becomes a convention of didactic poetry – although one could easily imagine an effective form of didactic that might incorporate dialogue.[6] But in the *Works and Days*, the silence of both Perses and the kings is by no means conventional. For Perses' vices and shortcomings, as they emerge in the course of the poem, manifest themselves in a kind of speech, precisely in the form of quarrels and disputes and in the lies and perjuries that accompany them. Similarly, Hesiod's indictment against the kings is primarily defined by their crooked decrees and pronouncements. Taking over the royal prerogative of pronouncing judgments and reducing his wayward brother to silence, Hesiod alone speaks in the *Works and Days*. Yet as Hesiod exhorts, cajoles, and harangues, spinning out the

---

[4] Cf. lines 202 and 248. An earlier attempt to understand the design of the poem traced the role of Perses in Clay (1993).

[5] Even if there is no genuine etymological connection, Hesiod may have linked νήπιος with ἔπος. For νήπιος, see Edmunds (1990).

[6] In his survey of ancient wisdom literature, West (1978) 3–25 mentions a few non-Greek examples that appear to have a dialogic form. The most common format involves advice from father to son and sometimes advice to princelings, but West cites no parallels for the brother-to-brother communication of the *Works and Days*. Martin (1984) 32 considers the *Works and Days* "the best surviving reflection of this genre in Greek." But the more equal fraternal relationship between speaker and addressee (we do not even know whether Hesiod was older than Perses) may be significant: what is the basis for Hesiod's authority to instruct his brother?

variegated fabric of his argument, we must imagine Perses mutely listening and absorbing his brother's message, a κωφὸν πρόσωπον, sometimes balking, sometimes assenting, and even at times in serious danger of backsliding. We may call this implied interaction between Hesiod and his silent brother the education of Perses. This process can be defined as a protreptic, first turning Perses onto the path of justice, then directing him to work as the sole legitimate means of gaining a livelihood, and, finally, bringing him to a comprehension of the ἐτήτυμα promised by Hesiod in the prologue. From the beginning, we the poem's audience, are silent observers of, and participants in, Perses' education. At times, Hesiod's exhortations even seem to address us directly when he addresses a nameless "you," while at others we distance ourselves to observe and judge his discourse and its impact on Perses. Ultimately, Hesiod's dramatic monologue is aimed, beyond Perses and the kings, at us, his audience, both as recipients and witnesses.[7]

To understand Hesiod's protreptic, we must first define its starting-point, that is, the situation of Perses and the relations between the two brothers. The question of Perses' fictionality or reality,[8] although long debated, is less important than the common claim that the presentation of Perses in the poem is inconsistent. West, for example, says: "it is apparent that Perses is a changeable figure that Hesiod stations in his poem as he chooses."[9] Perses does indeed change in the course of the poem as he absorbs Hesiod's teaching, but those changes represent the dynamic linear evolution of Perses' education.

The *communis opinio* holds that Perses had previously taken his brother to court and won his case, corruptly acquiring a larger share of the brother's estate by bribing the kings/judges. Now Perses threatens to haul Hesiod back into court in an effort to get even more, but Hesiod suggests an out-of-court settlement. The *Works and Days* has, in fact, been considered Hesiod's *plaidoyer* against his brother, trying the case, so to speak, in the court of public opinion.[10] Some scholars offer modifications of this basic scenario by arguing that Perses must have lost the first case; others deny

---

[7] Green (1984) 32–39 has rightly emphasized the dramatic character of Hesiod's discourse.

[8] On the reality or fictionality of Perses, see West (1978) 33–40; and Schmidt (1986) 19–21. The controversy is at least as old as the Scholia. See Pertusi (1955) on line 27.

[9] West (1978) 36–40. Schmidt (1986) 52 persuasively argues for a unified and consistent picture of Perses throughout the poem. See also Green (1984) 30–32; and Blümer (2001) 1, 5–17, who on the basis of the consistent portrayal of Perses illogically argues for his reality.

[10] Kirchhoff (1889), believed that lines 11–281 contained five separate songs concerning the brothers' court case; three additional songs (282–690) were composed under different circumstances and contain many later interpolations.

that a new trial is pending; but almost all seem to agree that the dispute centers on past or future litigation.[11]

These interpretations have evolved from an understandable desire to pin down Hesiod's rather elusive description of Perses' conduct and the differences that separate them. But it is safe to assume that, however elliptical, Hesiod gives us sufficient details within his poem for our understanding of the situation. Contrary to the views of many critics, I believe there is no unambiguous indication that Hesiod himself has been cheated or suffered any loss at Perses' hands.[12] Significantly, throughout the poem, Hesiod makes no demand for restitution of lost or stolen property, a demand that would be natural if Perses had in fact cheated him. Yet if we stick close to the text, a comprehensible scenario emerges. Apparently, the two brothers divided their father's κλῆρος, presumably land. Perses then proceeded to try to acquire by illicit means more property – not necessarily Hesiod's – in the form of chattel, with which he "conferred glory" on the gift-eating kings.[13] The probably sarcastic accusation, μέγα κυδαίνων, "greatly glorifying" the kings (38), is maddeningly vague; it could refer to court fees or to bribes, mere flattery, or to an intentionally muddy combination of all of these. Moreover, although Perses may have undertaken dishonest litigation (which, however, had not succeeded in enriching him), there is no clear evidence that such litigation ever involved Hesiod. At any rate, Perses is now nearly destitute; as we only learn later, he has recently come a-begging to Hesiod, evidently not for the first time (396). But now Hesiod refuses to bail his brother out.

It is this refusal, I suggest, rather than property loss, that triggers the dispute between the two brothers and provides the occasion for the poem, lending a tone of immediacy and urgency to the situation. The resolution to their quarrel is to take place here and now (αὖθι, 35) and in fact is the present poem. As Hesiod will later remark (286–92), Perses has come to the crossroads: he can either attempt to continue on the smooth easy road of κακότης or turn onto the rough, steep, and sweat-filled path of ἀρετή to

---

[11] In addition to the commentaries, see Latimer (1930); van Groningen (1957); Gagarin (1974); Lenz (1975); and Schmidt (1986) 21–28. But cf. Jones (1984) 315: "there is no real reason to think that these proceedings before the *basileis* were brought to completion – or, I would add, even initiated." Also Green (1984) 25: "there was no prior litigation;" and now Blümer (2001) 16.

[12] Cf. Schmidt (1986) 21: "In der Tat erfahren wir nicht einmal, worum der Streit eigentlich geht, ob um Land, Vieh, landwirtschaftliche Geräte oder andere Gegenstände, geschweige denn, welche Grösse oder welchen Wert der Streitgegenstand hat; ebensowenig hören wir über dessen Bedeutung für den Betroffenen selbst, über dessen Lage und Abhängigkeit von dem gefährdeten Besitz." Verdenius (1985) 37 is half right in observing that "[i]f ἄλλα referred to the property of other people, there would not be a quarrel among the brothers" – as though they could quarrel only over property!

[13] For the distinction between land and chattel, see Walcot (1963) 8; and Jones (1984) 315.

which Hesiod's protreptic points the way. The issue, then, between Hesiod and Perses is not merely a dispute over property, but the far more general question of how one should live.[14] While the *Works and Days* is addressed to the specific individual, Perses, its teaching casts a far wider net.[15] And it is precisely this combination of the general and the specific that gives the poem its validity as a protreptic.

Hesiod advises his brother that they should resolve their dispute on the spot rather than having recourse to the "gift-eating" kings who are quite "willing to pronounce the kind of judgment that is known here"[16] – since there is evidently something in it for them. Hesiod thus suggests that they by-pass such proceedings, because the judges are corrupt, judges who are immediately qualified as νήπιοι, fools, ignorant of fundamental human truths expressed in the two proverbial *sententiae* that follow:

νήπιοι, οὐδὲ ἴσασιν ὅσῳ πλέον ἥμισυ παντός,
οὐδ' ὅσον ἐν μαλάχῃ τε καὶ ἀσφοδέλῳ μέγ' ὄνειαρ.

Fools, nor do they know by how much the half is more
    than the whole,
Nor what great benefit there is in mallow and asphodel.

(40–41)

While the exact meaning of these sayings may be lost to us,[17] their general significance is clear enough. The first would appear to refer back to the κλῆρος the brothers shared. Perses, instead of being satisfied with his share, attempted to acquire more by improper means. But the kings too as gift-eaters – or bribe-takers – greedily try to get more by means of their unjust judgments. Both king and subject are guilty of the same charge: what appears to be more may not in fact be so, and what may seem less, but justly acquired, possesses lasting value. In the second case, mallow and asphodel, natural and uncultivated, may well have been the diet of mankind in the

---

[14] I am unable to follow the arguments of Rousseau (1996); and (1993), who makes of Perses a kind of Don Quixote devoted to a now outdated heroic ethos.

[15] Cf. Solmsen (1949) 96, who notes: "it is typical of Hesiod to see his own experience and situation *sub specie aeternitatis* as well as – and perhaps even more – *sub specie universi generis humani.*" For the structure of Hesiod's argument, see Benardete (1967).

[16] I follow the interpretation of Verdenius (1985) on τήνδε δίκην (39). Gagarin (1973) believes that *dike* always refers to a legal case. His conclusions are disputed by Claus (1977); and Dickie (1978). The Scholia at 279a (Pertusi) note that *dike* has several meanings in Hesiod: ποτὲ μὲν ἐπὶ τῆς σωματοειδοῦς θεᾶς, ποτὲ δὲ ἐπὶ τοῦ δικαίου, ποτὲ δὲ ἐπὶ τῆς κρίσεως, ποτὲ δὲ ἐπὶ τῆς τιμωρίας.

[17] Cf. West (1978) 152–53, who believes the two sayings are parallel; also Tandy and Neale (1996) 56: "the point here being that it is better to have simple things earned by honest work than to enjoy luxuries gotten dishonestly." That paraphrase works well for the first saying, but not the second; mallow and asphodel grow wild and require no work; they would seem to be appropriate feed for animals. Cf. Wilamowitz (1928) on line 41.

golden age long ago, when men were closer to the gods and before the invention of agriculture.[18] Nowadays, however, the "great benefit" in these weeds lies not in their being good to eat,[19] but on the contrary, in recognizing that they offer a poor diet for human beings of the present.[20] The beneficial lesson they provide derives from their revealing the unpleasant – and unappetizing – alternative to agricultural labor. Thus the two proverbs adumbrate the two great themes of work and justice that inform Hesiod's poem.

Two myths will take up these themes in reverse order. Introduced by the explanatory γάρ, the Prometheus story that immediately follows explains the human imperative to work. Since we will study the myth later in greater detail, let me here only summarize its beginning and end. The gods "have hidden and keep hidden men's livelihood" (42).[21] The ultimate consequences of the confrontation between Prometheus and Zeus are first, that men must work to eat, and second, that human life is full of countless invisible and unpredictable evils. Both are the results of Zeus's intentions and are henceforth inescapable for mankind:

οὕτως οὔ τί πη ἔστι Διὸς νόον ἐξαλέασθαι.

Thus, there is no way to escape the intention of Zeus.

(105)

A second account (*heteros logos*) of the human condition, addressed to a nameless singular "you," whom we may take to be Perses,[22] describes the successive stages in the history of mankind, from an original closeness to the gods to its present distance. Hesiod depicts two phases of the present and final age of iron: the first, in which "good things are mixed with evils" (179)

---

[18] Cf. Rousseau (1996) 155–56; and Ballabriga (1998) 318–19. Detienne (1972) 90–93 points out that the vegetarianism of the Pythagoreans and Epimenides – which included mallow and asphodel – represented the primeval diet that human beings once shared with the gods in the golden age.

[19] Line 822 offers a perfect parallel to the sense here. Hesiod concludes his list of good and bad days with: "These days are a great benefit (μέγ' ὄνειαρ) for men who live on earth." He does not mean that all the days he has mentioned are lucky; rather *knowing* which are propitious and which are not is a great benefit. See also *Theogony* 871. Rousseau (1996) 156 incomprehensibly translates μέγ' ὄνειαρ as "grande jouissance."

[20] Cf. Virgil, *Georgics* 1.158–59; although Virgil does not mention mallow and asphodel, but rather the other component of pre-agricultural food, acorns, these lines would seem to support this interpretation: Ceres first transformed the human diet from acorns to wheat (*Georgics* 1.8), but without unrelenting labor, you will again be reduced to that primitive nutrition.

[21] The expression κρύψαντες . . . ἔχουσι is significant. Otherwise, men could have found their livelihood once and for all and be done with it. But it eternally remains hidden and thus requires constant human toil to gain it.

[22] I have suggested (Clay [1993] 27) that Perses is to recognize himself in the μέγα νήπιοι of the Silver race. That the first argument on the necessity of justice should be addressed to Perses rather than the kings, who are always referred to in the plural, is significant.

and a final one, of irremediable evils. The description of the estrangement of brothers and the lack of respect given the just man or the one who keeps his oath resembles the conduct of Perses (184, 190–94). We are, then, at a pivotal moment of human history; unless Perses can be won over to the side of justice, disaster is imminent. Hence the urgency of Hesiod's message which ends with an apocalyptic vision into the future where man's complete alienation from the divine, signaled by the departure of all sense of shame and moral outrage (Aidos and Nemesis), will lead to mankind's annihilation at the hands of Zeus.[23]

While superficially quite different, the two stories share a certain common framework: both recount a previous happier state of human life and its demise; and in both cases, Zeus is the moving force behind that decline. But beyond their shared bleak picture of the human condition, the two myths incorporate somewhat different messages concerning how men must live and what remains in their power to ameliorate their situation. The Prometheus story teaches that men must work to live, while the myth of the races instructs human beings about the necessity of exercising proper conduct toward each other and toward the gods; both imperatives derive ultimately from the authority of Zeus. The human need to gain a livelihood (food, and, beyond mere subsistence, prosperity) must therefore be moderated and informed by the rules of just behavior.

In general, Hesiod subscribes to the notion of what we would call a zero-sum economy, i.e. that the total amount of wealth is finite and that, to get more, you have to take it away from another.[24] But since taking from another is unjust, the only source for the production of just wealth, according to Hesiod, is agriculture. The wealth thus gained from excess agricultural production may ultimately permit the acquisition of another's property (cf. 341). Hesiod, however, accuses Perses of rejecting the only just route to prosperity and, with the connivance of the kings, resorting instead to both theft and bribery, the first strategy unjust, and the second a foolish and short-sighted misuse of any wealth he may have had. Perses fully lives up to his name that derives from πέρθω, "to lay waste," "to plunder." In the process of attempting to plunder the property of others, he has managed – fool that he is – to lay waste his own. Both methods of acquisition, however, are doomed to failure because Perses does not understand the way the world works – in other words, the *etetuma* that Hesiod sets out to expound both in these introductory myths and throughout the rest of his poem.

Alternately addressed to the kings and to Perses, the following sections set out the argument for just behavior and, equally forcefully, exhort against

[23] Cf. Rousseau (1993) 70–71.   [24] Cf. Millett (1984) 95–96.

injustice. Hesiod proceeds *hysteron proteron* to launch his great protreptic toward justice. His discourse is what I would call triangular, directed in turn to the kings and to Perses.

Hesiod's discourse, then, is twofold, as is his strategy, which has aptly been likened to the so-called Prisoner's Dilemma in modern game theory, which has aptly been summarized as follows:

> Each of two agents, A and B, who are unable to communicate with each other, has to choose for his part if he is going to (i) obey a moral norm or (ii) act against it in such conditions that if A and B both chose (i) they both would get fairly good results, and if they both chose (ii), they both would get essentially worse results, and if A (or B) chose (ii) while B (or A) chose (i), A (or B) would get the best possible result for himself, while B (or A) would get the worst possible result for himself . . . It can be claimed that moral education consists of convincing people in one way or another that they should make type (i) choices in all situations, since type (ii) choices, which seem prima facie [to] give best results to each individual's own advantage, bring disastrous results if universalized.[25]

Perses' activities, which he believes are advantageous to himself, are not only unjust in themselves, but require for their success the connivance of the kings, who likewise consider only their immediate advantage in accepting Perses' bribes and proffering their crooked judgments. Both must be persuaded simultaneously that not only does justice serve both their interests, but that its contravention leads to punishment and universal disaster.

Hesiod begins, then, with the fable of the hawk and the nightingale addressed to the kings. The nightingale caught in the hawk's talons cries out piteously only to be told that the hawk, insofar as he is the stronger, can do anything he wants to her, even make her his next meal. The fable would seem to indicate that might makes right, but no explicit moral is given. If, as is usually thought, the hawk resembles the kings and the nightingale Hesiod himself, then Hesiod would seem to indicate that *eris* between king and poet is a waste of time.[26] At any rate, the nightingale does not respond. The kings are left to ponder the meaning of the fable. Singer can only compete with singer and, presumably, king with king. But the nightingale

---

[25] Sihvola (1989) 51. While stating the general principle as relevant to Hesiod's strategy, Sihvola does not identify the participants A and B as Perses and the kings.

[26] Wilamowitz (1928) 64 believes the point of the fable is that Hesiod will suffer the fate of the nightingale if his lawsuit comes before the kings. Bonnafé (1983) points out the parallels between the nightingale and the subsequent description of Justice outraged. For recent "revisionist" interpretations, see Perysinakis (1986) 106, who equates the hawk with Zeus and the nightingale with the kings. Nelson (1998) 77–81 (similarly, Nelson [1997–98]); and Leclerc (1992) argue for two levels: both kings and poet, and kings and Zeus. Cf. Beye (1972) 39. Lonsdale (1989) argues that the fable may also be understood as an omen. Hubbard (1996) sees Perses as the nightingale and Zeus as the hawk.

will soon recover her voice; if the poet can manage to ally himself with the *demos*, those who depend on the kings, the contest may even out. Perses stands for all those who foolishly believe that the corrupt kings benefit them. Hesiod's strategy requires winning over Perses so that the kings can then be confronted with a united front.

At this point, Hesiod turns away from the kings, who will not listen, to address Perses: "But you, Perses, you hearken to justice" (213).[27] The nightingale, silenced by the hawk, now begins to sing with a new voice: the voice of Justice.[28] Perses must not cultivate Hybris, "for hybris is burdensome for a δειλὸς βροτός (like Perses), but even for an ἐσθλός (that is to say, a king) she is a heavy burden" and leads to certain disaster. Hesiod here deploys figurative language, which we would call allegorical. He describes a race in which Hybris, Dike, and Horkos (Oath) are the runners, a race that Dike will inevitably win in the end.[29] A second image follows, one involving the rape of Dike by gift-eating kings, which is accompanied by "the murmur of protest that spreads among the people".[30] This outcry reveals that the unjust actions of the kings do not ultimately meet with popular approbation. And for a good reason: Dike will unleash her revenge upon the city as a whole. It will engulf the innocent as well as the guilty.

Concluding this part of his protreptic, Hesiod presents two opposing tableaux, one of the just, and the other of the unjust city (225–47). While the latter is marked out for destruction through hunger, disease, and war, the former in its peaceful abundance and prosperity resembles the luxuriant fecundity of the Golden Age and the distant islands of the Blest. But this idealized picture would seem to contradict Hesiod's earlier teaching in his account of the succession of races. Or are we to think that mankind will survive on acorns and honey and renounce agriculture?[31] The vegetarian diet and absence of sailing point to the Golden Race and pre-Promethean

---

[27] Both West (1978) 209 and Mazon (1914) 78 note that we expect here a direct address to the kings, which is deferred: "c'est à Persès qu'il donnera des conseils faits pour les plus grands que lui."

[28] I would argue that Dike is already personified here; the genitive is ambiguous. Arrighetti (1998) prints it with a capital letter.

[29] The difficult allegory in 219 is important for Hesiod's argument. The crooked judgments, here as elsewhere, belong to the kings; but Horkos, Oath – and also the punishment attendant upon perjury – falls upon those like Perses who forswear themselves before the judges. Cf. 282–85. Not only the crooked judges, but also their collaborators, the perjurers, will be punished.

[30] West (1978) on 220.

[31] West (1978) struggles with the acorn diet in line 233. Cf. Knox (1982) 326–27: "Hesiod is here posing the results of communal justice and injustice against each other in the extreme form appropriate for moral examples and such dramatic pictures tend to take mythical shape. In real life nothing is so clear cut; but the plea for justice is best served by the pushing of the contrast to extremes."

man, but, according to Hesiod, the city comes into being only with the race of heroes (cf. 162 and 165).

Throughout this section, while adopting the voice of Justice, Hesiod speaks *about* the kings but his harangue is directed at Perses. It is Perses who must be persuaded that his interest lies in promoting justice among the kings rather than in encouraging their greed through flattery and bribery. Otherwise, the whole community will inevitably suffer, including finally Perses himself. The contrasting visions of the idealized just and unjust city demonstrate how the welfare of the city as a whole depends on the justice dispensed by its kings. Yet there is an asymmetry in the two descriptions: while the good king will make his people prosper, the injustice of even one man – whether king or commoner – brings Zeus's wrath down upon the whole community.[32] The point of this rhetorical ploy is to suggest to Perses that not only must he behave justly, but that he has a positive stake in the righteousness of the kings as well as of the commoners. Only when Perses has been persuaded that his prosperity cannot depend on unjust judges – their very corruption poses a threat to him – and becomes convinced of the communal punishment meted by Zeus, that is, when Perses has been won over to the cause of justice, for himself and others, can Hesiod turn his attention back to the kings.

Now the poet/nightingale adopts a new and menacing voice. Addressing the kings directly with threats of divine punishment, Hesiod launches the heavy artillery of his rhetoric, warning the kings that their injustice cannot escape detection: 30,000 guardians of Zeus watch over their actions as does Dike herself, who complains to her father; and finally, nothing escapes the eye of Zeus himself, which sees and observes all (πάντα ἰδὼν Διὸς ὀφθαλμὸς καὶ πάντα νοήσας, 267). The evil done by the kings will crash down upon their own heads. Not only their own status, but the survival of the entire community depends on the quality of justice that the kings dispense and promote. Indeed, without justice, the kings will not even have a city to regulate. The prayer with which the poem opened (9) is assumed fulfilled.

Hesiod here expresses an enigmatic wish to which we will later return: he would not be just, nor want his son to be so, since it is a bad business to be just if injustice carries the day.[33] But Hesiod adds: "I still hope that

---

[32] Erler (1987) 20, who believes that Hesiod here modifies an Oriental notion of sacral kingship, notes that the injustice of one man can bring down the (unjust) city; but he does not seem to recognize that, in Hesiod's portrayal, the blessings of the just city are more intimately bound up with the righteousness of the kings.

[33] Mazon (1914) 84 cites *Odyssey* 2.230 and 5.8 as parallels.

Zeus will never bring about such a state of affairs" (270–73). One cannot practice justice by oneself; justice is a communal affair and demands the cooperation of the *polis* as a whole, both kings and *demos*. The kings will suffer directly from Zeus's inescapable punishment; the *demos* will suffer the destruction of their city. The self-interest, the self-preservation, of both kings and Perses demand not only the practice of justice, but its mutual reinforcement.

Suddenly, Hesiod turns away from the kings and returns to Perses; he must hearken to Dike and "altogether forget *bie.*" Now at long last we get an explication of the fable with which Hesiod began his discourse on justice. The previously helpless nightingale has found her voice, or rather, joined her voice to that of Dike and Zeus's 30,000 guardians to form a mighty chorus that can respond to the hawk. The *nomos* that Zeus imposed upon men does not permit them to eat each other, like birds and fishes, because he has given men *dike*. Zeus granted *dike* to men after the bronze race completed its mutual annihilation and the Olympian introduced communal life as we know it. The *dike* of Zeus embraces the great (the kings) as well as the lowly, such as Perses, that is to say, the entire community. The necessary association, the alliance, of great and small in sustaining justice is expressed in the following passage (280ff.): he who knows and speaks justice (the kings), to him Zeus gives prosperity; but he who forswears himself and lies (Perses), his line will diminish while, on the contrary, the family of the man who keeps his oaths faithfully will increase and flourish.[34] King and peasant must, each in his own fashion, support justice in their own interests, interests that ultimately coincide with the preservation of the *polis*.[35] The just speech of kings emerges in their straight judgments; that of Perses, in his keeping his oath. The *Works and Days* themselves constitute the just speech of Hesiod.

Between lines 213 and 285, words containing the root *dik* occur no less than 27 times. Only afterwards does Hesiod take up the theme of work and agricultural work in particular. It seems quite fair to ask – although few critics do – why he chooses this order rather than its opposite, that is, why does he place the argument for work after the argument for justice, for this decision has a profound impact on the whole design of his poem. Work, which the Greeks did not find intrinsically ennobling, comes after Dike. Justice involves and defines the entire community, whereas

---

[34] Mazon (1914) 85, n. 5 aptly cites Antiphon 5.11 on "the greatest and mightiest oath: the destruction of oneself, one's family, and one's house."

[35] One could say that the whole second book of the Plato's *Republic* is dedicated to refuting this self-interested argument for justice.

work need not; one can labor alone or in the relative isolation of the *oikos*;[36] but, as Hesiod makes eminently clear, you cannot practice justice alone.[37] Dike is personified as a mighty goddess and daughter of Zeus; work, however, receives no such hypostatization. That Hesiod begins from the higher before taking up the lower is critical to an understanding of his argument.

After the protreptic toward *dike*, in which he deploys the full panoply of his rhetoric, Hesiod caps his demonstration with the famous allegory of the two ways, the broad and easy road leading to *kakotes*, while the narrow, steep path leads to *arete*.[38] Directly thereafter, Hesiod himself likewise reaches the high point of his demonstration as he expounds his own excellence – for the *panaristos* who can figure things out on his own and therefore can instruct and command others is none other than Hesiod himself. Adopting the thundering voice of a god, he issues commands to the previously foolish Perses, who is – momentarily – elevated to a heroic level:[39]

> ἀλλὰ σύ γ᾽ ἡμετέρης μεμνημένος αἰὲν ἐφετμῆς
> ἐργάζεο, Πέρση, δῖον γένος.
>
> But you, being always mindful of our commands,
> Work, Perses, scion of Zeus.   (298–99)

Here Hesiod himself accomplishes what Zeus was said to do in the proem, namely to raise up the obscure (ἄδηλον ἀέξει, 6), i.e. the wretched Perses. From this height of excellence, Hesiod modulates into the next transitional section with its advice, *gnomai*, and exhortations that weave together the poem's two main themes: work and justice. Echoes of the poem's opening and Perses' circumstances punctuate the transition to a new phase of Hesiod's argument, and wealth as the reward for work makes an emphatic return (22, cf. 313, 377, 381). The last occurrence in the poem of a word with

---

[36] Consider, for instance, Laertes in the *Odyssey*.

[37] Note line 270: ἐν ἀνθρώποισι δίκαιος. Note also that at the poem's opening (33–34), Hesiod holds out the possibility to Perses that, once he has acquired sufficient sustenance, he can go ahead and indulge in quarrels to gain the property of others. Later on (341), the possibility of buying another's property depends on the good will of the gods.

[38] Many scholars define κακότης and ἀρετή here pragmatically as "failure" and "success" (Tandy [1996] 81–82) or, with West ad loc., "inferior and superior social standing." Yet the close connection between the allegory of the two ways and the *panaristos* passage that follows cannot be ignored and demand an ethical interpretation: the former describes the path to human excellence, while the second defines it.

[39] δῖον γένος also reminds us of the connection between gods and men established in the race of heroes. The ancients were puzzled by the expression and interpreted it to mean that a certain Dion was Perses' father! Others believe it means "of noble birth," which blunts Hesiod's word play and ignores his irony.

the root of *dik* in it comes here, and both kings and *polis*, so prominent before, disappear from the poem,[40] while words connected with work and the roots *erg-* and *erd-* move to the fore. But the protreptic toward Dike is presupposed, as is Perses' successful conversion; for the alternative to work is no longer quarrels in the *agora*, but begging (394–404).

If the poem's first half concentrates on justice within the *polis*, its second half presents a narrowing of perspective focusing on the *oikos*, the family farm, and neighbors rather than on the larger community. In the almanac of the farmer's year, seasonable work correctly done holds out the prospect of success (383–617). The natural world, the rising and setting of the stars, the song of the cuckoo, swallow, and cicada, provide signals for the activity appropriate to each part of the yearly cycle. Even while recognizing that Hesiod provides no manual for farming, many critics have considered this section the core of the poem. To be sure, Hesiod views agriculture as the defining activity of post-Promethean man, but farming is only part of his message. The farmer's year occupies but one -third of the composition, and as critics, we too must respect due measure.

While beginning and ending with the critical fall plowing and sowing and generally following the yearly cycle, the "Calendar," on closer examination, nevertheless frequently interrupts the orderly catalogue of seasonal chores by anxious glances both forward to the hopes and fears for the resultant harvest and backward to the preparations required for each task. In fact, right at the beginning, Hesiod backtracks a month to give a list of all the chores – wood-cutting, the making of tools, plows and wagon, choosing the proper oxen and farmhand – that must be completed before the fall plowing can even begin (414–47). This jerky technique creates a sense of urgency and haste during the busy periods of the year, spring and fall, and emphasizes the farmer's dependence on the imperatives of time. Yet such periods are interrupted by seasons of enforced inactivity during the cold of winter and the heat of mid-summer. In the extended description of winter, the bitter weather and the suffering of the exposed beasts frame the vignette of the maiden bathing and napping indoors, who is contrasted to the shivering octopus in his fireless house. Likewise, the crushing and parching summer heat dictates a respite from toil and allows shady feasting on meat and wine.[41]

---

[40] Fränkel (1962) 145 notes the absence of descriptions of public life in the *Works and Days*, but his suggestion that Hesiod lived in a pre-*polis* society can no longer be maintained. See, for instance, Raaflaub (1993).

[41] For a sympathetic discussion of this part of the poem and its structure, see Nelson (1998), especially 44–58; and Riedinger (1992). See now also Marsilio (2000).

Two contrasting images punctuate these scenes of enforced repose: the pampered girl still innocent of sex (519–23), and randy women rendered lubricious during the dog days that enervate men and make them dry, shriveled, and impotent (586). Both vignettes suggest the complexity of the relations between human beings and nature. The first depicts the human capacity to fabricate a defense (ἔρυμα) against the cold by sewing together the hides of beasts and to protect even the most vulnerable member of the family in the face of a hostile natural environment. The marriageable maiden is valued and protected because she will become a means of uniting one *oikos* with another.[42] In the latter image, nature affects male and female in opposite ways, so that human sexuality is eternally at odds with the natural cycle. These two images of the female, the one positive in that it binds human society together, the other, the source of perennial tension and disjunction, reminds us of the ambiguities of Pandora, the necessary evil of human life.

Be that as it may, Hesiod's pleasant mid-summer feast is suddenly interrupted – as if too much dawdling might lead Perses back into his lazy ways. Here again Hesiod backtracks a whole month to the critical time of threshing and storing the year's grain, the culmination of the process that began with fall plowing (597–608). The watchword throughout has been timeliness, timely preparations, timely reading of the appropriate signs, and timely completion of chores.[43]

To the farmer's calendar Hesiod appends – with apparent reluctance – a section on the appropriate seasons for sailing (618–93), introducing the whole subject in disparaging terms: "If a passion for inhospitable sailing seizes you" (εἰ δέ σε ναυτιλίης δυσπεμφέλου ἵμερος αἱρεῖ, 618).[44] That desire appears literally untimely, since it takes hold of Perses just when the season for navigation has come to a close (619–30). Apparently, as the two reproving addresses to Hesiod's brother here suggest (633, 641)[45], he might be especially prone to the seduction of quick profits that seafaring offers.[46] Hesiod, however, confesses to little personal knowledge of sailing and must rely on the Muses for his information. The absence of sea travel

---

[42] Cf. Lévêque (1988) 52.

[43] ὡραῖος, ὥρη, and ὥριον occur no less than 16 times in this section.

[44] δυσπέμφελος occurs again at 722 to describe surly behavior at a feast; in Homer, it is also used of the sea.

[45] In 633 Perses is again reduced to being a "big idiot" (μέγα νήπιε Πέρση, cf. ἀεσίφρονα θυμόν, 646), while at 641, Hesiod impresses on his brother the critical need for timeliness, especially in relation to seafaring.

[46] κέρδος, a term which Hesiod uses twice in this passage (lines 632 and 644) and only twice elsewhere in the poem (lines 323 and 352), always has negative connotations.

from the golden age and the just city (226–37) may account for his low opinion of the whole business in which risks outweigh possible gains. If your wagon breaks down, you can repair it, but if something goes wrong on the sea, you may lose not only your cargo, but also your life. In any case, only a pauper or a gambler would risk his life on the sea. Such, Hesiod declares was their father, who took to sailing out of penury; and even he finally settled down in Askra, despite its general wretchedness and, we may add, worked hard enough to leave behind a κλῆρος for his two sons. In fact, Hesiod recommends navigation only as a *supplement* to agricultural work, not as a substitute. For this reason he reserves his special distaste for spring sailing (lines 682–83): at this critical moment, you should be home bringing in the harvest; if you have none, you must be a desperate man indeed. Summer sailing, however, interferes only with the summer lull and feasting, although one must rush home in time for the *vendanges* and autumnal rains (line 674). But Perses, as his brother well knows, is by nature a gambler, one who prefers a quick fix to steady application. His quarrels and litigation, in fact, constituted nothing more than bad gambles, which he lost. Throughout the navigational calendar, Hesiod has taken pains to underline the dangers and risks. In moving from land to sea, we palpably progress from the more certain to the less.

The *Works and Days* continues for nearly 200 lines, but after the sailing calendar the name of Perses disappears from our text as Hesiod addresses his teaching only to a nameless "you." It has been suggested that Perses' disappearance signals a shift from the specific situation of the poem (whether real or fictive) to a more general public.[47] This may be partially true, but it ignores the fact that most of the poem has contained general verities, not tied to Perses' specific circumstances, and it overlooks the dynamics of Perses' education. In the course of the poem, Hesiod has stated and presumably won over his feckless brother to his doctrine of justice and labor. Yet right at the beginning, Hesiod had promised to tell ἐτήτυμα to Perses, the way things really are. Throughout his work, Hesiod has given subtle indications of these realities, but the role of chance in human life – or is it the gods? – increases toward the end of the poem.[48] Perses, I submit, is incapable of absorbing such ἐτήτυμα and still practicing hard work and justice. At best, he can assimilate Hesiod's explicit counsel and become, if not an ἐσθλός, at least a decent member of the human community. The

---

[47] Cf. e.g. Calame (1996) 181.

[48] Cf. Benardete (1967) 166; and Gagarin (1990) 177–78 and 181: "The surface message is essentially the 'ethical' lesson, 'follow certain rules and you will achieve prosperity'; but the sub-text is a new, more complex lesson of ambiguity and arbitrariness."

deeper truths – that the practice of justice may not always be rewarded and that even hard work may come to naught – are reserved not for Perses, but for Hesiod's ideal addressee, ὁ πανάριστος, like Hesiod, "the man who can think for himself and sees how things will turn out in the end".[49]

If the poem's first peak asserted Hesiod's authority to speak, its second peak occurs in the "autobiographical" discursus where Hesiod describes his poetic victory at Chalcis and the dedication of his prize tripod to the Muses of Helicon (654–59). The reference to the Heliconian Muses links this passage closely to the proem of the *Theogony*, where Hesiod first encountered his patron goddesses. It suggests further that his prize-winning composition was none other than the *Theogony* itself.[50] From those heights, a precipitous descent to the depiction of human vulnerability at the poem's close.

The progressive darkening of vision becomes even more evident if one compares the two gnomic passages that flank the calendars (327–80, 706–64). Some of the *gnomai* in the latter section actually contradict the advice given earlier; in one case, neighbors are better than relatives (345); and neither a friend nor a brother is to be trusted (370–71); later on, however, we are instructed not to treat a friend as an equal to a brother (707). Blood has become thicker. While the principles of reciprocity and even generosity in human interactions dominated the earlier series,[51] the latter is characterized by a kind of negative reciprocity and avoidance, finally culminating in the emergence of Gossip as a powerful quasi-divine force in human life (761–64). Moreover, in the earlier set of prohibitions against abusing guests, parents and orphans, Hesiod warns of strict retribution from Zeus for specific unjust deeds that can be avoided (333–34), but the second group concentrates on various religious taboos and superstitions involving natural physical functions whose infraction incurs vague and nameless punitive measures (724–56). At the same time, the focus narrows even further to the human body, now truly viewed as a mere belly producing waste products and defilement. Here Hesiod describes a world filled with nameless dread; the human body has become a veritable cesspool of pollution, and the most one can hope for is the avoidance of defilement and disaster in the face of mysterious and hostile forces beyond man's control or comprehension.

From the yearly cycle of the seasons with their appropriate signs and labors, Hesiod proceeds to the more limited and less predictable compass of

---

[49] Translation by Athanassakis (1983) 74.
[50] Cf. Wade-Gery (1949) 87.   [51] Cf. Millett (1984) 96–103.

the month with the catalogue of the Days.[52] He thus documents a decrease in human certainty and a corresponding increase in the precariousness of human existence. The overall trajectory of his argument can already be traced: an ascent (the argument for Dike) culminating in Hesiod's self-representation as the *panaristos*, followed by a gradual descent (the argument for work), interrupted by a second peak (Hesiod at Chalcis) before the final and definitive decline.

The massive differences between the *Theogony* and the *Works and Days*, both in their structure and their content, should be clear from the preceding synopsis, which has attempted to lay bare the organizing principles of the two compositions. Their contrasting dynamics, that is, the linear movement of each work, constitutes perhaps the most striking result of our analysis. The *Theogony* presents a positive progression of generations leading to the establishment of Zeus's eternal rule and a stabilized cosmos. The *Works and Days*, however, involves more complex modulations. Its progressive constriction reveals itself temporally in the movement from the defining epochs of human history, in the myths of Prometheus and the races of mankind, to the cycle of the year and the days of the month.[53] Spatially too there is a narrowing of horizons from the city to the *oikos* to the human body viewed from its lowliest physiological needs, which brings the work to a close on a far more pessimistic note. Thus the orientation of the two poems suggests the existence of irresolvable tensions between the divine and the human cosmos, which the next chapters will seek to elucidate.

---

[52] The authenticity of 724–64 as well as of the following "Days" has been denied by many scholars, most influentially by Wilamowitz, whose edition (1928) ends at line 760; cf. also Fränkel (1962) 124, 143–44; and Solmsen (1963), for whom "the 'Days' are best thought of as a wild growth, proliferating without control and direction and reflecting the equally uncontrolled wildfire spread of superstition" (314); also Samuel (1966). West (1978) sets out the problems in this section, but defends its genuineness, as does Schwabl (1970) 468–70, who notes: "Die Athetese der Reinheitsvorschriften und Tage beruht bislang m.E. auf . . . dem Versuch, die hesiodische Deisidaimonie in eine ethisch bedeutende (und daher akzeptable) in eine abergläubisch-kleinlich (und daher für ihn unwahrscheinliche) Komponente zu zerlegen." But even if one confronts the underlying prejudices, the function of these passages within the poem requires interpretation. Pellizer (1975) argues for the unity of the "Days", while Lardinois (1998) shows convincingly that the "Days" cohere closely with themes and motifs found elsewhere in the poem.

[53] Cf. Leclerc (1994).

CHAPTER 3

Overtures

THEOGONY

τοὺς θεοὺς αὐτούς . . . ἐρομένου τοῦ Διός, εἴ του δέοιντο, αἰτῆσαι
<τὸ πᾶν ἄρτι κοσμήσαντα> ποιήσασθαί τινας αὐτῷ θεούς οἵτινες
τὰ μεγάλα ταῦτ' ἔργα καὶ πᾶσάν γε τὴν ἐκείνου κατασκευὴν
[κατα]κοσμήσουσι λόγοις καὶ μουσικῇ.

When Zeus had newly completed the arrangement (κοσμήσαντα) of
the universe, he asked the gods if anything was lacking; and they in
turn asked him to make for himself some divinities who could adorn
(κοσμήσουσι) with words and music his great works and the whole
of his arrangement.

Pindar, fr. 31 (Snell–Maehler)

The Bible begins, *Berayshit*; the Gospel of John, ἐν ἀρχῇ ἦν ὁ λόγος; the
Enuma Elish, "When on high . . ." These accounts of beginnings just begin; they do not account for themselves, nor explain the source of their
accounts. How can we know these first beginnings before there was anything, certainly, before there were human beings to record them? In these
texts, the question is never posed. The early Greeks, however, fretted about
it and insisted on accounting for the source of their knowledge of first
beginnings. Thus for example, Parmenides recounts his journey to a goddess who reveals to him the nature of the cosmos. Empedocles identifies
himself as a fallen god who thus has access to the origins and workings of
the cosmos. Hesiod, too, who offers us the first systematic account of the
genesis of the cosmos and its evolution to its present state, likewise prefaces
that account with a lengthy prologue of 115 lines that authorizes his ability
to speak on such matters, matters well beyond ordinary human ken. That
prelude to cosmogony self-consciously raises the epistemological question
of how to begin an account of beginnings.

A Greek proverb declares, ἀρχὴ ἥμισυ παντός: the beginning is half of
the whole. The *Theogony* is a poem of beginnings, of *archai*, the principles

49

of the world and the origins of those principles. According to Aristotle,
Greek archaic thought, that is, Pre-Socratic philosophy, consisted of speculation on principles, on the origins of things.[1] From this perspective, one
would have to include the poet Hesiod in the company of the Pre-Socratic
philosophers since he too seems obsessed with the question of beginnings.
Or, perhaps more accurately, one could consider Pre-Socratic thought as
both a continuation and a response to the issues raised by Hesiod concerning the origins of the gods and the cosmos.[2]

Let us begin, then, methodically, from the beginning:

Μουσάων Ἑλικωνιάδων ἀρχώμεθ' ἀείδειν.

Let us begin to sing from the Heliconian Muses.

(1)

The opening of the *Theogony* has often been called a "Hymn to the Muses,"
and, in fact, as Friedländer, Minton, and others have observed,[3] its structure closely resembles Greek hymns, especially, the collection known as the
Homeric Hymns. Some of these common features include the immediate
naming of the divinity to be celebrated, followed by a relative clause characterizing the god, a description of the epiphany of the divinity, his gifts to
mankind, his characteristic functions and activities, and often an account
of his birth.

But upon further reflection, the first line of the *Theogony* turns out to be
less typical than it might first appear. Unlike those Homeric Hymns that use
the first person singular of the present tense of ἄρχομαι ("I begin"),[4] Hesiod
employs the first person plural subjunctive, ἀρχώμεθα, "let us begin." This
form is not simply the equivalent of "let me begin" or "I would begin";[5]

---

[1] Aristotle, *Metaphysics* A *passim*. This interest in origins can be traced even farther back to Homer,
who habitually describes objects not so much in terms of their finished form as through their genesis
or making (e.g. Agamemnon's scepter, Pandarus' bow, Achilles' shield, Odysseus' bed). For ἀρχή as
meaning not just "beginning," but "from the beginning and continuing until the present," hence
"origin" and "principle," see Classen (1996).

[2] For Hesiod's influence on individual Pre-Socratics, see, for instance, Diller (1946); Stokes (1962) 1–37;
Heitsch (1966b); and Hölscher (1968).

[3] Friedländer (1914); van Groningen (1958) 258–60; Büchner (1968); Minton (1970); Lenz (1980) 127–81;
Janko (1981) 20–22; and Thalmann (1984) 134–39. The overly schematic interpretations of Walcot
(1957); Bradley (1966); and Schwabl (1963) do not give due weight to the dynamics of the proem. For
Verdenius (1972), association of ideas without a fixed scheme characterizes the proem. Of the many
discussions of the form and structure of the proem, I find Thalmann's (134–52) most congenial. See
also Clay (1988).

[4] *Homeric Hymns* 2, 11, 13, 16, 26, 28; with a slight variant, 22. Cf. Hymn 25, which contains lines 94–97
of the *Theogony* and begins Μουσάων ἄρχωμαι.

[5] As West (1966) 152; Verdenius (1972) 226; and Podbielski (1994) 175 claim. Cf. Kambylis (1965) 46:
"Am Anfang seines Gedichtes . . . ruft er sich selbst eine Aufforderung zu." Cf. p. 35. But see Schwyzer

rather, it implies the presence not only of the speaker but also of another, or others, who are invited or exhorted to share in the action. But who are these others? In choral poetry, the hortatory form is typical and readily comprehensible since the chorus in some sense represents and co-involves the community that makes up the audience.[6] Homer, however, uses the plural "we" to refer to himself on only two occasions, and, interestingly enough, both contexts involve the Muses. In the tenth line of the *Odyssey*, the poet concludes his invocation by asking the Muse to begin her tale and includes himself in the poem's audience:

> τῶν ἁμόθεν γε θεά, θύγατερ Διός, εἰπὲ καὶ ἡμῖν.

> Of these things, from some point at least, goddess,
> daughter of Zeus, tell us too.

In the *Iliad* before launching into the daunting task of enumerating the Greek forces, the poet enlists the help of the Muses:

> ὑμεῖς γὰρ θεαί ἐστε, πάρεστέ τε, ἴστέ τε πάντα,
> ἡμεῖς δὲ κλέος οἶον ἀκούομεν οὐδέ τι ἴδμεν . . .

> You are goddesses, are present, and know all things;
> But we hear only rumor and know nothing . . .
> (*Il.* 2.485–86)

Here, Homer's "we" refers to the ignorance he shares with all human beings that are not privy to the Muses' knowledge. In both cases, the Homeric "we" stands in opposition to a clearly defined "you," the Muse or the Muses. The first verse of the *Theogony*, however, does not fit this pattern.[7] As he begins his song, Hesiod neither identifies himself with his audience nor with mankind in general; nor does he appear to create an opposition between himself and the Muses.[8] Rather, he *includes* the Muses in his exhortation.[9] From the beginning, then, the poet considers his song a

---

(1950) 2: 315; and Goodwin (1889) 88. *Iliad* 22.392–93, often cited as an exception, in fact proves the rule. For after urging the Greeks to sing a paean and bring the slaughtered Hector back to the ships, Achilles, perhaps uncharacteristically, shares the glory of the triumph with all the Greeks.

[6] For the differing patterns of enunciation in epic and lyric poetry, see Calame (1995a) 27–57.

[7] As Wackernagel (1981) 1, 100 maintains.

[8] Maehler (1963) 43 argues that τύνη and ἀρχώμεθα at *Theogony* 36 are addressed to Hesiod's audience: "Durch das direkte 'Du' und den Plural der Aufforderung durchbricht er [Hesiod] die epische Anonymität auch in der Richtung auf den Hörer hin. . . . Damit tut Hesiod einen entscheidenden Schritt vom Epos fort zur Lyrik." Cf. Sellschopp (1934) 45–46; and Lenz (1980) 141, n. 1. The evolutionary scheme that positions Hesiod between Epic and Lyric lurks beneath such interpretations. Schadewaldt (1926) 201 takes τύνη as Hesiod's self-exhortation. Similarly, Theraios (1974) 136 calls it a "Mahnung des Dichters an sich selbst."

[9] Cf. *Epigoni* fr. 1 (Bernabé): Νῦν αὖθ' ὁπλοτέρων ἀνδρῶν ἀρχώμεθα, Μοῦσαι; and Theocritus 17.1: ἐκ Διὸς ἀρχώμεσθα καὶ ἐς Δία λήγετε Μοῖσαι; but see also the opening of Aratus, *Phaenomena*,

collaborative production; it is not simply his alone, but, insofar as his is an inspired voice, it is joined with, and indissociable from, the voice of the Muses. In the sequel, Hesiod will describe the genesis of his collaboration with the Muses, when he narrates his encounter with the goddesses and his *Dichterweihe*.

I may seem to have made fairly heavy going of what may appear to be a minor grammatical detail, but it is germane to Hesiod's central endeavor in the *Theogony*: to describe the beginnings of things from their first beginnings. Yet the *Theogony* itself cannot begin with the beginning, since it presupposes an earlier beginning, i.e. Hesiod's initiation into the art of poetry by the Muses, who on the occasion of that first encounter commanded Hesiod always to begin with them:[10]

> τόνδε δέ με πρώτιστα θεαὶ πρὸς μῦθον ἔειπον.
>
> On that first occasion, the goddesses addressed me – the
> very one here.   (24)

The first verse of the *Theogony* proper describes what came into being "first of all," πρώτιστα (116). At the conclusion of the proem, when Hesiod invokes the Muses to sing for him the song of beginnings, he uses the words "begin(ning)" or "first" five times; similar terms likewise occur at the beginning of the proem to describe his initiation.[11] The "first of all" of Hesiod's poetic initiation precedes and presupposes the "first of all" from which Hesiod insists the Muses begin their theogonic account. It is hardly surprising that Hesiod, who sets himself the task of describing the origins of the cosmos, should reflect on the problem of origins, more particularly on the origins of his own divinely inspired ability to enunciate them. The proem of the song of beginnings, thus even as it makes its beginning, attempts to give an account of its own beginning. The results of these reflections surface in the peculiar but nevertheless logical structure of the proem, a structure which in fact contains three beginnings: first, the account of the origins of Hesiod's poetic skill (1–35);[12] second, the

---

where the plural "we" refers to the speaker and mankind in general. Calame (1995a) 46 and 63–67 rightly speaks of "a doubling of the *I*" in line 36; but in line 1 Calame believes the "we" is "probably associated" with the public (p. 73). However, Calame (1995b) 18 speaks of "un *nous* englobant." This ducks the question of when the collaboration of Hesiod and his Muses begins – or began.

[10] Cf. Brague (1990).

[11] ἀρχώμεθα (1, 36); πρώτιστα (24, 116); πρῶτον (34, 115); τὰ πρῶτα (108, 113); ἐξ ἀρχῆς (105).

[12] The meaning of line 35, which breaks off the narration of Hesiod's meeting with the goddesses, has long been subject to debate. See West (1966) 167–69. The Scholiasts gloss the phrase as ἀρχαιολογεῖν; *Odyssey* 19.163 gives παλαίφατος as an epithet for an oak tree. Nagy (1990) takes Hesiod's proverbial oak and rock to refer to "ancient myths of anthropogony" (182), and paraphrases the line

fulfillment of the Muses' command always to begin to sing from them (36–103); and finally, the invocation which introduces the *Theogony* proper (104–15). While resembling the formal elements of a hymn, Hesiod's proem actually obeys an inner logic of its own that draws self-conscious attention to the problematic character of his undertaking as a prelude to cosmogony.

Hesiod's opening line reveals yet another grammatical anomaly. When the formulaic phrase ἄρχομαι ἀείδειν occurs in the Homeric Hymns, it is always followed by the name of the divinity in the accusative, that is, as the object of the verb "to sing." The scholiast had it right when he paraphrased: ἀπὸ τῶν Μουσῶν ἀρχὴν ποιούμεθα τοῦ λέγειν.[13] Hesiod does not simply propose to sing the Muses; rather, he undertakes to begin to sing *from* the Muses.[14] The distinction may seem trivial, but it is not, for two reasons: first, to my mind it settles the old issue of the proem's organic link to the *Theogony* and disproves the view of those critics from antiquity to the present who considered this "hymn to the Muses" to be tacked on to the *Theogony* proper;[15] second, it reveals that the Muses constitute the appropriate or even necessary starting-point for Hesiod's song, but that they are not its object. It is only via the mediation of the Muses that Hesiod can sing his *Theogony*. But, as we shall see, the proem that describes the path of that mediation requires us to take considerable detours before reaching its goal.

Attempts to describe the plan of the proem are often overly schematic, offering a static architectural model dominated by the notion of ring-composition. Others find an absence of plan, but rather a movement based

as "the equivalent of asking why he has lingered at the beginning of beginnings" (199). The phrase would then appropriately draw attention to primal origins: this time, to the problematic origins of Hesiod's song. For other recent interpretations, see Hoffmann (1971); Schmoll (1994); and O'Bryhim (1996). West (1966) insists that "περί with the accusative in early epic always has a local sense so that the phrase is not simply 'about', i.e. concerning, tree and rock, but 'round'." But cf. *Iliad* 3.408: περὶ κεῖνον ὀΐζυε; and the phrases περὶ δόρπα . . . πονέοντο (*Iliad* 24.444) and περὶ δεῖπνον . . . πένοντο (*Odyssey* 4.624 and 24.412). The Hesiodic expression may in fact contain an ellipsis of πενέσθαι, "to busy oneself with," "engage oneself about." A possible translation of the general sense: "to beat around the bush."

[13] Scholia to line 1 (Di Gregorio): "We make the beginning of our speech from the Muses."

[14] Cf. the genitives in line 36 and *H. Hom.* 25.1, which appears to be an abbreviated version of the Hesiodic proem. However, the genitive plus ἄρχομαι is common at the *ends* of the Homeric Hymns in the transitional formula σεῦ . . . ἀρξάμενος or, more explicitly, ἐκ σέο δ' ἀρξάμενος (*H.H.* 5, 9, 18, 31, and 32). Cf. Apollonius Rhodius, *Argonautica* 1.1. But the clearest example of the distinction between the genitive and the accusative comes from Theocritus 22 (*Dioscouri*) 25–26: Κάστορος ἢ πρώτου Πολυδεύκεος ἄρξομ' ἀείδειν; | ἀμφοτέρους ὑμνέων Πολυδεύκεα πρῶτον ἀείσω. Cf. van Groningen (1958) 256: "le premier vers . . . prouve déjà que le poète considère ses louanges des Muses comme un début, ἀρχή, un prélude à une matière différente."

[15] Cf. West (1966) 150 for details of the controversy. Lamberton (1988) 45–48 believes that the proem was added in the Hellenistic period.

on the association of ideas. The first approach neglects the dynamics and
linear progress of performance, while the second attributes an "archaic"
mindset to Hesiod and the lack of overall organizing principles. Yet, within
the proem itself, Hesiod seems to provide us with meaningful categories
of space and time that shape the progress of the proem in an intelligible
fashion.

Let us begin, then, on Helicon, where the Muses dance and sing in
their secret rites, secret because up there on the "god-haunted" (ζάθεον)
summit no one – or at least no human being – can observe them. Hesiod's
uncertainty concerning the bathing-places of the Muses seems to indicate
as much: they wash themselves either at Permessus or at Hippocrene or at
Olme (5–6).[16] ἀκροτάτῳ Ἑλικῶνι, on the summits of Helicon, they dance,
or rather, they circle around a spring or the altar of Zeus. But, suddenly,
their movements change: forming a line, they begin to march, στεῖχον.
From the peaks of Helicon, they marched, or rather were marching in the
imperfect (10). This imperfect does not appear to fit into the usual rules
of Greek grammar,[17] but it expresses temporally what has already been
expressed spatially through the Muses' descent from the sacred locales of
the gods to the habitations of mortals. In effect, the imperfect στεῖχον
conveys precisely and vividly the moment of transition from the eternal
time of the gods to the temporality of mankind.

Descending from Helicon at night, the Muses sing; only their voices
betray their presence. In nocturnal darkness, shrouded in mist, that is,
invisible, they sing of the gods (11–21). This first catalogue of nineteen divinities has been called a table of contents in reverse order to the *Theogony*.[18]
A closer look, however, quickly reveals that the principles of organization
differ from Hesiod's;[19] in fact, the catalogue presents several peculiarities
and obscurities.[20] The priority of Zeus does not surprise, nor that of his
consort/sister Hera, although it is noticeable that she is not specifically

---

[16] Marg (1970) 87 claims that "die drei Stellen sind weit voneinander entfernt," which Hesiod's audience
would of course know, and would emphasize Hesiod's ignorance of the Muses' exact location. This
list of alternatives is not quite parallel to the common cataloguing of a god's favorite haunts, for
instance *H. Dem.* 490–91 and *H. Ap.* 141–45.

[17] Cf. West (1966) 156 and Verdenius (1972) 229, who seems to believe that the Muses are headed
for Olympus; cf. *H. Ap.* 5 and Clay (1989) 23–29. The discussion of Kambylis (1965) 50–53 is not
convincing.

[18] By, for example, Aly (1913a) 54, n. 1: "eine Inhaltsangabe der Theogonie in umgekehrter Reihenfolge."
Cf. von Fritz (1956) 301; Kirk (1960) 84–85; and Büchner (1968) 21.

[19] Hamilton (1989) 12 calls it "chaotic" and "probably meant to be chaotic." Snell (1975) 55 suggests
that the order is not genealogical but based on status.

[20] Some of these are enumerated by Schlesier (1982) 152–53. Cf. Clay (1989) 325–27 and Rudhardt (1996)
33–34.

designated as such. While Athena's relationship to Zeus is explicitly stated (κούρην . . . Διός, 13), that of Apollo and Artemis is not. With Themis we appear to move from Zeus's offspring and contemporaries to an earlier generation of gods, but the mention of Aphrodite seems out of place; Dione's presence in the following verse invites us to suppose that this Aphrodite is the daughter of Zeus of the Homeric tradition,[21] as does the proximity of Hebe, his daughter by Hera. After Leto, however, some semblance of order seems to reassert itself: two Titans are followed by the most prominent meteorological figures, Sun and Moon, and then by what West calls "elemental divinities":[22] Earth, Ocean, and Night.

A comparison of the song of the Heliconian Muses with Hesiod's own reveals a number of striking differences. First and most obviously, the list in lines 11–21 generally proceeds backwards from the Olympians to earlier deities, whereas Hesiod's theogony begins ἐξ ἀρχῆς. Furthermore, except in the case of Athena, relations between the named divinities are not clarified. Any simple chronological scheme seems to be jettisoned in the catalogue's middle section, nor does any other clear principle of ordering emerge. Moreover, Aphrodite's implied genealogy contradicts the one Hesiod gives in his subsequent theogony (188–200); Dione, her mother in Homer, does reappear later (353) but merely as one of the Oceanids. Also, the celestial bodies occupy a more conspicuous position here than in Hesiod's later account; and the primacy of Night, found also in so-called Orphic theogonies, seems here to be a feature of traditional or perhaps even competing theogonies.[23] Finally, line 21 makes clear that this enumeration of the gods remains incomplete, while Hesiod at least suggests that his will be exhaustive.

Another significant point of contrast is perhaps less evident at first glance. In Hesiod's own account of the gods, he appears to avoid local cult epithets. The apparent exception, Aphrodite, proves the rule; for Hesiod goes out of his way to derive her epithets, "Cyprian" and "Cytherean," from the circumstances of her birth rather than from any specific and local cultic associations.[24] In general, the epithets used here by the Muses of Helicon to describe the gods seem fairly conventional. But one stands out, not only because it occurs only here in the Hesiodic corpus, but also because it differs in kind from the other divine epithets: Ἥρην Ἀργείην.[25] Hera is

[21] The Scholia ad loc. emphasize that this Dione cannot be Aphrodite's mother.
[22] West (1966) 156.   [23] See Ramnoux (1986) 177–230.   [24] Cf. Nagy (1990) 46.
[25] Judet de la Combe (1993) 29–30 believes the catalogue represents "the theological universe of the *Iliad*" (29). But Hera is called Argive only twice in Homer (*Iliad* 4.8 and 5.908). The epithet is far more commonly used of Helen.

appropriately called Argive because one of her oldest and most important shrines was located in Argos. The Heliconian Muses, themselves localized divinities, preserve traces of localized cult in their song, whereas Hesiod's song, inspired by the Muses of Olympus, is consciously Panhellenic.[26]

To summarize, the catalogue contained in the nocturnal song that accompanies the Muses' descent from Helicon appears neither strictly speaking chronological nor does it follow a clearly articulated genealogical scheme. Moreover, it does not take its start from the first gods, ἐξ ἀρχῆς, as Hesiod will in his theogony, but begins instead from Zeus and the Olympians, the present generation of gods, i.e. those most apparent and closest to us, and then proceeds backward to earlier deities, but their interrelationships are left oddly obscure. Finally, it is local and incomplete while Hesiod's theogony appears to be Panhellenic and comprehensive.[27]

Accompanying the Muses' descent from Helicon, this first catalogue takes as its point of departure what is closest to us, *to proton pros hemas*, as Aristotle would say. In the *Nicomachean Ethics*, Aristotle distinguishes two kinds of argumentation when he says: "one must not forget that arguments (*logoi*) proceed either *from* first principles or *toward* first principles"; and he then goes on to explain: "there are in fact two kinds of principles: those that are known to us, and those which are principles simply."[28] The Heliconian song of the Muses belongs to the first category.[29] In addition, its beginning from the *hic et nunc*, its incompleteness and genealogical obscurities, and the absence of any clear principles of ordering, represent what later thinkers would call *doxa*, possibly even *ortha doxa*: neither completely true nor completely false, yet perhaps a necessary preliminary for arriving at a more complete and accurate account.[30]

Making their way down the holy mountain, the Muses have arrived at the habitations of men, Ἑλικῶνος ὕπο ζαθέοιο (23) – or rather, at the limit of the world of men, *ta eschata*, the high pastures where notoriously gods and human beings may encounter each other. Simultaneously, we enter human time with the temporal aorist (αἵ νύ ποθ'. . . ἐδίδασκαν, 22); and

---

[26] Nagy (1990) 57–59.

[27] Hesiod draws attention to both of these characteristics of his theogony when he apologizes for not enumerating all the rivers: τῶν ὄνομ' ἀργαλέον πάντων βροτὸν ἄνδρα ἐνισπεῖν, | οἱ δὲ ἕκαστοι ἴσασιν, ὅσοι περιναιετάουσι ("To enumerate their names would be difficult for a mortal man, but each of those men who lives nearby knows them," 369–70).

[28] *Nicomachean Ethics* 1095b.

[29] This may explain the prominence of Dawn, Sun, and Moon in the often athetized line 19 (omitted from one papyrus and one MS and placed before 18 or 15 in others), a prominence which contrasts with their minor role in the *Theogony* (and in Greek religion generally). For human beings, at least, they are the most conspicuous of the heavenly phenomena.

[30] Cf. Arrighetti (1998) 311–12; and Leclerc (1993) 198–202, who detects a contrast between the nocturnal Muses of lines 1–21 and the "luminous" Muses of the rest of the proem.

it is an individual with a name, Hesiod,[31] who is the recipient of the goddesses' instruction. With the deictic τόνδε, Hesiod signals that we have
arrived *here*, at the known world, the world of men.[32] Moreover, the voice
that has been describing the Muses' nocturnal activities and their descent
from the holy mountain and to whom they entrusted their art turns out
to belong to none other than the speaker before us at the present moment.
In this "most explicit self-presentation of any narrator in all of Greek literature",[33] Hesiod links the present moment of performance to both the
near past of his poetic initiation and the mythical past of cosmogony. In
fact, the presentation of the remote past when the cosmos took on its
present and final form is only available to us here and now through the
mediation of that critical moment of Hesiod's personal encounter with his
goddesses.

The position of τόνδε in line 24 suggests that it modifies με,[34] but, strictly
speaking, it could also go with μῦθον; and because of the double function
of ὅδε, both deictic and cataphoric, τόνδε μῦθον can refer simultaneously
to the specific words of the Muses that follow (26–28) as well as to the poem
as a whole – including this primal scene of initiation. Again we are faced
with the *aporia*: when did Hesiod's collaboration with his patron goddesses
begin?[35]

In the meantime, the change in the Muses' name and address – from
Heliconian to Olympian – underlines the movement from a localized,
epichoric, perspective to a Panhellenic one.[36] This movement reinforces a
parallel progression from the limitations of human vision to the Olympian
perspective of the gods. At any rate, the epithet "Olympian" emphasizes
the unbridgeable distance between mortal beings and the immortal gods at
the very moment the Muses address Hesiod. Their first words, both brutal
and condescending, reveal the distance that separates immortal goddesses
from the shepherd Hesiod and his ilk, "mere bellies," who can scarcely be
distinguished from the sheep they graze.[37]

---

[31] On Hesiod's name, see Introduction, n. 6.
[32] Cf. the Scholium at line 23: αἱ Μοῦσαι <ἐν> ἀκροτάτῳ Ἑλικῶνι ὡς θεαί, αὐτὸς δ᾽ ὑποκάτω τοῦ ὄρους ὡς βροτός.
[33] Bakker (1999) 10. Bakker goes on to point out that "[w]hat Hesiod talks about, the reign of Zeus, the honors of the gods, or the agricultural calendar, is an important part of everyday reality" (10–11).
[34] Cf. Verdenius (1972) 233, n. 2.
[35] Rudhardt (1996) 28–29 indirectly puts his finger on the problem: "En se nommant, il ne désigne pas en lui un poète fameux – il n'est pas encore." But could the preceding lines have been sung by one uninitiated?
[36] Nagy (1990) 58: "the local goddesses of Helikon are assimilated into the pan-Hellenic goddesses of Olympus." Cf. Latte (1946b).
[37] The plural, I take it, is contemptuous and simultaneously characterizes the general brutishness of humans. Cf. *H. Dem.* 256–57.

The cryptic words that follow have provoked floods of controversy:

ἴδμεν ψεύδεα πολλὰ λέγειν ἐτύμοισιν ὁμοῖα,
ἴδμεν δ' εὖτ' ἐθέλωμεν ἀληθέα γηρύσασθαι.

We know how to compose many lies indistinguishable from
    things that are real;
And we know, when we wish, to pronounce things that are
    true.   (27–28)

Commentators have traditionally interpreted these enigmatic lines as Hesiod's proclamation of the truth of his song as opposed to the songs of other poets who only pronounce *pseudea polla*. Accordingly, the Muses' declaration should be understood as a polemic directed at Homer or perhaps at heroic epic in general.[38] Svenbro views Hesiod's polemic in social terms as an attack on those poets who depend on their aristocratic patrons, as opposed to Hesiod himself, who prides himself on his autonomy.[39] According to Nagy, on the other hand, Hesiod's targets are the poets who perform theogonies of only local interest, whereas his own is Panhellenic in its scope.[40] Recently, Arrighetti has proposed another interpretation of the Muses' mysterious statement: the object of Hesiod's polemics is not Homer, but his character, Odysseus, or indeed anyone like him, who may possess the ability to persuade and even enchant his audience, but who has not received from the Muses the gift of truthful song.[41]

To offer an exhaustive doxography of the Muses' enigmatic statement would lead too far afield.[42] Nevertheless, the importance of these verses for any reading of the *Theogony* requires us to grapple with their implications. But before doing so, I would draw attention to the hidden, even unconscious, prejudices that have influenced many commentators: Hesiod must be convinced of the absolute truth of his message and therefore his reference to "lies like the truth" must refer to something outside his own text.[43] The need for discovering an external object for Hesiod's supposed polemic

---

[38] Cf. Puelma (1989) 75.

[39] Svenbro (1976) 46–73. For a critique of Svenbro, see Judet de la Combe (1993) 26–28.

[40] Nagy (1990) 45. Neitzel (1980) believes lines 27 and 28 refer to other poets who composed competing but inferior accounts of the gods. Otto (1952) 51–52, while regarding the lines as Hesiod's claim for the veracity of his song, detects in the *pseudea polla* not polemic, but the "Bezauberung durch die lebensvollen Bilder der Phantasie" which are also part of the Muses' domain.

[41] Arrighetti (1996) 53–60.

[42] For a summary of views, see Svenbro (1976) 46–49; Stroh (1976) 90–97; and Neitzel (1980).

[43] Cf. Arrighetti (1996) 54, whom I cite, not in a polemical spirit, but because he expresses clearly the problem that every critic must confront: "If we do not establish a precise reference, *outside of Hesiod's work*, for *Theogony* 27, we must then accept as a fundamental presupposition for any interpretation of his work that it is impossible for him to escape from a condition of uncertainty between falsehood and truth, since the Muses can inspire the one as well as the other. This would

arises from the conviction that Hesiod could not possibly cast doubt on the veracity of his own poem. Even those scholars who recognize the ambiguity inherent in the Muses' declaration, at the last minute side-step the consequences of their interpretations. Thus Heitsch first allows that "the gift of the Muses was not unambiguous; the Muses endow the poet's activity with truth, but also deception, which as such cannot be detected by human beings – nor indeed by the poet himself." But Heitsch later retreats by claiming: "Hesiod is only certain of the truth of his own inspiration because the Muses explicitly reassure him that they speak the truth to him as opposed to other rhapsodes."[44] Such reassurances, however, are nowhere to be found in our text. Even Pucci, who thoughtfully analyzes the ambiguity of the Muses' declaration, finally rejects the inevitable conclusions of his own analysis by attributing a naiveté to Hesiod that permits the poet to exempt his own discourse from the intrinsic doubleness of the Muses' *logos*.[45] It is time, I think, to discard the antiquated notion of Hesiod's primitive simplicity and to accept the possibility that he may be fully aware of the implications of his own words.

To return to our passage: we must first acknowledge what the Muses do not say. It is precisely the absence of a polemical tone in their declaration that is striking – especially since Hesiod elsewhere alludes to the possibility of a *Dichterstreit* (cf. *Works and Days* 26), and has ample opportunity in the sequel to suggest a distinction between truthful and lying poets when he describes the Muses' gifts to mankind (94–103).[46] In addressing Hesiod, however, the Muses do not designate the object of their polemics. One

be a perfectly legitimate position if *in Hesiod as a whole*, i.e. from the first verse of the *Theogony* to the last verse of the *Works and Days*, *a clear and certain conscience of knowing the truth did not manifest itself* . . . (Italics and translation mine.) Cf. Leclerc (1993) 71: "Il serait en effet paradoxale de supposer qu'au moment même de son initiation, le poète prête aux Muses qui le légitiment une intention aussi manifestement contraire aux prétentions véridique qu' il affiche." To refuse to accept the paradoxical character of the text will not make it go away; better to confront it and live with the consequences.

44 Heitsch (1966b) 199 and 233 (translation mine).

45 Pucci (1977) 1: "Hesiod, however, is convinced that such a dangerous *logos* is administered by the Muses to other poets, not to himself."

46 There, Hesiod explicitly mentions epic poetry as one facet of the Muses' gift to mankind, thereby precluding Homer or epic as the object of any polemic. Stroh (1976) 85–112 effectively refutes the traditional polemical interpretations of line 27; poetry contains plausible lies as well as truth. But according to Stroh, Hesiod's claim on behalf of his own plausibility is very limited in scope, for instance in his assertion that Cronus swallowed rather than ate his children (p. 108). Like many critics, Stroh ignores εὖτ' ἐθέλωμεν in line 28. Rudhardt (1996) 30 also thinks Hesiod does not condemn lying poets, but only that he enumerates two types of poetry "entre lesquels il [Hesiod] établit simplement une hiérarchie: le second est supérieur au premier." West (1966) also denies any generic opposition, but paraphrases: "'Admittedly, we sometimes deceive; but when we choose, we can reveal the truth, and we are going to reveal it to you.'" The last clause is not in the Greek.

might wonder at a polemic that shies away from naming its target. And, finally, the goddesses do not say that they will entrust the truth to Hesiod, which would have been easy enough to do in a brief line. But if the Muses' words do not have a polemical tenor, they nevertheless insist on the contrast between the brutishness of mortals and their own divine superiority. It would seem that the Muses simultaneously lay claim to, and boast of, their peculiar expertise that manifests itself in two kinds of speech. Their repeated ἴδμεν ("we know") most closely resembles the boast of the Sirens to Odysseus:

> ἴδμεν γάρ τοι πάνθ' ὅσ' ἐνὶ Τροίῃ εὐρείῃ
> Ἀργεῖοι Τρῶές τε θεῶν ἰότητι μόγησαν·
> ἴδμεν δ' ὅσσα γένηται ἐπὶ χθονὶ πουλυβοτείρῃ.

> We know all that the Argives and Trojans
> Suffered in wide Troy through the will of the gods;
> And we know whatever happens on the much-nourishing earth.
> (*Odyssey* 12.189–91)

But it also recalls Demeter's declaration of her skill as a (benign) sorceress (*H. Dem.* 229–30):

> οἶδα γὰρ ἀντίτομον μέγα φέρτερον ὑλοτόμοιο,
> οἶδα δ' ἐπηλυσίης πολυπήμονος ἐσθλὸν ἐρυσμόν.

> For I know an antidote much stronger than the woodcutter's spells,
> And I know an excellent shield against painful attack.

Here, as in the Muses' words, the incantatory repetitions appear additive rather than contrastive: what is emphasized is the assertion of expert knowledge in two kinds of speech. The Muses first claim their expertise in composing[47] many falsehoods that are similar or equal to real things. ὁμοῖα embraces both the sense of "identical" and that of "similar"; to preserve its range of meaning, it should here be rendered as "indistinguishable," the vanishing point between identity and similarity.

The difference between ἀληθέα and ἔτυμα, while often ignored, is crucial not only for this passage, but for Hesiod's entire undertaking.[48] *Aletheia* exists in speech, whereas *et(et)uma* can inhere in things;[49] a complete and accurate account of what one has witnessed is *alethes*, while *etumos*, which

---

[47] Wakker (1990) 87, n. 8 points out that in early Greek epos "ist λέγω nicht ein wirkliches *verbum dicendi*: es hat immer die Nuance 'Reihe von Tatsachen erzählen die in sich zusammenhängen.'" See also Krischer (1971) 151–58, who defines λέγειν as both "to collect" and "to select" and notes that λέγειν is more closely allied to the sphere of lies, whereas καταλέγειν is used in relation to the truth.

[48] At *Works and Days* 10, Hesiod claims to speak ἐτήτυμα to Perses. See below.

[49] Note *Odyssey* 3.241, where ἐτήτυμος is used of νόστος.

perhaps derives from εἶναι ("to be"), defines something that is real, gen-uine, or corresponds to the real state of affairs. A passage in the *Odyssey* offers a useful example of the distinction (*Od.* 19.535–69); even though the word *aletheia* is not explicitly present, it is surely implied. The disguised Odysseus and Penelope have been conversing with increasing intimacy late into the night. Suddenly, Penelope asks the charming stranger to interpret her disturbing dream in which an eagle swoops down and kills her favorite geese. The eagle then announces himself as her husband Odysseus who will soon slaughter all the suitors. Odysseus responds that it is imposs-ible to interpret the dream by "bending it in some other direction" (ἄλλη ἀποκλίναντ') since the eagle-Odysseus himself has interpreted it. In other words, any interpretation Odysseus might give would be *alethes* if it did not deviate in any way from the eagle's; it would be accurate and hit the mark, so to speak. But this assertion is not enough for Penelope: what if the dream as a whole was deceptive? Did it come through the gates of ivory whence emerge the false dreams that will not be fulfilled or through the gates of horn that send forth dreams that really come true and are realized (ἔτυμα κραίνουσι). *Etuma* refer to things as they really are and hence cannot be distorted; *aletheia*, on the other hand, insofar as it is a full and truthful account, can be willfully or accidentally deformed through omissions, additions, or any other distortions. All such deformations are *pseudea.*

Aletheia, then, consists of "the truth, the whole truth, and nothing but the truth".[50] The legal terminology readily springs to mind, since *aletheia* involves a complete and veracious account of what one has witnessed. If the archaic Greek conception of *aletheia* has a far narrower range than our "truth," then the Greek *pseudos* has a wider range of meaning – to which the Muses' assertion of the multiplicity of lies (*pseudea polla*) draws attention – in comparison to our notion of falsehood.[51] *Pseudea* embrace not only consciously misleading statements intended to deceive, but also unwitting errors, omissions, and inaccuracies, as well as additions, embroideries, and

---

[50] Cf. Cole (1983) 12: "What is involved is strict (or strict and scrupulous) rendering or reporting – something as exclusive of bluster, invention or irrelevance as it is of omission or understatement." Also Krischer (1965) 167 for the distinction between ἀληθής and ἔτυμος relevant to the Hesiodic passage: "der Anwendungsbereich von ἀληθής ist im wesentlichen auf den Augenzeugenbericht beschränkt, also den Fall, in dem der Sprecher aus genauer Kenntnis spricht und nur darauf zu achten braucht, dass ihm kein Lapsus unterläuft; wird hingegen eine Aussage als ἔτυμος bezeichnet, so ist es ganz gleichgültig, woher der Sprecher seine Information hat: er mag Vermutungen angestellt haben, geträumt haben, er mag Wahrheiten in eine Lüge streuen, was zutrifft, ist ἔτυμος. Cf. Pratt (1993) 96 defines *aletheia* as "an accurate account of what really happened provided to a reliable reporter by honest eyewitnesses."

[51] Cf. Luther (1935) 80–90 for the wider range of Greek *pseudos*; also Levet (1976) 201–14.

even figurative speech. While the Muses would seem to be immune from simple mistakes, they seem quite proud to lay claim to all other kinds of *pseudea*.[52]

It may again be useful at this point to turn to a line in the *Odyssey* which may help us to explicate the Muses' riddling words. The issue of priority need not concern us here.[53] Still cloaked in his beggarly disguise, Odysseus recounts his adventures to Penelope, who has yet to recognize her husband. His tale is full of apparently truthful and circumstantial details that manage to convince Penelope that he met Odysseus in Crete on his way to Troy. But Homer tells us:

ἴσκε ψεύδεα πολλὰ λέγων ἐτύμοισιν ὁμοῖα.

Composing many lies, he likened them [so as to render them]
indistinguishable from real things.   (*Odyssey* 19.203)

Unlike Odysseus' other Cretan tales that we can compare to the stories he tells the Phaeacians and thus seem *prima facie* to be false, the beggar's account here offers a possible farrago (λέγων) of truth and falsehood. We have no way of verifying whether Odysseus did actually stop in Crete on the way to Troy. But the description the stranger provides of Odysseus' dress and appearance at any rate seems to be genuine (cf. ἐτεόν, 19.216) and convinces Penelope of the rest of the story. Part of it is true and the rest probably false, but persuasive, even if unverifiable, just like the Muses' boast.[54] To discern which remains beyond human ken.

The multiple paradoxes of the Muses' cryptic statement are further underlined by their claim to speak the truth "whenever we may wish" (εὖτ' ἐθέλωμεν, 28). In drawing attention to their capricious nature, the Muses reveal themselves to share a trait that elsewhere too characterizes the attitude of the gods vis-à-vis the human race. If the Muses have the capacity to declare[55] the truth, if they want, we mortals cannot know when they do so, nor can we distinguish their lies from their truths. To paraphrase Detienne: "Les maîtresses de vérité sont aussi des maîtresses de tromperie."[56] The

---

[52] For a clearly positive valuation of the ability to make ψεύδεα . . . ἐτύμοισιν ὁμοῖα, see Theognis 713, where after listing various kinds of human excellence – the *sophrosyne* of Rhadamanthus and the cleverness of Sisyphus – Theognis ascribes this skill to Nestor.

[53] See the discussion of Neitzel (1975) 8–10. Russo (1992) 87 suggests that "the phrasing is traditional." In addition to Theognis 713, see Xenophanes fr. 35 (DK).

[54] Cf. Pucci (1977) 10: "Odysseus' stories are subject to verification by a search of evidences and witnesses; but the Muses' song about the past and future lies beyond the limits of any inquiry."

[55] Note the difference between the rare verb γηρύσασθαι (28) and the unmarked λέγειν (27). The former is used of Dike's denunciation of human injustice to her father Zeus (*W&D* 260).

[56] Cf. Detienne (1967) 74.

words the smooth-talking (ἀρτιέπειαι, 29)[57] Muses address to Hesiod put us on notice that we too cannot distinguish the truth in what follows, that is, in the *Theogony* itself. While Hesiod may well be the Muses' spokesman, and the voice (*aude*) that they breathed into him possesses their authority, nevertheless, he does not and cannot guarantee the absolute truth of his song.[58]

The importance of the Muses' remarkable declaration of their own ambiguity cannot be over-emphasized. At first glance, it appears to be a decisive break with Homeric poetics. But it is equally important to recognize how it evolves from reflection on passages like the invocation preceding the Catalogue of Ships:

> Ἔσπετε νῦν μοι, Μοῦσαι Ὀλύμπια δώματ' ἔχουσαι –
> ὑμεῖς γὰρ θεαί ἐστε, πάρεστέ τε, ἴστέ τε πάντα,
> ἡμεῖς δὲ κλέος οἶον ἀκούομεν οὐδέ τι ἴδμεν . . .

> Tell me now, Muses who inhabit Olympian halls –
> For you are goddesses, are present, and know all things;
> But we hear mere report, and know nothing. . .
>
> (*Il.* 2.484–86)

While declaring his total dependence on the Muses to tell his story, the epic poet draws attention to the gap between human and divine knowledge. But in Homer, that gap is immediately bridged as the Muses speak through the poet and share their knowledge with the audience. With Hesiod, the consciousness of that gap widens, and the poet's dependence on the Muse becomes problematic.[59] By the very fact that Hesiod depicts the Muses as addressing him, he separates himself from them in a way that Homer never does. This interjection of himself as the object of the Muses' discourse defines the nature of that separation. The unbridgeable gap between the Muses and their pupil is constituted by the difference between divine and human knowledge, more specifically, that knowledge, which is available to

---

[57] The word may mean "speaking clearly, precisely" and "speaking glibly." Perhaps the ambiguity of the word here is intentional. See Pucci (1977) 18–19; and Pratt (1993) 110.

[58] Cf. Thalmann (1984) 151: "the Muses never explicitly promise to convey the truth to Hesiod; and this inconclusiveness in their speech, as well as other more subtle indications, hints that the *Theogony* will, after all, be a way of speaking humanly about the world and not necessarily an absolutely faithful representation of it." See also Wade-Gery (1949) 86; Stroh (1976) 97–112; Wilamowitz (1916) 473; Judet de la Combe (1993) 31–32; and Pratt (1993) 106–13.

[59] Cf. Thalmann (1984) 149: "It is with the dependence on the Muses that the possibility of error or delusion enters. . . The truth or falsehood of the song they give depends ultimately on their own caprice." Walsh (1984) 22–36 seems to believe that the audience will somehow be able to discern the truth or falsehood of song by its effect on them. But the effect of the Muses' song, whether true or false, is always pleasure.

the gods alone, that can discern truths from falsehoods that masquerade as truths and human knowledge that cannot.

It is, however, equally important not to lose sight of the context of the Muses' declaration to Hesiod. Many critics take their words as a general statement of archaic Greek poetics or of the deceptive nature of rhetoric or of all speech *per se*, or equate them with the later saying that "poets always lie."[60] Yet such a global interpretation ignores Hesiod's exploitation of rhetoric and his claim to speak the truth in the *Works and Days*. With the Muses' statement, Hesiod introduces an important, perhaps even revolutionary, but nonetheless qualified, skepticism, but he does not claim that all poetry is false, far less that all language inevitably distorts the truth.[61] Hesiod is not a Derridian *avant la lettre*. His Muses insist both on their capriciousness in dispensing and withholding the truth and on the impossibility of distinguishing their lies from things as they truly are, an impossibility, to be sure, for *human beings*. And no wonder: the things recounted in the *Theogony*, the origins of the cosmos and the gods, are beyond human ken and hence unverifiable. Moreover, even the Muses themselves might have difficulty narrating their own begetting, not to speak of the primordial events preceding their birth. Hesiod, who must have pondered the question of beginnings, draws attention to this contradiction when he narrates the Muses' origins twice, once in the proem (53–60) and again in their proper temporal sequence toward the end of his poem (915–17).[62] In so doing, he also fulfills the goddesses' command to "sing them first and last" (34). The Muses are in a sense both the necessary beginning and the culmination of the *Theogony*.

In this context, we might well recall another version of the Muses' birth recounted in Pindar's Hymn to Zeus, which evidently stood first in the collection of his Hymns. Only a few scraps of this famous poem survive, but a summary of its contents, which I have used as the epigraph to this chapter, has come down to us:

---

[60] Cf. Arthur (1983) 104–6; and Pucci (1977) 12–13.

[61] Against the deconstructionist interpretation of Pucci and Arthur, see Ferrari (1988). Cf. Detienne (1967) 76: [The statement of the Muses] "est remarquable d'abord parce qu'elle représente un stade intermédiaire entre le plan mythique, celui de la double *Apaté*, et le plan rationnel, celui d'*aléthés et pseudés*."

[62] Cf. Heitsch (1966b) 197: "Die Musen, deren Lied Hesiod wiederholt, erzählen von der Vergangenheit, von den Anfängen der Welt und den Anfängen der Götter. . . . Wer hätte das alles gesehen, daß er davon wissen und berichten könnte? Die Musen jedenfalls nicht, sie die späten Kinder von Zeus und Mnemosyne." The double narration of the Muses' birth, according to Heitsch, is Hesiod's attempt to disguise the difficulty, of which he thus must have been aware.

. . . when Zeus had newly completed the arrangement (κοσμήσαντα) of the universe, he asked the gods if anything was lacking; and they in turn asked him to make for himself some divinities who could adorn (κοσμήσουσι) with words and music his great works and the whole of his arrangement.

Pindar, fr. 31 (Snell–Maehler)

The tattered fragments of the Hymn to Zeus seem to outline that first cosmogony sung by the Muses. Zeus's disposition of the cosmos is evidently not complete until it can be celebrated in song. That song can only be sung after the theogonic process has been completed; and its singing, in turn, brings it to completion.[63] Zeus's cosmos is mirrored in the cosmos of the Muses' song, a cosmos of words.

Along with their order to sing them first and last, the Muses endow Hesiod with a twofold gift: they give him a scepter of laurel,[64] and they breathe into him *thespis aude*, a "divine human voice," an expression that "approaches a paradox or oxymoron".[65] It is this human voice (*aude*), but one imbued with the divine (*thespis*), that allows Hesiod to fulfill the Muses' demand that he celebrate (κλείοιμι) "the things that will be and those that were before" (τά τ᾽ ἐσσόμενα πρό τ᾽ ἐόντα, 32).[66] Hesiod's claim to receive from the Muses the power to sing of "the things that will be" constitutes an old *aporia*, since nowhere in the *Theogony* does he exercise this prophetic capacity. Already in the second century, Lucian mockingly took Hesiod to task for not fulfilling his promise to prophesy the future; after a rather sheepish response by Hesiod, Lucian concludes that the poet did not know what he was doing anyway, but that the Muses, capricious and unreliable as gods are, reneged on their promise to him.[67] The scholiasts side-step the problem by equating poetry and prophecy, but although the two have a great deal in common, they are not identical. Moreover, the expression

---

[63] On the Pindaric poem, see Snell (1975) 82–94. Compare the *Hymn to Hermes*, where the newborn god sings a theogony in which his own birth constitutes the culminating event. Cf. Clay (1989) 138–39. Also Arthur (1983) 97: "the Prooemium is, at one and the same time, both a coda and an overture to the *Theogony* proper: it is located, in narrative time, after the consolidation of Zeus's reign, and so at the end of the *Theogony*; but it is also a story of beginnings – of Hesiod's initiation as a bard, which in turn endorses his authority to transmit a tale of origins." Cf. Hamilton (1989) 40.

[64] I prefer to read δρέψασθαι at line 31. The combination of passive inspiration and active plucking resembles Phemius' description of his own art in *Odyssey* 22.347–48. Cf. Jacoby (1930) 78–79; Friedländer's (1931) review; Kambylis (1965) 65–66; and Marg (1970). *Contra*, see Rzach (1912); West (1966) 165; and Arrighetti (1998).

[65] Ford (1992) 186. Ford's discussion of this peculiar collocation takes up pp. 172–97.

[66] On the interpretation of line 32, see Neitzel (180) 396–98, who correctly notes that it makes no sense to celebrate (κλείοιμι) the future and that "what was and will be" constitute a single category.

[67] Lucian, *Hesiodus*.

in line 32 does not refer to two distinct categories, "the things that will be and the things that were before," which would require the repetition of the article.[68] The Hesiodic phrasing refers to *one* category of things that both will be and were before. When the goddesses require Hesiod to celebrate what was and will be, they command at the same time that he hymn the "race of the blessed ones who are forever" (μακάρων γένος αἰὲν ἐόντων, 33). These two expressions are parallel and have the same referent; the things that will be in the future and have been in the past are the eternal things, that is, the *genos aien eonton*.[69]

To celebrate the beings that are eternal is the task that the Muses require of Hesiod and the one he will accomplish in his *Theogony*. But that is not the whole of the Muses' knowledge. After Hesiod's initiation, the goddesses leave the liminal space at the foot of Helicon, where men and gods encounter each other, to ascend to Olympus where they sing to "delight the mind" of their father, Zeus. There, their song is more extensive, embracing not only τά τ' ἐσσόμενα πρό τ' ἐόντα, but also τὰ ἐόντα. Most scholars equate lines 32 and 38 and assume that the former is simply an abbreviated variant of the latter.[70] However, what is meant by *ta eonta* is clarified a few lines later when Hesiod outlines the full contents of the Muses' Olympian song: the human race, the ἀνθρώπων γένος (50). This equation of *ta eonta* and ephemeral human things will strike students of Greek philosophy as most peculiar. In subsequent philosophical thought, that which is eternal becomes *to eon*, Being, while the Hesiodic ἐόντα correspond to Becoming. This fundamental ontological shift may, in fact, have arisen precisely from a

---

[68] Cf. Sophocles, *Ajax* 34–35: τά τ' οὖν πάρος | τά τ' εἰσέπειτα; and Plato, *Timaeus* 37e: τό τ' ἦν τό τ' ἔσται.

[69] Note the chant of the priestesses at Dodona: Ζεὺς ἦν, Ζεὺς ἐστίν, Ζεὺς ἔσσεται (Pausanias 10.12.10); and the riddle in the *Certamen Homeri et Hesiodi* 95–101. Cf. Neitzel (1980) 397–98: "Wenn wir jetzt fragen: was ist das 'was sein wird *und* vorher war'? . . .Von keinem Zustand in der menschlichen Geschichte kann man also sagen, daß er war und auch in Zukunft sein werde. Das 'was sein wird und vorher war', ist also durch die Zeit hindurch daurend, d.h. es ist immer. Folglich bezieht sich der Ausdruck τά τ' ἐσσόμενα πρό τ' ἐόντα nicht auf Menschliches und Zeitliches, sondern auf das ewige Göttliche." Cf. Wismann (1996) 19–20.

[70] For example, West (1966) 166; Neitzel (1980) 396; Lenz (1980) 151; Stroh (1976) 89; and van Groningen (1958) 257, n. 2. But note Pucci (1977) 22, who observes that in line 32 "the absence of the 'present' is indeed shocking, especially in view of line 38 when the Muses, teachers of Hesiod, are described as singing '*present*, future and past.'" Arrighetti (1998) 315–17 connects the absence of *ta eonta* with Hesiod's confession of ignorance in connection with the names of the rivers (*Theog.* 369–70) and the rules for navigation (*W&D* 649, 660). But in the latter case, it is precisely the Muses that have taught him those rules! Schlesier (1982) 164 notes: "si les Muses proclament ce qui est, ce qui sera, ce qui a été . . . elles ne chargent le poète que de chanter le passé et le futur (v. 32); le présent temporel semble en être exclu." In this connection, one should perhaps reinterpret the description of Calchas in *Iliad* 1.70 to mean that the seer "knew both the divine and the human things" and understood their interconnection. See also the discussion below, in the Conclusion.

radical questioning of the notion of theogony: for how can what is eternal, i.e. the gods, have come into being?[71]

However that may be, in Hesiod the Muses' knowledge, which comprehends both truths and falsehoods that cannot be distinguished from truths, embraces both the eternal gods and ephemeral mortals; the divinities may grant such knowledge to their ministers, the bards, who likewise sing both the "human race" (ἀνθρώπων γένος) and the "blessed gods who inhabit Olympus" (μάκαράς τε θεοὺς οἳ Ὄλυμπον ἔχουσιν, 100–101). But on the occasion of the *Theogony*, at least, the goddesses transmit to Hesiod only part of their expertise: the knowledge of eternal things. In other words, Hesiod limits himself in the *Theogony* to speaking of the eternal things. He will speak of the world of men elsewhere, but as we shall see, this division is emblematic of his whole *œuvre* and a fundamental part of his poetic program.

To delight Zeus on Olympus, the Muses hymn the race of the gods in genealogical order from the beginning, ἐξ ἀρχῆς (45): first the primordial divinities, Earth and Sky, then the Olympians who are born from them. Second, they celebrate Zeus and his supremacy (46–47). This ordering inverts the human order, the order of *doxa*, which begins from the present and works back to the origins (cf. 11–21). It is an ordering from an Olympian perspective and resembles the song that Hesiod will request of the Muses at the end of his proem (105–15). Hesiod's *Theogony* will be a version of the song that the Muses sing on Olympus. But before beginning his own account, Hesiod will delineate a complex trajectory of the Muses' movements. To trace that trajectory both spatially and temporally reveals how the Muses mediate between past and present, between earth and Olympus, and the divine and the human.

After a description of their timeless activities on Helicon's peaks and their descent to its slopes, when they met Hesiod at a unique historical moment in the past, the Muses now re-ascend to Olympus, where they are eternally present in the halls of Zeus (36–51). On each occasion, they sing, and their song is suitably modulated to their spatial and temporal

---

[71] Cf. Parmenides, B 8.5–6 (DK); Xenophanes, B 14.1 (DK); and especially Epicharmus B 1.3–6 (DK), which explicitly alludes to Hesiod: – ἀλλὰ λέγεται μὰν Χάος πρᾶτον γενέσθαι τῶν θεῶν. – Πῶς δέ κα; μὴ ἔχον γ' ἀπό τινος μηδ' ἐς ὅ τι πρᾶτον μόλοι. – οὐκ ἄρ' ἔμολε πρᾶτον οὐθέν; – οὐδὲ μὰ Δία δεύτερον. . . ("But indeed it is said that Chaos came into being first of the gods." "How could that be? Since it would possess nothing from which or to which it might first come forth." "Then in fact did nothing come forth first?" "Not even second, by Zeus!" Whether the decisive break was made by Parmenides or by one of his precursors, perhaps Anaximander, remains unclear. See Kahn (1973), esp. 454–57. M. Kraus, *Name und Sache: Ein Problem im frühgriechischen Denken* (Amsterdam 1987) sees the crucial shift occurring in Parmenides' singular τὸ ἐόν as opposed to the plural τα ἐόντα.

surroundings. What they sing on Helicon's summit is hidden from us; the only sound heard is the footfalls of their dancing (8). Yet uninitiated, Hesiod can give no report of their song. Their descent is accompanied, as we have seen, by a catalogue of divinities that is incomplete and that mirrors the human perspective on the gods (11–21). Although the Muses sing repeatedly in the course of the proem, only once, in their address to Hesiod (26–28), are their words directly quoted. On all other occasions, Hesiod mediates their song.[72]

From Olympus in the timeless present, where the goddesses entertain their father with the song that most resembles Hesiod's own – although his would appear to exclude the "race of human beings and giants" – Hesiod takes us back in time to the site of the Muses' birth, to Pieria, "not far from the topmost peak of snowy Olympus" (62), where even now they have their homes and dancing-places and "celebrate the laws and goodly ways of all the immortals" (66–67). It was there in Pieria that Memory bore them to Zeus as a "forgetfulness of woes and an end to cares." In paradoxically linking the daughters of Memory with oblivion, here viewed not as amnesia, λήθη, or a negation of truth, ἀλήθεια, but as a healing power, Hesiod reinforces the ambiguity of their nature. When, one might ask, were the gods who "live easy" in need of such therapy? Perhaps only once, after the defeat of the Titans, when the other gods had to become reconciled to Zeus's rule, as their next song (71–74) indicates. But, as we shall see, the uniting of the daughters of Memory with the healing powers of oblivion centrally defines their efficacy in the human realm. Despite her fundamentally negative character, Lethe, like Eris, a daughter of Night, acquires positive features in the realm of the human.

Immediately after their birth, the goddesses, singing and dancing all the while, made their ascent to their father.[73] But here something quite extraordinary happens.[74] Hesiod's narrative of the Muses' progress to Olympus moves seamlessly into a description of Zeus's might and present reign, how he acquired it through his victory over Cronus, and his establishment of ordinances and honors among the immortals (71–74). But, suddenly, we learn that:

---

[72] A special case is lines 71–75, where we only discover afterwards that Hesiod was relaying the Muses' song. Similarly, the songs of the bard, described as the "servant (*therapon*) of the Muses," mediate the renditions of the goddesses (98–103).

[73] νισομένων in line 71 means that the Muses are going to their rightful abode on Olympus, hence are Olympian, and to their father's house, hence are daughters of Zeus. The first arrival of a new divinity on Olympus is a common hymnic motif.

[74] West (1966) cites *Od.* 8.83, 367, and 521 as parallels, but they also serve to bring out the difference between Homer and Hesiod here.

ταῦτ᾿ ἄρα Μοῦσαι ἄειδον Ὀλύμπια δώματ᾿ ἔχουσαι.

These things the Muses, who inhabit Olympian homes, sang.

(75)

Thus Hesiod not only incorporates this first song of the Muses, the account of Zeus's victorious kingship, into his own composition, but his voice has become indistinguishable from that of the Muses. Their singing in unison again raises the question of when their collaboration began.

Only now, when they have taken up their Olympian abodes as daughters of Zeus, does Hesiod catalogue the goddesses' names, musical names that they have acquired and exercised in the course of the proem.[75] Striking is the omission of any reference to their truth-telling, which suggests that it may not be part of their essential nature.[76] Their names emphasize not the content of their songs, but the pleasure their songs provide.

Having now arrived at the Olympian heights and having acquired their eternal identity and function as singers, the goddesses send down (again in the present tense) their divine gifts to mankind. To favored kings they dispense the mollifying rhetoric that has the power to resolve even a great quarrel; those who have been wronged are soothed and reconciled.[77] To their human servants and counterparts, the bards (ἀοιδοί), the goddesses grant sweet song that produces forgetfulness of woes and alleviates even fresh grief.

Both kings and singers, then, mediate the Muses' gifts to mankind, and what they offer is not truth, but distraction. In both cases, the goddesses' blessings distract from a painful present by soothing injured parties at odds with one another, and, as we have already seen, by bringing oblivion from care, a turning away from hurt and sorrow, a forgetfulness of suffering (μαλακοῖσι παραιφάμενοι ἐπέεσσιν, 90; ἐπιλήθεται, παρέτραπε, 102, 103; cf. ἄλλη ἀποκλίναντ᾿, *Od.* 19.556). Again Hesiod revels in the double paradox that the daughters of Memory produce forgetfulness and that forgetfulness (*lethe*, see also 54–55) constitutes the negation of truth (*a-letheia*). Here too Hesiod makes abundantly clear that what the Muses offer to mankind cannot simply be *aletheia*, for *aletheia* cannot be bent in any direction or distorted. Rather, the efficacy of their gift lies in its power

---

[75] Already noticed by Klaußen (1835) 443–44. Cf. Friedländer (1931) 114–15; and Thalmann (1984) 138: "With the transformation of descriptive verbs, nouns, and adjectives into proper names, Hesiod virtually summons these goddesses into existence through language."

[76] Cf. Marg (1970) 95.

[77] West (1966) at 89 notes that βλαπτομένοις "is best taken as passive." Apparently, those who commit wrongs do not require such therapy. Throughout, I have used the term "kings," although Hesiod seems to refer only to their juridical functions.

to heal and soothe and bring relief from the unceasing cares that are coeval with the human condition.[78]

The goddesses' powers on earth cannot reproduce the undiluted pure pleasure that delights the mind of Zeus and gladdens all of Olympus. Of course, like their father and the rest of the Olympians, the Muses themselves have no need of the therapy they dispense, for their own hearts are free of divisions and cares, ὁμόφρονας, ἀκηδέα θυμὸν ἐχούσαις (60, 61). The twofold gifts of the Muses to kings and poets serve to alleviate the harshness of human life and to reconcile ourselves to our situation. In presenting Hesiod with both the laurel scepter and a divine voice, the Muses would appear to unite in the person of their human favorite their double powers.

Finally, Hesiod outlines the bards' twofold responsibilities: to hymn the "famous deeds (κλεῖα) of men of the past and the blessed gods who inhabit Olympus" (100–101). Hesiod's subject matter clearly sets him apart from other poets who sing of the heroes or who hymn the present Olympian pantheon. Hesiod thus differentiates his theogonic song from both epic and hymn poetry.[79]

Through a complex series of parallels, juxtapositions and contrasts, the various songs the Muses either sing or inspire in the course of the proem serve to define the unique character of Hesiod's own theogonic song that follows. At the same time, the goddesses' displacements in time and space – from the distant past of their birth in Pieria and first arrival on Olympus, to their more recent encounter with Hesiod on the slopes of Helicon, where heaven and earth meet, to their eternal activities, both on the heights of Helicon and Olympus, and in their unceasing gifts to mankind – represent their mediating function between past and present and between the human and the divine.[80]

Such a use of dramatic movement to map a divinity's characteristic function or mode of action, his *timai*, seems to be a typical feature of divine narratives. In the *Homeric Hymn to Hermes*, for example, the newborn god's zigzag course to Olympus testifies to his characteristic prerogative as a god

---

[78] On the Muses' distracting powers, see Pucci (1977) 17–29. Cf. Lamberton (1988) 68: "Both king and bard emerge as therapists functioning in the context of the general misery of the human condition." Ledbetter (2003) demonstrates how Hesiod's therapeutic poetics differs from Homer's poetics of truth.

[79] For the generic distinctions and complementarities of these three different types of *epos*, see Clay (1989) 15 and 267–70.

[80] See Clay (1989) *passim*. Thalmann (1984) 143 also notes the progression from the Muses' initial isolation on Helicon to their role within the divine and human community, which reveals the civilizing power of poetry.

of passage. Similarly, the plot of the *Hymn to Demeter*, which traces the movements of Demeter and her daughter between heaven, earth, and the nether realms, reveals the role of the two goddesses as mediators between these cosmic spheres; and the many geographical catalogues of the *Hymn to Apollo* emphasize the god's universality.[81] In the case of Hesiod's Muses, their oscillations encompass not only divine and human geographies – Olympus, Helicon, and the world of men on earth below – but also divine and human temporalities – past and present, eternal, and ephemeral – and convey by means of dynamic reenactment their mediation between gods and men, present and past.

The request with which Hesiod concludes the proem constitutes the invocation properly speaking (104–15). It parallels the various songs the Muses sing on Olympus, but combines them into one. Hesiod first asks the Muses to begin ἐξ ἀρχῆς, from the beginning, as they do on Olympus, and to recount in order the generations of the gods from Gaia and Uranus (106, cf. 45); in addition, he requests an account of the Olympians, "givers of good things" (δωτῆρες ἑάων (111, cf. 46);[82] how they divided their wealth and *timai,* a clear allusion to Zeus's dispensation (112, cf. 73–74); and how it was that they first gained possession of Olympus, a reference to Zeus's victory over the Titans (113, cf. 71–73). But, more interestingly, Hesiod's request also embraces some items not included in the goddesses' Olympian songs: he asks them to include, in addition to Earth and Sky, the origins of natural phenomena like the rivers, the sea, and the stars (108–10).[83] Significantly, toward the end of his poem, Hesiod takes leave not only of "those who have Olympian homes," i.e. the gods, but also "the islands, mainlands, and the salt sea," the cosmos as it has achieved its final disposition (963–64). Hesiod's song, then, differs from its divine counterpart by offering simultaneously a cosmogony as well as a theogony. Furthermore, Hesiod seems to include Night and Pontos among the first gods (107). Neither was named by the Olympian Muses, although the Heliconian goddesses assigned Night the last place in their catalogue (20). In fact, the position of Nyx there suggested that she might be the first of the primal gods.[84] As it turns out, Hesiod's theogony reveals that this

---

[81] Cf. Clay (1989); and Vernant (1965b).

[82] West (1966) 190, following Rzach (1912), ejects line 111, which cannot, however, be dispensed with. The Olympians, δωτῆρες ἑάων, have not yet been mentioned, and they are not "comprised in θεοί in 108," as West claims.

[83] In his edition, Solmsen (1970) brackets 108–10, but see Marg (1970) 102–03 for a defense of these verses.

[84] Ramnoux (1986) 177– 231 discusses several ancient theogonies in which Night is the first of the gods. Cf. Ballabriga (1986) 276–78.

notion is mistaken. Neither Night, nor Ocean, nor Pontos are the earliest divinities – nor, for that matter, are Gaia and Uranus the primordial couple, as the Olympian Muses appeared to suggest. Hesiod himself begins by naming Chaos first of all (πρώτιστα, 116). In fact what is striking is Hesiod's repeated insistence (τὰ πρῶτα, 108, 113; πρῶτον, 115; ἐξ ἀρχῆς, 115) on the correct beginning; he demands of the Muses that they begin at the absolute beginning and proceed in a strictly chronological fashion.

In adopting the song of the Muses on Olympus and making it his own, Hesiod likewise adopts their Olympian perspective and distances himself from the human perspective adumbrated in the first catalogue (11–21) in which the gods are viewed not in the order of their birth and genealogy, but in the order of their proximity to mankind. Only by keeping this divine viewpoint in mind can we begin to understand the *Theogony*.

WORKS AND DAYS

The opening of the *Works and Days* also begins with the Muses and thus conforms to their programmatic demand enunciated in the *Theogony* that Hesiod always begin with them. But the most obvious feature of the proem to the *Works and Days* is its brevity in comparison to the extensive prologue to the *Theogony*: ten verses as opposed to 115. Why this brevity? Apparently, the subject-matter of the *Works and Days* does not require such a lengthy introduction: no detailed description of the meeting of Hesiod and the Muses on Helicon, nor an account of his initiation, nor their demand that he sing a theogony, which they inspire and even dictate. Without the authorization of the Muses, no *Theogony*. But in the *Works and Days*, Hesiod takes as his subject not the gods and their origins, subjects far beyond the normal ken of mortals; rather, he sings of contemporary human affairs, human life on earth, how one should live and act towards one's fellow men and the gods, and how to work and prosper within the limits imposed on mortals by the eternal gods and the laws laid down by Zeus.

Understandably, to describe the human world does not require the authorization of the Muses to the same degree as the *Theogony*. The absence of the Muses, one might even say their superfluousness, in Hesiod's present enterprise is indicated in an almost comic fashion when he later invokes their authority, not for their knowledge of matters beyond human ken, but in order to explicate the rules for navigation, rules to which Hesiod, for want of practical experience, is not privy. Yet, paradoxically, the aid of the Muses *is* critical to the task Hesiod sets himself in the *Works and Days* and to the way he carries it out. To understand the nature of that task, we must refer back to a puzzling passage in the proem of the *Theogony*, where the Muses gave Hesiod a *skeptron* of laurel at the same time that they inspired him with a divine voice (30–32). Pausanias and others in antiquity thought that this scepter was the equivalent of a *rhabdos*, the staff carried by the rhapsodes, and they therefore concluded that Hesiod was unable to play the lyre. West does not offer a parallel for a *skeptron* being equivalent to the rhapsode's staff and notes that Hesiod himself associates bards and lyre-playing in line 95. Nevertheless, he accepts the old argument that "if Hesiod bore a staff instead of a lyre, it was . . . because he could not obtain a lyre or could not play one."[85]

The significance of Hesiod's *skeptron* lies elsewhere: it most closely resembles the function Achilles attributes to the scepter upon which he swears his great oath in book 1 of the *Iliad*:[86]

> . . . υἷες Ἀχαιῶν
> ἐν παλάμῃς φορέουσι δικασπόλοι, οἵ τε θέμιστας
> πρὸς Διὸς εἰρύαται.

> . . . the sons of the Achaeans
> Carry it in their hands, those who dispense justice
> (*dikaspoloi*) and who uphold the
> Ordinances of Zeus.   (*Il.* 1.237–39)

The scepter is the emblem of royal authority, an authority which ultimately derives from Zeus; to possess it entails the maintenance of his ordinances and the dispensation of justice.[87] As Hesiod has explained in the *Theogony*, singers come from the Muses and Apollo, but kings from Zeus (94–96). But the king whom the Muses honor receives the gift of eloquence, which permits him to resolve disputes peacefully:

[85] West (1966) 164. Østerud (1976) 27 is on the right track when he remarks: "Surely the staff is chosen because it . . . anticipates the association of poets with kings in lines 80–103."

[86] Arthur (1983) 106 also compares Hesiod's *skeptron* to Achilles': "Like the sceptre of Achilles 'which will never again bear leaf or branch . . . nor will it blossom' (*Il.* 1.234–37), the δάφνης ἐριθηλέος ὄζον is wrenched from its inscription within the cycle of nature to become fixed within the cultural order."

[87] van Wees (1992) 276–80 argues that there are only three kinds of scepters in Homer: the staff or walking-stick, the scepters of the *basileis*, and those carried by priests (Teiresias, Chryses). In fact, the only occurrence of the first kind, where *skeptron* is used of a common staff with no connection to status or authority, is (perhaps significantly?) the staff of the disguised Odysseus (13.437; 14. 31; 17.199). Frequently in Homer the *skeptron* is explicitly linked to *themistes*: *Il.* 2.206; 9.99, 156, 298; *Od.* 11.569. Combellack (1948) examines those Homeric scenes where a speaker is said to hold a scepter and concludes that on such occasions, his "words are of special significance and solemnity" (215).

οἱ δέ νυ λαοὶ
πάντες ἐς αὐτὸν ὁρῶσι διακρίνοντα θέμιστας
ἰθείῃσι δίκῃσιν· ὁ δ᾽ ἀσφαλέως ἀγορεύων
αἶψά τι καὶ μέγα νεῖκος ἐπισταμένως κατέπαυσε.

The people all
Look to him as he discerns the ordinances
With straight judgments; and he, speaking without stumbling,
Quickly and expertly makes an end, even to a big quarrel.
(*Theog.* 84–87).

Solmsen has noted that the inclusion of political rhetoric in the Muses' domain appears to be a Hesiodic innovation.[88] For Hesiod, all those whom the Muses favor, whether poets or kings, share a "sweet voice" (*Theog.* 96–97) that has the power to sooth and divert (παραιφάμενοι, 90; cf. παρέτραπε, 103)[89] both the aggrieved and the grieving. But according to Solmsen and others, this positive valuation of royal eloquence and its connection with the Muses was only a passing phase, belied by Hesiod's indictment of the crooked judgments of the kings in the *Works and Days*.[90] Yet it is within the *Theogony* that the picture of the persuasive power of the *basileis* constitutes an apparent digression, seemingly tangential to the central concerns of the poem.[91] Only in the *Works and Days* does the full significance of this Hesiodic innovation emerge. For there, Hesiod exercises the royal prerogative whose emblem is the laurel scepter that unites the authority of Zeus with Apollo's emblematic branch. It is in fact Hesiod himself who proposes to resolve his dispute with Perses on the spot:

---

[88] Solmsen (1954). But Thalmann (1984) 140 rightly draws attention to *Iliad* 1.249, describing Nestor's eloquence in similar terms and notes that "Nestor is attempting to pacify the partners to a public quarrel." Still, his rhetoric is not explicitly connected with the Muses. For the old question of the relation of *Theogony* 84–93 to *Odyssey* 8.166–77, see Neitzel (1977); and Braswell (1981). Both argue for the priority of the *Odyssey* passage, but a second parallel, not usually cited, from *Odyssey* 7.71–74 suggests to me that these descriptions are traditional. See also Arrighetti (1998) 321–22.

[89] Cf. Pucci (1977) 17–18. Roth (1976); Duban (1980); and Brillante (1994) emphasize traditional parallels between poet and king. But Gagarin (1992) rightly, I think, stresses Hesiod's innovation, and rejects the notion of the Hesiodic *basileis* as repositories of orally transmitted laws or divine pronouncements. Cf. Laks (1996) 83–86.

[90] Solmsen (1954) 13–15. Cf. Wilamowitz (1916) 477, who considers the passage a *captatio benevolentiae* aimed at the audience of kings; also West (1966) 44, who believes the *Theogony* was performed in front of kings. Puelma (1972) 94–95 rejects the idea that Hesiod's apparently contradictory judgments of the *basileis* can be accounted for biographically or through the development of his thought. In the *Works and Days*, Hesiod reserves his hostility for the kings because they are corrupt, not merely because they are kings.

[91] Cf. West (1966) 181, who speaks of "a somewhat contrived transition to the subject of kings" and an "even more awkward transition from kings to singers" and then asks (182): "Why are the kings introduced at all?" Stein (1990) 14–18 argues that Hesiod depicted the kings in a positive light in order to enhance his own status and that of his poetry: the Muses favor not only poets, but even kings.

... ἀλλ' αὖθι διακρινώμεθα νεῖκος
ἰθείῃσι δίκῃς, αἵ τ' ἐκ Διός εἰσιν ἄρισται.

... but let us decide our quarrel here and now
With straight judgments, which from Zeus are the best.

(35–36)

Hesiod's language here echoes his earlier evocation of the equitable ar-
bitration of the just king (*Theogony* 84–87). In the *Works and Days*, the
kings are no longer those "who wield the scepter" or "who dispense the
themistes": they have become the "gift-eating kings."[92] Since the kings have
abdicated their responsibilities and are corrupt, Hesiod must take justice
into his own hands. The vacuum of authority and rectitude obliges Hesiod
to appropriate royal authority and rhetoric and to wield the scepter.[93]

One may recall a somewhat analogous situation where a political vacuum
demands intervention; in the second book of the *Iliad*, after Agamemnon
has precipitated the flight of the Greek army by his ill-advised test of
their morale, Odysseus restores order among the troops (*Il.* 2.183–332). He
snatches up the scepter of Agamemnon, the same scepter whose history
Homer had earlier traced all the way back to Zeus (2.101–8). Quickly and
efficiently, Odysseus manages to impose his authority and stops the army's
headlong flight. The end of the episode is well known: after encouraging
the princes with gentle words and the general ranks with threats, Odysseus
uses the scepter to beat the rebellious Thersites. In this scene, Homer seems
to intend to depict for us what it means to rule.[94]

Armed with both the eloquence of the Muses and the authority of Zeus,
Hesiod sets out to accomplish a similar feat in the *Works and Days*. Even if
Hesiod does not have recourse to physical violence, nevertheless his royal
discourse threatens, commands, and exhorts far more often than it cajoles
and soothes his auditors, the kings and his brother Perses. Neither king
nor commoner is addressed with gentle words (cf. *Iliad* 2.189); both are
νήπιοι, fools who resemble the big babies of the silver race who gave no
heed either to the gods or to other men, and who were destroyed by Zeus's
anger. If anything, Hesiod seems to invert Odysseus' strategy, reserving his
most violent threats for the kings, all the while presenting himself as the
mouthpiece of Zeus. In this way, too, the *Works and Days* completes the

---

[92] Von Fritz (1956) 312 recognizes the link between the two poems here and believes that when Hesiod
composed the *Theogony*, he already foresaw the inevitable quarrel with Perses and therefore inserted an
idealized portrait of a king who would be able to resolve such a quarrel. If von Fritz is right, Hesiod
would indeed have been prescient! It is surely easier to suppose that each composition was revised
in the light of the other, or that they were from the outset conceived as complementary works.

[93] Cf. Laks (1996) 91: "L'aède hésiodique est l'ancêtre du philosophe-roi platonicien."

[94] Reinhardt (1961) 113.

program outlined in the opening of the *Theogony*. For Hesiod's initiation
there embraced not only the Muses' inspiration that allowed him to sing of
the eternal gods, but also their gift of the laurel scepter that unites the authority of Zeus with the poetry of Apollo. In a sense, then, Hesiod's double
initiation that opens the *Theogony* supplies not only the introduction to the
Theogony itself, but already foreshadows his role in the *Works and Days*.

The invocation to the Muses that introduces the *Works and Days* is not
only much shorter; it also differs from the *Theogony*'s in its form. If the
latter exhibits some of the formal elements of the hymn, the proem to the
Works and Days resembles the characteristic features of prayer.[95] Hesiod
calls on the Muses to come from Pieria, Πιερίηθεν, to descend from their
celestial habitations, more precisely, from their birthplace as described in
the *Theogony* (53). While the latter composition is characterized by its ascent
from the vales of Helicon to the heights of Olympus, the *Works and Days*,
on the contrary, begins with a descent toward the world of mortals.[96] In
addition, Hesiod asks that the Muses do what they always do, that is,
celebrate their father in song. But the subject of the requested song here
also differs from the one they sing on Olympus. They do not celebrate the
greatness of their father and his superiority over all the other gods (ὅσσον
φέρτατός ἐστι θεῶν κάρτεϊ τε μέγιστος, *Theog.* 49), nor his victory over
Cronus (*Theog.* 71–74). Instead, with a pun on Zeus's name that emphasizes
his mediation (ὅν τε διά, "through whom," 3), they hymn a function of
Zeus, which is in fact normally attributed to the Muses themselves:[97] the
power to confer fame or repute, and its opposite, on men.

> ὅν τε διὰ βροτοὶ ἄνδρες ὁμῶς ἄφατοί τε φατοί τε,
> ῥητοί τ' ἄρρητοί τε Διὸς μεγάλοιο ἕκητι.
>
> . . . through whom mortal men are both disreputable and reputable,
> Famous and infamous,[98] through the will of great Zeus.   (3–4)

Right from the outset, then, the Muses, so essential to the project of the
Theogony, are short-circuited in favor of Zeus. His control over human fame
or obscurity, in turn (γάρ), derives from his general and absolute power
over mankind, an omnipotence he wields easily and without effort:

---

[95] Cf. Rousseau (1996) 103–4; and Race (1992) 32. Calame (1996) 174 calls it a cletic or cult hymn. Cf.
Livrea (1966) 444.

[96] Cf. Rousseau (1996) 95–96.

[97] The phrase ἀοιδῇσι κλείουσαι, "who grant *kleos* in song" (1), without an object (cf. *Theogony* 44–49)
draws attention to this function. Cf. Pucci (1996) 192.

[98] It is difficult to distinguish the two pairs of adjectives. In both cases, the negative forms are easier to
understand than the positives: ἄφατον means "what cannot be expressed"; ἄρρητον, "unspeakable."
For a discussion, see Mancini (1986). Mancini himself renders the latter pair "ben regolato oppure
no," which I find unconvincing.

ῥέα μὲν γὰρ βριάει, ῥέα δὲ βριάοντα χαλέπτει,
ῥεῖα δ' ἀρίζηλον μινύθει καὶ ἄδηλον ἀέξει.

Easily he gives strength, and easily trips up the strong;
Easily he diminishes the great and makes great the obscure.

(5–6)

But the next line suggests that this power is not exercised randomly, but involves a normative and punitive dimension.[99]

ῥεῖα δέ τ' ἰθύνει σκολιὸν καὶ ἀγήνορα κάρφει
Ζεὺς ὑψιβρεμέτης ὃς ὑπέρτατα δώματα ναίει.

Easily too he makes the crooked straight and shrivels the proud,
High-thundering Zeus, who inhabits the most exalted halls.

(7–8)

And with that, the Muses more or less disappear.[100] We cannot even be sure that they have hearkened to Hesiod's request, nor, for that matter, whether the words of praise for Zeus in the opening lines are to be assigned to their voice or to Hesiod's.[101] Nevertheless, their royal rhetoric is far more centrally present in the *Works and Days* than in the *Theogony*. At any rate, the poet abruptly turns away from them to address Zeus directly. And what he addresses to the highest god is a fairly brusque prayer: "hearken, watching and listening "(κλῦθι ἰδὼν ἀιών τε, 9).[102]

The beginning of the *Works and Days* with its prayerful attitude clearly differs from the hymnic note struck at the opening of the *Theogony*. Hymns can be sung even on Olympus, but prayers originate on earth. The Muses further emphasize the distance separating gods and men in the *Works and Days* by concluding their celebration of their father with the phrase: "high-thundering Zeus, who inhabits the most exalted halls" (Ζεὺς ὑψιβρεμέτης, ὃς ὑπέρτατα δώματα ναίει, 8). Now suddenly, and even more abruptly, Hesiod breaks off a second time, without even the usual hymnic salutation (χαῖρε) to Zeus:

---

99 For the shift to an ethical perspective in these lines, see Rousseau (1966) 102; and Muth (1951). Mazon (1914) 36 correctly sees that these lines reveal Zeus in his role as "Justicier, qui frappera les rois pour leur 'fausseté' et leur 'orgueil'" and adds that "Zeus est pour lui [Hesiod] le Vengeur plus encore que le Sauveur."

100 Verdenius (1985) 2–3 and 9 mistakenly believes that the Muses continue to sing through the poet's mouth.

101 As we have seen, something similar happens in the opening of the *Theogony*. At line 75, we learn that the preceding lines celebrating Zeus's power among the gods were sung by the Muses; here also, we cannot determine which of the preceding lines celebrating Zeus's power over mankind can be ascribed to the goddesses and which to Hesiod. The momentary melding of the two voices must be intentional in both places.

102 Cf. Verdenius (1985) 9: "κλῦθι. The epic introduction of a prayer." Cf. Kerschensteiner (1944) 153. Calame (1996) 175 sees the shift here as one from the hymnic to the lyric mode of enunciation.

δίκη δ᾽ ἴθυνε θέμιστας
τύνη· ἐγὼ δέ κε Πέρσῃ ἐτήτυμα μυθησαίμην.

Yours to make straight the decrees with justice,
But, as for me, I would declare to Perses the way things are.
(9–10)[103]

Here again a significant difference between the *Theogony* and the *Works and Days*. In the former, Hesiod could indeed transmit the words of the Muses, but he could not guarantee the truth of those words, because of his inevitable mortal incapacity to distinguish *aletheia* from *pseudos*, that is, to ascertain the correspondence between the words of the Muses and reality. But in the *Works and Days,* where he speaks of human things whose knowledge is granted to men through their own experience, Hesiod can declare to Perses his intention to tell him *etetuma*, "things as they are."[104] Hesiod will immediately offer an illustration of the differences between the human and divine perspectives that inform the two compositions. In speaking about Eris, he revises the earlier teaching of the Muses by telling us that "on earth, it turns out that there are two Erides" – not one, as claimed in the *Theogony*. What this means is that from the point of view of the gods, there is only one Eris, whereas for mankind, there are two.

To summarize the complex scenario of the proem to the *Works and Days*: the Muses are to celebrate, i.e. praise their father Zeus and his power over mankind, more specifically, his power to punish. Zeus is to listen, observe and act. Zeus's actions, it becomes clear, affect specifically those who would pronounce crooked decrees, i.e. the kings; Hesiod, for his part, will tell *etetuma* to his brother.[105] This cooperative undertaking and its division of labor, outlined in the proem, will structure the poem that follows. If in the *Thegony* Hesiod takes up the Muses' instructions to celebrate, i.e. praise the gods, here he pointedly does not praise; he tells things as they are.

Both the formal elements and the contents of the opening lines of the two Hesiodic poems reveal their respective orientations. On the basis of our foregoing analysis of the two proems, we can now offer an admittedly schematic but perhaps still useful diagram that plots the coordinates of the two compositions and demonstrates their complementarities (see the table).

---

[103] Rousseau (1996) 106–10 notes the urgent tone here and understands the phrase as "straighten the decrees which are crooked."

[104] Cf. Rousseau (1996) 113–15. Nagy (1990) 68, n. 84 and (1996) 50–52 conceives of ἐτήτυμα μυθήσασθαι as an earlier expression, which becomes an unmarked member as opposed to the newer, marked ἀληθέα γηρύσασθαι. This diachronic interpretation would blur the important distinction Hesiod makes between the contents of the two poems.

[105] Cf. Mazon (1914) 36.

Poem	Theogony	Works and Days
Authorization	Super-human authorization	Authorized by human experience
Proem form	Hymnic	Prayer
Subject-matter	Genesis of the gods; Zeus's order	Human life within Zeus's order
Register	Celebratory	Non-celebratory (telling it like it is)
Truth claim	Mixture of lies and truth	Things as they are (*etetuma*)
Emblematic gift	*thespis aude*: Muse-inspired song	*skeptron daphnes*: Muse-inspired eloquence
Role of the poet	Servant of the Muses: *aoidos* (Hesiod in *Theog.*)	Muse-honored king – or his surrogate (Hesiod in *W&D*)
Function	Pleasure	Resolving quarrels
	Diversion from human pain	Alleviation of human pain
	Forgetfulness of human condition	Reminding of human condition

To conclude: from its beginning, the *Works and Days* characterizes itself in opposition to the *Theogony*: the latter, through the mediation of the Muses, offers an Olympian perspective on the cosmos; the *Works and Days*, by contrast, directly and without the need for a divine intermediary, presents the human viewpoint. The task these two poems set for us entails highlighting these two visions and, while respecting their differences, integrating their perspectives into a larger whole. The best way to accomplish this goal would appear to be to examine the presentation of human beings in the *Theogony* and, conversely, the role of the gods in the *Works and Days*. But we must admit right at the outset to a certain lack of symmetry between the two compositions. That the gods should play an important role in human affairs is not surprising; their crucial presence in the *Works and Days* is hence predictable. But given the announced subject-matter of the *Theogony*, to sing the immortal gods and the "race of those that are forever," the γένος αἰὲν ἐόντων, seems rather to exclude mention of the mortal race of men, which is, by definition, ephemeral. But if mankind is doomed to die and inevitably evanescent, the human condition, as established by Zeus through his eternal decrees, is nevertheless eternal. Consequently, we may nevertheless discover within the confines of the *Theogony* an exploration of those eternal laws that determine the human condition. That condition, in turn, derives from the genesis of mankind and the circumstances surrounding its origins, which constitute the focus of the next chapter.

CHAPTER 4

The origins and nature of mankind

As I have tried to demonstrate, from its beginning, the *Theogony* opens an Olympian perspective on the cosmos. Human beings, ephemeral creatures that they are, are necessarily confined to its margins. To study the origins and nature of mankind in Hesiod, we must, at least temporarily, turn our backs on the heights of Olympus and return to the more terrestrial level of the *Works and Days*, where the origins of mankind constitute the focus of Hesiod's myth of the five races.

Hesiod's account of the progressive decline of the human race, symbolized by the succession of metals, from the paradisiacal race of gold to our wretched age of iron may ultimately derive from Near Eastern or Indo-European traditions.[1] But Hesiod's version substantially modifies what was originally a straightforward pattern of decline. For one thing, the decline is dramatically arrested by the insertion of the race of heroes, for which there appear no Oriental parallels, between the race of bronze and the iron race. Most scholars explain the inclusion of the heroes by the practical necessity of incorporating these legendary figures who play such an important role in Greek mythology.[2] But in his influential interpretation, Vernant forcefully demonstrated that the presence of the heroes is not simply due to the pressure of tradition.[3] In fact, their presence radically changes the structure and hence the meaning of the myth. (One consequence of the insertion of the

---

[1] See West (1978) 172–75; and Gatz (1967) 7–27. See also Koenen (1994). Most (1997) 120–27 has recently argued that Hesiod may be far less influenced by non-Greek traditions than has usually been claimed and may have extrapolated his scheme on the basis of what the epic recounted about the human prehistory. Ballabriga (1998) believes the myth is Hesiod's invention used as a "critique sociale et religieuse" (333) of the Prometheus myth, which embodies an "idéologie aristocratique" (334).

[2] As argued, for example, by Fränkel (1962) 133. But note that the heroic age is omitted from the versions of Plato, Aratus, and Ovid. Matthiessen (1977) argues that even the heroes have Near Eastern precedents, for instance in the *nephelim* of Genesis 6.1–6. Nelson (1998) 72–74 argues, I think wrongly, that the Iron race is better than that of the Heroes.

[3] Vernant (1965a); and (1985). See also Goldschmidt (1950).

heroes, whose full meaning has been overlooked, is the fact that it places the race of bronze in the central position of the myth's architecture.[4] The centrality of the bronze race will occupy us later.) Moreover, even without considering the interruption caused by the heroes, the myth, as Hesiod presents it, does not depict a simple decline, but reveals a far more complex structure. For example, as Hesiod himself emphasizes, the race of silver and the race of bronze are totally different from one another, yet there are no obvious criteria for deciding which is the better and which the worse: both are marked by *hybris* – although to be sure in somewhat divergent forms.[5] As the central axis of his structural reading of the myth, Vernant posited the alternations of *hybris* and *dike*; the golden and heroic race symbolized the reign of *dike*, whereas both the silver and the bronze were marked by *hybris*.

On a general level, Vernant's structuralist analysis consciously underplays the importance of the narrative sequence or, rather, the narrative logic in the ordering of contiguous races.[6] Moreover his interpretation suffers, I think, from a fatal objection: *dike* has no place in the golden age.[7] The race of gold was indeed peaceful and content, but since it enjoyed an abundance of goods, there was no need for work or private property or competition for limited resources – via either the good or the bad Eris. Nor, consequently, was there any need for *dike*. Hesiod's conception of *dike* is evidently not a natural state of tranquility; for that apparently did obtain in the golden age. Rather, *dike* involves equitable division, whether of power or honor among the gods or of the scarce resources of human life. At the beginning of the poem, Zeus is asked to straighten the *themistes* by means of *dike*. It follows that *dike* is corrective, straightening what is crooked. And we should not forget that Hesiod's dispute with Perses centers on the unjust division of *property*, which did not even exist in the golden age. To speak

---

[4] Cf. Gatz (1967) 32; also Rudhardt (1981) 252 remarks on the "singularité de la race de bronze" and that it "occupe une situation médiane entre deux groupes de races apparentées."

[5] Cf. Nelson (1998) 71, who thinks otherwise: "by any traditional standards, the earlier Silver Age, which honors neither the right nor the gods, is far worse than the Bronze."

[6] Cf. Vernant (1985) 43: "Dans le cas du mythe des races, il s'agissait pour rendre intelligible un récit dont les séquences narratives, mal articulées, ne permettent pas de saisir l'ordonnance et la signification globales, d'en chercher la clef dans une structure." Yet the sequence of alternations, *dike/hybris/hybris dike*, in the first four races, followed by the "more just" first race of iron and finally the "less just" second race of iron, seems to have no inner necessity. Revealing the same structure, the simple alternation of *dike/hybris* throughout would have been more intelligible.

[7] The point is also made by Crubellier (1996) 451; Redfield (1993) 47; and Carrière (1986) 204: "la justice fait une entrée discrète dans l'histoire." Similarly, Pindar's Hyperboreans (*Pythian* 10.43–44) live free from ὑπέρδικον Νέμεσιν (I owe this reference to A. Bernadini). Aratus' adaptation, *Phaenomena* 96–136, reduces the number of races to three and makes Dike the focus throughout. See the recent discussion of Schiesaro (1996).

Hesiodically, Eris and Hybris precede the birth of Dike. *Dike* enters the world of men only much later, with the fourth race, the age of heroes. It is precisely Dike, daughter of Zeus and Zeus's gift to mankind, that renders the heroes better than both the races of bronze and silver that preceded them.

Drawing on the myth in Plato's *Statesman*, Vernant also claimed that the temporal framework of the Hesiodic myth, that is, the succession of races, is not linear but cyclical; at the end of the age of iron, which he divides into two, the cycle of races starts again with a new golden age or, more likely, a new age of heroes as the sequence reverses itself.[8] Vernant finds confirmation for his interpretation in Hesiod's declaration at lines 174–75:

> μηκέτ᾽ ἔπειτ᾽ ὤφελλον ἐγὼ πέμπτοισι μετεῖναι
> ἀνδράσιν, ἀλλ᾽ ἢ πρόσθε θανεῖν ἢ ἔπειτα γενέσθαι.

> Would that I were not among the fifth [race of] of men,
> But either died before or were born hereafter.

"Before" would indicate the race of heroes; "hereafter" would mean – with the renewal of the cycle – either the return of the golden age or that of the heroes. Although many scholars have not found Vernant's cyclical scheme persuasive, the meaning of these enigmatic words remains obscure.[9] Vernant himself offers a solution when he remarks that "there is not in reality *one* age of iron but two types of human existence."[10] I would rather insist on two phases of the Iron Age. In the first, the one in which we find ourselves, even if human life is full of misery and suffering, "nevertheless, still they [human beings] have good things mixed with their evils" (179). But in the following phase, described in the future tense, only "baneful woes will abide for mortal men, and there will be no remedy for evil" (200–01). Hesiod's wish at lines 174–75 to be born either later or earlier can, I propose, be paraphrased as follows: "It would have been better to be born in the preceding age (the age of heroes), *or* in the final phase of the age of iron, but the worst eventuality is to live at present when good and evil are still mixed."

---

[8] Mezzadri (1988); and Carrière (1986) 228–29, elaborate on Vernant's cyclical scheme. Gatz (1967) 25 gives a summary of earlier scholarly opinion.

[9] Verdenius (1985) 105 argues that "the whole phrase means that Hes. would have preferred to live at any time but the present one." Rudhardt (1981) 280–81, while rejecting a cyclical scheme, believes that Hesiod here expresses a more optimistic view of the future.

[10] Vernant (1965a) 20. Admittedly, for his scheme of alternations, Vernant must divide the iron race into two. See also Martin (1942–43).

To understand Hesiod's meaning, we must consider another passage:

νῦν δὴ ἐγὼ μήτ᾽ αὐτὸς ἐν ἀνθρώποισι δίκαιος
εἴην μήτ᾽ ἐμὸς υἱός, ἐπεὶ κακὸν ἄνδρα δίκαιον
ἔμμεναι, εἰ μείζω γε δίκην ἀδικώτερος ἕξει.

Now, I myself would not be just among men,
Nor have my son just, since it's a bad thing to be a just man
If the unjust will have greater right.   (270–72)[11]

Nun de, that is, in our era, when good and evil are still mixed, to be just among the unjust is the worst of all possible worlds. Among the heroes, apparently, the just composed the majority. But in the future, Hesiod predicts, justice will disappear and injustice will triumph and become universal.[12] The most painful situation, in fact, is exactly the one in which Hesiod finds himself: a just man surrounded by the unjust, including his own brother. What makes our age so difficult is its intermediate status between justice and its opposite, *hybris*. Difficult and painful, yes, but not, according to Hesiod, altogether hopeless, as he immediately states: "but I hope that Zeus will not bring these things to pass" (273). Here, in fact, lies the task Hesiod sets himself in the *Works and Days*: to strengthen justice so that *hybris* cannot completely hold sway over human society. To convert his erring brother and the gift-eating kings, Hesiod must demonstrate that justice is not only preferable to *hybris*, but that the exercise of justice serves the interests of both Perses and the kings, while its rejection will lead inevitably to certain destruction and divine punishment.

The progression of the races, as Falkner has aptly observed, mirrors the stages of human life: from the childishness of the silver race, to the violent adolescence of the bronze men, to the balanced maturity of the heroes, followed finally by the senescence of the final phase of the iron age when babies are born gray-haired.[13] The threat that Zeus will destroy mankind when wizened infants arise suggests that the pattern ends not in a new cycle but in death.[14] Furthermore, the assumption of a cyclical interpretation would completely undermine the paraenetic character and urgency of

---

[11] Wade-Gery (1949) nicely translates 270–71 as: "O who'ld be just, in such a world? not I / nor son of mine." Cf. the perceptive interpretation of Lamberton (1988) 123–24: "In a world where success is closely linked to corruption, should we raise our children to be corrupt successes or honest victims of the successful tactics of the corrupt? The only alternative is to remake the world – and that, finally, is the implicit project of this poetry."

[12] Cf. Rousseau (1993) 69 on Hesiod's "souhait paradoxal": "Et l'on verra alors le poète lui-même renoncer à agir selon la justice."

[13] Falkner (1989); cf. also Smith (1980), for a more psychological interpretation.

[14] Against a cyclical view: Rosenmeyer (1957); Smith (1980) 155; Bona Quaglia (1973) 119. The cyclic view can already be found in the Scholia ad 160–61 (Pertusi).

Hesiod's message. Why worry if better days are undoubtedly ahead? Why change one's evil ways? Indeed, Hesiod's repeated insistence on mankind's – and Perses' – critical choice, his ethical responsibility, and the proximity of catastrophe would merely constitute empty blather.[15] Moreover, if justice, as I have suggested, did not yet exist in the golden age, the relation between the adjacent pairs of races cannot, as Vernant maintains, be sufficiently explained by the opposition *dike/hybris*. Finally, to complicate matters still further, even excluding the race of heroes, the progression from the silver to the bronze race does not seem to fit the pattern of a straightforward decline.[16] Nor would a scheme of unbroken degeneration fit Hesiod's needs; why attempt to dissuade Perses and the kings from their wicked ways if the end is not only near but inevitable?[17] The whole project of the *Works and Days* would constitute a fool's errand.

Some earlier critics detected two different strands in Hesiod's myth: a philosophic or mythical view of mankind's degeneration, contained in the progression from the golden to the silver race, to which was attached a "historical" view of mankind's development from the bronze to the iron age.[18] Another line of interpretation emphasizes that Hesiod had attempted to graft the Oriental myth of the decline of the human race from an earlier felicity to its final decadence to a Greek conception which insisted that the heroes were superior both to the present age and to their predecessors.[19] The synthesis of such heterogeneous elements inevitably occasioned anomalies and contradictions. Yet the very fact that Hesiod so radically refashioned a straightforward account of man's decline suggests that Hesiod thought deeply about the origins of humanity; it is up to us to discover the myth's underlying coherence.

To begin an analysis of the myth afresh,[20] I would start from a very simple observation. Unlike the genetic origins of the gods, Hesiod's myth of the human races is radically discontinuous, but nevertheless sequential. The order matters and it entails the presence of an ordering principle. The races – with one exception to which we shall return – do not spring from

---

[15] Cf. Bianchi (1963) 193. Neschke (1996) 477 points out that the poem would likewise lose its paraenetic function if disaster is inevitable.

[16] Bianchi (1963) 145 aptly notes: "non si tratta . . . di una linea discendente univoca, continua, essendo ogni razza un po' un caso e un problema a sè."

[17] Cf. Most (1997) 108.

[18] Cf., for example, Bamberger (1842); and Roth (1860). Similarly, Meyer (1910) sees two parallel developments: the reign of Cronus: gold – silver; the reign of Zeus: bronze – iron, with the second in each sequence representing the decadence of the first. For an overview of older interpretations of the myth, see Gatz (1967) 1–6, and, more recently, Smith (1980) 145–53.

[19] E.g. Reitzenstein (1924); and Heubeck (1955).

[20] My interpretation is most indebted to Benardete (1967) 156–59; Rudhardt (1981b); and Sorel (1982).

their predecessors, but they are made (ποίησαν, ποίησε) by the gods or Zeus. Human beings are not generated by chance or at random (and for Hesiod even generation is not without a *telos*); nor are they autochthonous, sprung from the earth, but men are made, manufactured one might say, for some purpose, a purpose that emanates from the gods.[21] Moreover, in the case of the first three races, each attempt on the part of the gods to produce a race of men fails either for internal reasons, that is, because of some shortcoming or infirmity within the race itself, or for external reasons, through destruction at the hands of the gods. We seem to be dealing with a series of experiments that proceeds on the basis of trial and error. It then becomes crucial to determine at each stage the flaw that precipitates the destruction of one race and the attempt to correct that imperfection in the following one. For the manufacture of each successive race is not the product of a random process but the result of a purposeful undertaking on the part of the gods, one aimed at a comprehensible goal.

At first glance, the race of gold seems to enjoy complete perfection:

> ὥστε θεοὶ δ' ἔζωον ἀκηδέα θυμὸν ἔχοντες·
> νόσφιν ἄτερ τε πόνου καὶ ὀιζύος, οὐδέ τι δειλόν
> γῆρας ἐπῆν, αἰεὶ δὲ πόδας καὶ χεῖρας ὁμοῖοι
> τέρποντ' ἐν θαλίῃσι, κακῶν ἔκτοσθεν ἁπάντων·
> θνῆσκον δ' ὥσθ' ὕπνῳ δεδμημένοι· ἐσθλὰ δὲ πάντα
> τοῖσιν ἔην· καρπὸν δ' ἔφερε ζείδωρος ἄρουρα
> αὐτομάτη πολλόν τε καὶ ἄφθονον· οἳ δ' ἐθελημοὶ
> ἥσυχοι ἔργ' ἐνέμοντο σὺν ἐσθλοῖσιν πολέεσσιν.

> They lived like gods, possessing hearts without cares,
> Far removed from toil and woe, nor did wretched old age
> Weigh them down, but with hands and feet unchanging,
> They took their pleasure in feasts, remote from all evils.
> They died as if overcome by sleep; all good things
> Were theirs; the fertile earth brought forth fruit
> In abundance and unstinting; compliant and peaceful
> They looked after their works with many good things.
>
> (112–19)

---

[21] Most critics in fact ignore the implications of the divine fabrication of mankind. Typically, Nelson (1998) 68–69 plays down the intentionality of the gods' "making" and considers it "colorless." But compare Gaia's "making" (ποιήσασα) of "the race of adamant" and "fashioning" (τεῦξε) of the great sickle (*Theogony* 161–62) or the gods' fabrication of Pandora (*Works and Days* 69–82). As Sorel (1982) 27 notes, both creations involve a separation, first of Earth and Sky, and then of human beings from the gods. Preller (1852) 43 speaks of "ein wiederholtes experimentieren der gottheit." For the purposefulness of the gods, see Sorel (1982). Loraux (1996) 9–11 divides myths of the origins of mankind into "born from earth" or "produced by artifice." See also Guarducci (1926).

Line 108 is generally regarded as spurious, and indeed it does not fit the scheme of races created by the gods. It is, however, appropriate to the conception of mankind's origins in the *Theogony*, where, like the other gods, human beings spring from Gaia and Uranus. See below.

Where in this paradisiacal state can one detect a flaw or imperfection? Of course, the golden men were mortal, but death came upon them as gently as sleep. Here indeed their sole imperfection surfaces: the men of the race of gold (and they appear indeed to have been males, since otherwise they could not have lived in such a state of bliss!) did not have the ability to reproduce themselves;[22] and without this ability, they quickly became extinct. Without any intervention on the part of the gods, the men of gold died out within one generation.

The second race of silver, also manufactured by the gods, is as Hesiod tells us explicitly worse than the preceding one both in its appearance and its intellect:

> δεύτερον αὖτε γένος πολὺ χειρότερον μετόπισθεν
> ἀργύρεον ποίησαν Ὀλύμπια δώματ' ἔχοντες,
> χρυσέῳ οὔτε φυὴν ἐναλίγκιον οὔτε νόημα.
> ἀλλ' ἑκατὸν μὲν παῖς ἔτεα παρὰ μητέρι κεδνῇ
> ἐτρέφετ' ἀτάλλων, μέγα νήπιος ᾧ ἐνὶ οἴκῳ·
> ἀλλ' ὅτ' ἄρ' ἡβήσαι τε καὶ ἥβης μέτρον ἵκοιτο,
> παυρίδιον ζώεσκον ἐπὶ χρόνον, ἄλγε' ἔχοντες
> ἀφραδίῃς· ὕβριν γὰρ ἀτάσθαλον οὐκ ἐδύναντο
> ἀλλήλων ἀπέχειν, οὐδ' ἀθανάτους θεραπεύειν
> ἤθελον οὐδ' ἔρδειν μακάρων ἱεροῖς ἐπὶ βωμοῖς,
> ἣ θέμις ἀνθρώποισι κατ' ἤθεα.

> Thereafter in turn a second race, much inferior,
> The silver one, the inhabitants of Olympus made,
> Resembling the golden neither in appearance nor mind;
> But for a hundred years a child was nursed by its mother,
> Playing at home, a big baby;
> But when finally it grew up and reached adulthood,
> They lived but a short time full of grief
> Because of their mindlessness; for they couldn't refrain
> From reckless violence against each other, nor were they willing
> To attend to the gods or to sacrifice on the holy altars of the gods,
> As is the proper rule for human beings according to their customs.
>
> (127–37)

The silver race presents a dramatic decline from golden bliss, from physical perfection to prolonged childhood, from peaceful contentment to mindless violence. Nevertheless, the flaw that doomed the race of gold to rapid

---

[22] Cf. Wilamowitz (1928) 48. Brown (1998) 388 believes that Zeus "brought the golden race to an end," but it is clear that Zeus comes to power only in the course of the silver age. For Ballabriga (1998) 321–22, the gods allowed the golden race to disappear because they were too much like the gods themselves.

extinction has been corrected; the gods appear to have discovered a means to allow the human race to reproduce itself. In spite of its serious faults, the silver race represents a significant progress through its correction of the sole shortcoming of the preceding race. The presence of mothers and children indicates as much.[23] The introduction of women in the silver age also marks a fall from an idyllic time when only males existed, yet the invention of sexual reproduction creates a mechanism for ensuring the autonomous survival of the human race without divine intervention.

But if the gods discovered the means to continue the human race, they have yet to perfect it; for the silver race suffers from excessive infantilism. Children for a hundred years, they are cared for by their mothers at home like big babies, but their infancy is followed by a very brief period of adulthood marked by grief and violence because of their lack of reason (cf. *aphradies*), that is, their stupidity, a continuation of their prolonged childishness.[24] As a result, they ignore the gods and cannot control their violent impulses. To honor the gods requires at the very least a comprehension of the difference or the distance that separates gods and men. The big dummies (*mega nepioi*) of the silver age are simply too childish and too stupid since, like babies, they possess neither self-consciousness nor consciousness of their superiors. Now, such consciousness of being a human being and not a god, and the capacity to perceive the distance between the two, sets human beings apart from the beasts; it is this that constitutes the θέμις ἀνθρώποισι (137). One begins to suspect that the gods' purpose in making human beings aimed at creating a human awareness of that distance. At any rate, Zeus in his anger "hid" the silver race because it refused honors to the blessed gods. In the course of the silver age, then, Zeus has apparently come to power and deposed the preceding generation of gods. There is already a hint here of a pattern that will emerge more clearly later: the succession of generations among the gods has a positive direction from disorder to order, whereas the succession of the human races seems to move in the contrary direction.

The two first races also receive a special status after their death. In accordance with Zeus's will, the δαίμονες ἐσθλοί (the race of gold) become benevolent guardians of mortals and grant them prosperity (121–26). They are in all probability the same as the 3,000 guardians who observe the

---

[23] The word φυή at line 129 already implies this change, since it connotes growth and development as opposed to unchanging limbs of the golden race.

[24] West (1978) at 130 believes that the original myth had the silver race retain their youth, which "originally represented a blessing; Hesiod has lost the sense of this, giving them a long childhood instead of a long ἥβη."

judgments and evil deeds of men in a later passage (254–55). Both times, their activities are closely linked to Zeus and his dispensation for mankind, but the first passage emphasizes their benign aspects while the second dwells on their punitive powers.[25] If the post-mortem fate of the golden men seems appropriate to their nature, the destiny of the silver race has provoked considerable discussion. Rohde was the first to view them as the heroes of Greek cult;[26] in this he is followed by Vernant, who argues that both gold and silver *genea* embody Dumézil's first function, that of sovereignty, and offer two versions of the hero, the first in the context of *dike*, the second, of *hybris*.[27] But in the historic period, at least, heroes of cult are generally not anonymous; rather they are usually credited with a specific history and accomplishments that link them to their community. In the case of the silver race, it is difficult to see why, given their great inferiority to their predecessors, they should receive honor, even of a second rank.[28] And why, as silly overgrown babies, should they be honored specifically as heroes tied to their local communities as protectors? Finally, what should one make of the paradoxical label assigned to them: "subterranean blessed mortals"?

The answer, I believe lies in the meaning of *makares*, which I take to be euphemistic and apotropaic. At line 730, Hesiod warns of the taboo against urinating or exposing oneself en route or on the side of the road because "the nights belong to the blessed ones" (μακάρων τοι νύκτες ἔασιν). These are not, as de Heer points out, the Olympian gods, but the "powers of the dark like those associated with night, and they need to be placated in the same manner."[29] The honor these evil spirits or ghosts receive resembles not the honor of cult, as Rohde argued, but the honor paid to the bad Eris who rejoices in trouble (κακόχαρτος, 28) "by necessity" (ὑπ᾽ ἀνάγκης . . . Ἔριν

---

[25] West (1978) brackets 124–25 as an interpolation from 254–55; nevertheless, the identity still holds.

[26] Rohde (1898) 1.95–102. Rohde insists on the absence of hero cult, or even the impossibility of hero cult, in Homer's view of the afterlife (but cf. p. 128). Yet Homer's downplaying of religious veneration of dead heroes (for he is not completely silent) points rather to the epic's affirmation that it alone can confer immortality. von Fritz (1947) 237–40 believes that Hesiod added the post-mortem fate of the silver race in order to accommodate local heroes as opposed to the heroes of Epic. Preller and Robert (1887) 1.1.91 represent the pre-Rohde view, with which I concur, that the silver men become some kind of demonic creatures of local popular belief. Preller (1852) 42, n. 107 aptly compares the post-mortem existence of the gold and silver race to the Italian Lares and Lemures. See also Roth (1860) 456–59. Burkert (1985) 180 notes that, with the exception of the *Agathos Daimon*, *daimones* are not usually the objects of cult. Rudhardt (1981b) 256 observes that the first three races have collective identities, whereas only the last two are composed of differentiated individuals.

[27] Vernant (1965a) 62. Vernant's attempt to impose Dumézil's tri-functionalism on Hesiod's myth has not won wide acceptance. Cf. the critique of Rudhardt (1981b) 246–47. Nagy (1979) 151–55 follows Vernant's interpretation closely, but breathes not a word about Dumézil.

[28] Cf. Bona-Quaglia (1973) 99–103; and Schoele (1980).

[29] De Heer (1969) 21–25.

τιμῶσι βαρεῖαν, 15–16), that is, in recognition of their power to harm, a power which is mitigated by calling them *makares*. Not the heroes of cult, but far closer to the genii of popular superstition, poltergeists, and things that go bump in the night, the mindless silver babies, in accordance with their terrestrial nature, become the somewhat malign uncanny forces beneath the earth, while the golden race become beneficent spirits on it.

Hesiod characterizes the succeeding race as radically different from the silver:

> Ζεὺς δὲ πατὴρ τρίτον ἄλλο γένος μερόπων ἀνθρώπων
> χάλκειον ποίησ᾽, οὐκ ἀργυρέῳ οὐδὲν ὁμοῖον,
> ἐκ μελιᾶν,[30] δεινόν τε καὶ ὄβριμον, οἷσιν Ἄρηος
> ἔργ᾽ ἔμελε στονόεντα καὶ ὕβριες· οὐδέ τι σῖτον
> ἤσθιον, ἀλλ᾽ ἀδάμαντος ἔχον κρατερόφρονα θυμόν·
> ἄπλαστοι· μεγάλη δὲ βίη καὶ χεῖρες ἄαπτοι
> ἐξ ὤμων ἐπέφυκον ἐπὶ στιβαροῖσι μέλεσσιν.[31]
> τῶν δ᾽ ἦν χάλκεα μὲν τεύχεα, χάλκεοι δέ τε οἶκοι,
> χαλκῷ δ᾽ εἰργάζοντο· μέλας δ᾽ οὐκ ἔσκε σίδηρος.
> καὶ τοὶ μὲν χείρεσσιν ὑπὸ σφετέρῃσι δαμέντες
> βῆσαν ἐς εὐρώεντα δόμον κρυεροῦ Ἀίδαο
> νώνυμνοι· θάνατος δὲ καὶ ἐκπάγλους περ ἐόντας
> εἷλε μέλας, λαμπρὸν δ᾽ ἔλιπον φάος ἠελίοιο.

> Father Zeus made another race of men, the third,
> Brazen, in no way resembling the silver one,
> From ash-tree nymphs, terrible and mighty, who occupied
>   themselves
> With the groaning works of Ares and deeds of hybris; nor
>   did they
> Eat any grain, but had brutal hearts of adamant;
> Rough creatures; and great force and powerful hands
> Grew from their shoulders on their mighty limbs.
> Their arms were of bronze, and their houses of bronze,
> And they worked in bronze; but they did not have black iron.
> Overcome by their own hands,
> They went into the moldy house of chilly Hades
> Nameless; and although they were terrible, black death
> Took them, and they left the bright light of the sun.   (143–55)

---

[30] West (1978) notes that Hesiod uses the genitive in -ᾶν in order to bring out the femininity of the Meliai, the ash-tree nymphs. The word should probably be capitalized as at *Theogony* 187. See also the Scholium at 145a. Appropriately, spears are made from ash trees, which brings out the warrior character of Bronze men.

[31] Solmsen brackets lines 148–49; West (1978) 188 finds lines 148–49 an "unfortunate" adaptation of *Theogony* 150–52 and 649 (cf. also 670–73), but fully worthy of Hesiod. But the similarity of the Bronze men to the Hundred-Handers may not be fortuitous.

The flaw in the silver age is indeed corrected, but it is, so to speak, over-compensated. While free of the childish weaknesses that characterized the silver race, the men of bronze possess an excess of physical strength that they exploit only to make war on one another. Unlike the Hundred-handers whom they resemble (cf. *Theogony* 151–52 and 649), the bronze men cannot channel their violence to useful ends. Moreover, as Hesiod remarks, they do not eat bread, i.e. they do not practice agriculture and hence are exempt from the need to cultivate the earth continually in order to eat.[32] One might well wonder what these bronze men ate. I would conjecture a diet of roast beef, nothing but meat, of which, however, they neglected to offer sacrifice to the gods.[33] Without the constant necessity of growing food to distract them and armed with weapons of bronze, they indulge in unrelenting mutual violence against each other until they manage to annihilate one another. They most resemble the armed warriors of Theban myth, the Spartoi, who sprang from the earth fully armed and quickly set about killing each other off.[34] The Homeric epic also seems cognizant of gigantic and savage warriors of an earlier era.[35] At any rate, the mutual destruction of the bronze warriors relieves the need for any intervention on the part of Zeus. The bronze race receives as its fate an anonymous death in the house of Hades. This is the first race that suffers the common fate of the human race. In this respect, the bronze race is already "like us";[36] it shares with us the specific character of human mortality. Perhaps we are closer to them than we think.

---

[32] Crubellier (1996) 458 implausibly believes that the Bronze men did not eat. Lines 146–47 in fact hint at a connection between the absence of agriculture and the bronze men's violence. Carrière (1986) 201–3 suggests that with the Bronze Age, work has made its entrance in human life. And indeed Hesiod stresses that they "worked in bronze," i.e. practiced metallurgy. Cf. Daudet (1972). For Fontenrose (1974) Hesiod's "myth of the five ages does in fact support the doctrine of work for mankind and illustrate the consequences of disobedience" (p. 5).

[33] The Scholia (146a) suggest cannibalism or hunting wild beasts.   [34] Richir (1995) 49–50.

[35] One thinks, for example, of Tityus and Orion, but also of the warriors of Nestor's youth. Nietzsche (1960) 2.787 considers the bronze and the heroic races to be one and the same; their differences are those of perspective.

[36] The namelessness of the bronze race after death reminds of Zeus's power to make men ἄφατοι and ἄρρητοι, of which the proem spoke. Wilamowitz (1928) 54 calls the bronze race "das erste wirklich menschliche Geschlecht"; see also p. 140; and West (1978) 187: "the Bronze race's origin from trees or tree-nymphs identifies them with the first men known to ordinary Greek tradition." Cf. Mazon (1914) 65: "C'est celle [la troisième race] dont descendent les hommes d'aujourd'hui." Tandy and Neale (1996) 68 define Meliae as "a group of nymphs here construed as the mothers of the Bronze Race." Also Most (1997) 109: "With the bronze race, however, a group of beings comes into existence which is biologically distinct from the first two races but which we can recognize as being much like ourselves." One might perhaps conjecture that the bronze women were the mothers of the heroes and hence that we are their lineal descendants.

The fourth race, that of the heroes and the only one not identified with a metal, is also made by Zeus:

αὐτὰρ ἐπεὶ καὶ τοῦτο γένος κατὰ γαῖα κάλυψεν,
αὖτις ἔτ' ἄλλο τέταρτον ἐπὶ χθονὶ πουλυβοτείρη
Ζεὺς Κρονίδης ποίησε, δικαιότερον καὶ ἄρειον,
ἀνδρῶν ἡρώων θεῖον γένος, οἳ καλέονται
ἡμίθεοι, προτέρη γενεὴ κατ' ἀπείρονα γαῖαν.
καὶ τοὺς μὲν πόλεμός τε κακὸς καὶ φύλοπις αἰνή
τοὺς μὲν ὑφ' ἑπταπύλῳ Θήβῃ, Καδμηίδι γαίῃ,
ὤλεσε μαρναμένους μήλων ἕνεκ' Οἰδιπόδαο,
τοὺς δὲ καὶ ἐν νήεσσιν ὑπὲρ μέγα λαῖτμα θαλάσσης
ἐς Τροίην ἀγαγὼν Ἑλένης ἕνεκ' ἠυκόμοιο.

But when the earth covered over this race,
Yet another one, the fourth, Zeus son of Cronus made
On the much-nurturing earth, one more just and better,
The divine race of hero men, who are called
Demi-gods, the previous race on the boundless earth.
Evil war and dreadful conflict destroyed
Some under Thebes of the seven gates in the Cadmean land
Fighting over the flocks of Oedipus;
And brought others in ships over the great expanse of the sea
To Troy for the sake of fair-haired Helen.   (156–65)

Whereas the gods', presumably the Titans' (the generation of Cronus), second attempt at producing human beings was less successful than the first, Zeus manages to improve on his second try.[37] As Hesiod insists right away, the heroes are more just and better than the preceding race, which suggests at least some link between the two.[38] But the comparatives are equally valid in respect to the following age of iron. In some sense, then, the heroic age looks both backward and forward. Moreover, along with the heroes, *dike*, justice, has entered the world of men.[39] The heroes themselves are produced by the intervention of the gods, specifically, through sexual intercourse between gods and human beings that generate the *hemitheoi*. In addition, a number of other innovations mark the heroic race. While war in some form – of all against all – may have existed in the era of bronze, here it is organized for a specific purpose with a well-defined beginning and end.[40] Moreover, cities, exemplified by Thebes, traditionally reputed to be the first city, and Troy, and all they imply for communal life

---

[37] Benardete (1967) 156; Rudhardt (1981b) 258.
[38] Cf. 129 and 144, where the discontinuity between *genea* is emphasized.
[39] Cf. Carrière (1986) 204.   [40] Cf. Rudhardt (1981b) 255.

and social organization, appear for the first time; likewise sailing and of course agriculture, which through the need for constant exertion domesticates the innate violence of human beings that marked the two previous races.

By definition, the heroes are a mixed race between men and gods that traces its origins to the mingling of divine and human blood. The dual parentage of the heroes is mirrored in their post-mortem fate. Some retire to the Isles of the Blest to enjoy a state that resembles the life of the gods as well as that of the golden race who lived "like the gods".[41] The rest simply die as we do. But if the gods intended to manufacture a race that could reproduce itself and prolong its existence independently, the heroes constitute a problem for them. Indeed, the production of heroes requires continual intervention on the part of the gods to preserve their mixed nature. And, in fact, the mythological tradition relates that from a certain moment on, the gods distanced themselves from intimate contact with human beings and refused to continue to bring forth such children of mixed parentage.[42]

No catastrophe or sudden destruction precipitates the end of the heroic age.[43] Instead, a gradual transition occurs as the gods withdraw from intercourse with mortals. Lines 173d–e, which most commentators – probably correctly – regard as interpolations, nicely express this shift when they say that Zeus did not make (ποίησε) the race of iron, but instead "established" (θῆκεν) it. Whether genuine or not, the term is well chosen, for the Iron Age is not created *de novo*. It represents not a total rupture but continuity with the preceding epoch. We, who belong to the race of iron, are the decadent heirs of the heroes, in whom the divine blood has become diluted, while our tendency to violent self-destructiveness, in part resembling that of the Bronze Age, increases.

In our age, the gods have distanced themselves, but their emissaries, Aidos and Nemesis as well as Dike and the good Eris, are still among us. As a result, we still enjoy good things mixed with the inevitable evils attendant on the human lot. But when children are born old with gray hair (the inverse of the silver age when childhood lasted a hundred years), then the goddesses, disgusted with the violence and injustice of mankind, will abandon the earth, and Zeus will annihilate the race. Still, the possibility of

---

[41] Carrière (1986) 206–12 clearly distinguishes between the epic heroes who die and those translated to the Blessed Isles while still alive, on the model of Menelaus (*Odyssey* 4.561–69).

[42] For the tradition of the end of the age of heroes, see Chapter 7.

[43] Cf. Benardete (1967) 156; Rudhardt (1981) 247–52; Bianchi (1963) 146.

stopping the progressive decline, which unchecked will lead to destruction, abides if men can be dissuaded from their violence and unjust ways.

The succession of races of mankind appears, then, to constitute repeated experiments involving trial and error by the gods or Zeus. But as we asked at the beginning of our inquiry: what was the purpose of the gods in fabricating the human race? For the *Works and Days* portrays the evolution of the human species not as a fortuitous accident, but rather as an action undertaken by the gods for a specific purpose. A cosmos that lacked mankind would somehow appear incomplete in the eyes of the gods. If only gods existed, there would be no creatures to honor them or to sacrifice to them. In short, without men, the gods would lack a sense of their own superiority.[44]

Of course, the primary difference between gods and men, immortality, already at the outset indicates the superiority of the gods. Human mortality is present in the very first divine attempt to fashion men in the golden age; while living like gods, they were nevertheless mortal. But without the ability to reproduce itself, the golden race would have required the constant intervention of the gods in every generation to renew itself. The gods then discovered a means to allow men to reproduce themselves: the gods invented woman. While, however, the human race could now reproduce itself autonomously, the silver folk were so infantile that they were incapable of recognizing the superiority of the gods. Hence Zeus's rage, their destruction, and a fresh attempt. But in correcting the childishness of the silver race, Zeus fashioned a race so violent that they annihilated themselves. The next age required the active participation of the gods to generate the heroes, who were thus of mixed origin and semidivine. At the same time, the gods tamed the innate violence of men in giving them justice and the communal life of the *polis* while simultaneously imposing upon them the need for work to feed themselves. Justice and agriculture enter the world together. Violence, however, does not disappear, but it is no longer gratuitous, but organized in the communal activity of war in the great expeditions against Thebes and Troy where the heroes demonstrate their valor – and perhaps provide entertainment for the gods.[45]

Why, then, did the gods not leave it at that? I think the answer lies in a fundamental instability that characterizes the heroic race. First, the

---

[44] Cf. Sorel (1982) 26: "L'humanité est créée, fabriquée par les Olympiens parce qu'elle leur est une nécessité." That the gods need human beings to honor them and to sacrifice to them is a major motif in the *Homeric Hymn to Demeter* and, in a comic mode, in Aristophanes' *Birds*. Consider also the song the Muses sing on Olympus in the *Homeric Hymn to Apollo* 190–93.
[45] Cf. Griffin (1980) 179–204.

production of the heroes again requires the constant active intervention of the gods to ensure continuity. But, secondly, these demi-gods were by definition too closely related to the gods. The purpose of the gods in fashioning mankind was to create a race not only inferior to the gods, but also conscious of that inferiority; without an awareness of their inferiority, human beings would not, as was the case with the silver age, see any reason to honor the gods. In this light, the semi-divine heroes pose a problem for, if not a potential threat to, the gods precisely because of their close familial ties to them. The danger, of which the tradition gives countless examples, is that the heroes, because of this intimacy, would attempt to challenge or even abolish the distance between gods and men – whose establishment was, after all, the reason that the gods fabricated human beings in the first place. Perhaps, then, this problematic proximity, which on occasion, as the epic tradition recounts, led to divine distress if not wrath, explains why the gods withdrew from intercourse with men.[46] The consequence of this withdrawal is the age of iron, our age, and human life as we know it.

Such, it seems, is the analysis of the evolution of the human race according to the *Works and Days*, that is, from the perspective of mankind. But if the *Works and Days* represents only a partial perspective on the cosmos, the account given there may only be part of the story. To supplement and even complement the story recounted in the *Works and Days*, we must examine the *Theogony* to see whether it offers an alternative version of the origin of mankind. To be sure, the origin of human beings may not play as central a role in the *Theogony*, whose announced intention is to recount the history of the gods and their *genos* (105–14). Within that framework, men necessarily occupy only a marginal place. Most scholars, in fact, deny that the *Theogony* contains an anthropogony at all.[47] I believe, however, that the *Theogony* does present an account of the origins of mankind but that the version it offers diverges substantially from the one given in the *Works and Days*.

Let us begin with a simple question: when in the chronological evolution of the eternal gods do men come into being? Human beings certainly play important roles in the so-called "Hymn to Hecate" as well as in the Prometheus story, where they are the passive victims of the contest between

---

[46] This withdrawal seems to be the theme of the *Homeric Hymn to Aphrodite*. See Clay (1989) 152–201.

[47] Most recently by Rotondaro (1997). But Klaussen (1835) 448 makes the interesting observation: "sehr mit Unrecht hat man die Theogonie beschuldigt, sie vernachlässige die Entstehung der Menschen: auf die einzelnen Menschen kommt es in einer Theogonie nicht an, sondern auf die Entstehung der in ihrem Herzen waltenden Geister; sobald diese da sind, wachsen die Menschen als ihre Zugabe aus der Erde hervor."

Prometheus and Zeus. But they are "already there" at an earlier period. A close examination of the text suggests that the appearance of the human race must pre-date the genesis of the children of Night (211–32). The catalogue of Night's offspring contains for the most part an unpleasant brood of negative forces, but many of these evils, as Hesiod explicitly says, exclusively influence human life.[48] Nemesis, for example, is a "bane to mortal men" (223); others, like Old Age, Hunger, and Toil do not touch the lives of the immortal gods, but constitute the eternal attributes of human life; and, finally, Oath, the last item in the catalogue, is said to "cause the greatest pain for men who inhabit the earth, whenever someone willingly swears falsely" (231–32).

It is important to account for the placement of the catalogue of Night's children within the overall architecture of the *Theogony*; from a purely "chronological" perspective, it could have been placed elsewhere.[49] For example, Hesiod could have immediately followed the birth of Night and her offspring, Day and Aether, through her union with Erebus (123–25), with the rest of the brood Night produces by parthenogenesis. But, as we have seen, Hesiod postpones that catalogue for 85 lines until he has completed his account of the emasculation of Uranus by his son Cronus. At that moment, Hesiod returns to the genealogical line of Night (211–32). The catalogue of Night's offspring, who are little more than personifications of sundry evils, is put off until the entrance of evil into the cosmos, that is, Uranus' abuses of Gaia and his consequent mutilation. Hesiod makes clear the connection by using words related to the personifications in the family of Night during the course of the preceding narrative: for example, Apate, "Deception" and Philotes (224), cf. ἐξαπάτας (205) and φιλότητα (206); Neikea, "Quarrels" (229), cf. νεικείων (208); and the whole brutal scenario embodies Eris (Strife), the spirits of revenge, violence, seduction, and trickery. (Hesiod has used this technique before, in the proem, when the names of the Muses emerge and derive from the preceding description of their activities.[50]) It now appears that the genesis of mankind occurs at the same time and is, in fact, intimately connected to that cosmic event. Hesiod describes how the drops of blood from Uranus' severed member fell upon Earth, who from them conceived the Giants and the Nymphs called

---

[48] To be sure, Eros (120–22), the principle of generation, is universal and affects proleptically both gods and mortals; but many of Night's offspring affect only humans. The high frequency of references to mankind in this catalogue suggests it has come into being.

[49] Cf. above, p. 19.

[50] Muellner (1996) 66–67 argues, on the contrary, that the personifications, in this case, the children of Night, prepare for events in the following episode. The naming of the Muses, however, would seem to argue the other way.

Meliai (185–87). From these, as the scholiast asserts, spring the ancestors of the human race (ἐκ τούτων ἦν τὸ πρῶτον γένος τῶν ἀνθρώπων, "from these came the first race of human beings").[51]

The proem of the *Theogony* lends support to this argument. There, the song of the Muses on Olympus embraced not only the genesis of the gods and the supremacy of Zeus (43–45), but also the "race of men and mighty Giants," ἀνθρώπων τε γένος κρατερῶν τε Γιγάντων (50). The phrase suggests the close relation, if not identity, of the race of men and that of the Giants.[52] Multiple traditions identifying aboriginal human beings with *Gegenes* are found throughout Greece. These local myths are closely linked to claims of precedence and autochthony on the part of individual *poleis*. Significantly, however, there exists no dominant Panhellenic tradition and no one universally accepted Greek Adam.[53] Nevertheless, Hesiod's claim that men and Giants have a shared ancestry by being descendants of the same *genos* would not surprise Greek hearers. Moreover, the Giants in the *Theogony* – huge and strong, gleaming in their armor and wielding their mighty javelins – are strikingly similar to the race of bronze, which was described in the *Works and Days* as ἐκ μελιᾶν, δεινόν τε καὶ ὄβριμον ("from the ash-tree nymphs, terrible and strong" 145). The Scholia to the *Works and Days* (143 b) gloss Hesiod's third race simply as τοὺς Γίγαντας. It would thus seem that the *Theogony* here alludes to an anthropogony in, one must admit, a fairly oblique manner. But it may indeed have been an old tradition and well known to his audience. At any rate, Hesiod's indirection here should not surprise us in a composition whose central subject is not mankind or its origins, but the coming-to-be of the gods.

According to the *Theogony*, then, it appears that human beings are descended from the union of the Giants and the Melian Nymphs, both of them, in turn, sprung from the bloody drops of the severed member of Uranus and incubated by Mother-Earth – a genealogy and birth as bizarre as it is unique, even for the *Theogony*.[54] The *Theogony*, accordingly, presents

---

[51] Scholia ad 187 (Pertusi). Cf. Wilamowitz (1928) 54: "das erste wirkliche menschliche Geschlecht stammt aus den Baümen."

[52] An obvious parallel for the construction: πατὴρ ἀνδρῶν τε θεῶν τε; "father of gods and men" implies only one father. Preller (1852) 40 says of the Hesiodic passage that "die menschen und die giganten ganz offenbar nur als zwei verschiedene generationen desselben geschlechts, nehmlich der γηγενεῖς, angesehen werden."

[53] The most thorough treatment is Preller (1852) 1–60. See also Preller and Robert (1887) 1.1.78–87; Guthrie (1957) 21–28; Vian (1952); and Lugenbühl (1992) 100–33. Loraux (1996) 20–26 observes the multiplicity of "first men" in Greek myth. Note that the mother of one of these primal men, Phoroneus, is named Melia: Apollodorus 2.1.1; cf. Pausanias 2.15.5 and 2.19.5, where Phoroneus replaces Prometheus as the discoverer of fire. For sundry claims to priority, see fr. ades. 67 *PMG*.

[54] See the remarks of the excellent Schoemann (1857a) 125–41.

the origin of the human race as the casual by-product of a violent cosmic drama that is simultaneously the first act of the myth of divine succession. Significantly, the birth of mankind there is more or less an accident; the violence of man seems to be due to the very circumstances of his birth. But most striking is the great disparity between the history of mankind in the *Works and Days* and the *Theogony*. In the latter poem, the generation of mankind is, as we have seen, almost a fortuitous accident, the by-product of a cosmic event which is not only the first act in the history of the king-ship of the gods, but also the primordial event of cosmogony that in a fundamental sense opens the very possibility of a cosmos; for without the separation of Heaven and Earth, the cosmos could not have come into being. The version recounted in the *Theogony* also reveals mankind as al-ready present from the earliest phase of the cosmos. This retrojection of the origins of human beings finds a parallel in Hesiod's treatment of the birth of Aphrodite that follows (188–206); he rejects the Homeric tradition that identifies her as a daughter of Zeus and Dione and presents her as a much older divinity, whose birth likewise coincides with the separation of Heaven and Earth. Significantly, the world defined by Aphrodite's emergence rep-resents a new cosmic order; spatially, it now resembles "our" world with its named islands distinct from both land and sea. Cosmologically, with the subordination of the primordial Eros to Aphrodite, generation is no longer an obscure process of "coming forth," but a regulated union of the sexes, henceforth Aphrodite's prerogative, which she exercises over both human beings and immortal gods (203–4).[55] Thus Hesiod presents the origins of the human race as coeval with the moment when cosmogony gives way to theogony properly speaking.

In the *Theogony*, the antiquity of mankind, its accidental origin, and its innate violence offer a very different picture from the origins outlined in the *Works and Days*: on the one side, the making of men through purposeful action on the part of the gods; on the other, a fortuitous accident. Each new race represented a fresh attempt by the gods to fashion creatures who were both independent of the gods and capable of ensuring their own continuity while also conscious of their inferiority to the gods and hence able to worship them. With the sole exception of the transition between the heroes and our Iron Age, the succession of races in the *Works and Days* is radically discontinuous. The primal happiness of mankind in the reign of Cronus cannot be recuperated. The primordial men of the *Theogony*, on the other hand, resemble most closely Zeus's first attempt to fashion human

[55] Cf. Vernant (1991b) 1.373; Bonnafé (1985) 31–32; and Rudhardt (1986) 17.

beings, the violent race of bronze of the *Works and Days*. It is significant that neither the race of gold nor that of silver find a place in the *Theogony*. This absence provocatively suggests that, from an Olympian perspective at least, no golden age of mankind ever existed. The *Theogony* also would appear to cast doubt on the role of the benign guardians of Zeus's justice, into which the golden race is transformed after their death – as well as the existence of the evil spirits arising from the silver race. Only with the bronze race do the two versions seem to coincide, the bronze race that occupied a central place in the anthropogony of the *Works and Days*. In fact, the rest of the two accounts could easily be harmonized to include the race of heroes and our age of iron. And, indeed, the *Theogony* speaks of the exploits of the heroes and describes, even if only in passing, the life of mankind more or less like our own in the "Hymn to Hecate." But if the *Theogony's* version can in some measure be accommodated to the last stages of the story told in the *Works and Days*, the two accounts of man's genesis, the circumstances surrounding it, and the human character arising from them nevertheless offer stark contrasts.[56]

Why did Hesiod present two such divergent versions of the origin of man? A simple, but certainly insufficient answer is to remind ourselves that the two compositions of Hesiod can be distinguished by their different perspectives. The *Theogony*, authorized by the Muses, treats mankind from an Olympian perspective, while the *Works and Days* offers a terrestrial view of human life. Olympus evidently regards mankind as a threat to divine supremacy, a threat that must be tamed and channeled into obedience; human beings look nostalgically to a golden age of happiness, which they set in an era before the reign of Zeus; over the course of time, they have become increasingly distant and subservient to the gods. Further elaboration and consequences of these divergent perspectives will emerge from an examination of the two versions of the Prometheus story presented in the two poems.

---

[56] Line 108 of the *Works and Days*, generally considered spurious, highlights these differences: ὡς ὁμόθεν γεγάασι θεοὶ θνητοί τ᾽ ἄνθρωποι (". . . that the gods and mortal men came into being from the same origin"). The verse seems wrong for the *Works and Days*, where men are made by the gods, but they would suit the account in the *Theogony*, where both gods and men spring ultimately from Gaia and Uranus.

CHAPTER 5

The two Prometheuses

ἐκρίνετο τί θεὸς καὶ τί ἄνθρωπος ἐν τῇ Μηκώνῃ.
In Mekone it was decided what is a god and what a human being.
(Scholium on *Theogony* 535)

If the anthropogonic myths we have examined trace the origins of mankind, the myth of Prometheus describes its condition. As a testimony to the signal importance he assigns to it, Hesiod relates the story twice, once in the middle of the *Theogony* (521–616), and again at the beginning of the *Works and Days* (47–105). This double telling, more or less contemporaneously, by the same poet offers a unique insight into Hesiod's myth-making; it also reveals how the story could be manipulated and adjusted to fit the very different contexts in which it appears. In the first case, the account, the longest sustained narrative in the *Theogony*, is placed in the middle of the poem between Zeus's deposition of his father Cronus and the Titanomachy, where the Olympians successfully defeat the gods of the previous generation. Thus the story patently – since Athena and Hephaestus, who are not yet born, take part in the action – breaks the expected temporal sequence. In the *Works and Days*, the myth, set close to the beginning, clearly serves as an introduction to Hesiod's exhortations to his brother Perses.

The narrative itself has frequently been viewed as a rather unsatisfactory synthesis of heterogeneous elements. West, for instance, sees the narrative as three disparate aetiologies: the first explains the division of the victim in Greek sacrifice, where men get the edible parts, but the gods receive only bones wrapped in fat; the second explains how human beings came into possession of fire; finally, we get an account of the origin of women and how they have made men miserable.[1] To this, according to West, the *Works and Days* add another element from yet another myth concerning

---

[1] Cf. West (1966) 305–7; he concludes, 307: "What we have in Hesiod, then, is a combination of three myths, all probably traditional, which could have been told separately . . ." Cf. Robert (1905) 170; Wehrli (1956) 415–18; Reinhardt (1960) 197; Philips (1973).

the release of human ills from a jar, which accounts for the presence of evils in human life.[2] Earlier critics attempted to reconstruct Hesiod's literary sources for the Prometheus narrative, perhaps a burlesque poem similar in tone to the humorous *Hymn to Hermes*, which Hesiod tried, without complete success, to exploit for more serious ends. Given its heterogeneous components and adaptation to a very different purpose, Hesiod's recasting of the Prometheus myth was almost inevitably doomed to be incoherent and contradictory.[3]

In the *Theogony*, however, the story is introduced under a unified rubric: "when gods and mortal men were in the course of distinguishing themselves at Mecone" (ὅτ' ἐκρίνοντο θεοὶ θνητοί τ' ἄνθρωποι | Μηκώνη, 535–36). The scholiast cited in the epigraph to this chapter grasped what it was that was being distinguished: what is a god and what is a mortal.[4] The account in the *Works and Days* also purports to have a unified theme: it explains how it came about that the gods hid and keep hidden human sustenance (κρύψαντες γὰρ ἔχουσι θεοὶ βίον ἀνθρώποισιν, 42). Hesiod, at least, believed, however naively, that each narrative, taken as a whole, made a meaningful and comprehensible statement.

The analysis of Jean-Pierre Vernant presented in a completely persuasive manner both the unity and the coherence of the myth.[5] Since this study builds on Vernant's interpretation, a brief outline may serve by way of orientation. The sequence of actions and counter-actions, ruses and counter-ruses, by both Zeus and Prometheus, from the sacrifice trick to the theft of fire and the fabrication of the Woman/Pandora, reveals a coherent narrative logic as well as a strict thematic and structural unity. The contest of wits between *metieta* Zeus (Zeus "who has *metis*") and Prometheus *ankulometis* ("of the crooked *metis*") is organized around the repeated motifs of giving and not giving, accepting and refusing, and revealing and hiding. What is given/accepted or refused or hidden is in each case a booby-trapped gift whose attractive exterior hides a destructive interior or, inversely, a less attractive exterior hides a human good (sacrificial portions, fire, Woman/Pandora). Finally each act of giving or refusing to give precipitates an equally deceptive counter-gift. As a result, "human existence through the operation of divine deception is characterized by the mixture of good and evil, by ambiguity and duplicity".[6] This underlying structural scheme informs the narrative sequence of the story that defines the human condition, uneasily poised between god and beast.

---

[2] West (1978) 155.   [3] See, for example, Aly (1913b); Wehli (1956); Lendle (1957); and Heitsch (1963). [4] Cf. Rudhardt (1981a) 214–16.   [5] Vernant (1974); and (1979).   [6] Vernant (1974) 190.

In the first act of this drama that outlines the progressive estrangement of gods and men, Prometheus divides up a sacrificial ox, assigning human beings the edible portions, but leaving only the bones and fat for the gods. Practiced solely by human beings, the act of sacrifice offers them a means of approaching and communicating with the gods, but at the same time it constitutes a tangible sign of their separation, since gods do not eat meat; rather, from their heavenly heights, they inhale the luscious aromas that arise from the cooking meat. Men, on the other hand, must constantly eat to live, and this necessity links them to the beasts. Zeus astutely responds to Prometheus' sacrifice trick by depriving men of fire. Without fire, human beings are compelled to consume raw food, just like the animals to whose level they are thus reduced. At the same time, mankind, barred from offering sacrifices, loses its means of communication with the gods. The loss of fire demotes mankind, allying it to the beasts and increasing men's distance from the gods. When, however, through his theft, Prometheus restores fire to men, their status is likewise restored for all time to its precarious intermediate position between god and beast.

In the final act in this drama of mutual deception, Zeus, suiting the punishment to the crime, creates woman – or, to be more precise, the Wife. For the anonymous woman of the *Theogony* and the Pandora of the *Works and Days* represent not merely the first "female woman," but the Bride, in all of her seductive splendor and adornment. Her arrival inaugurates the human institution of marriage, which like sacrifice serves to delimit the coordinates of the human condition. For as mortal beings, humans are compelled, like the beasts, to reproduce in order to continue the species. But unlike the promiscuous beasts who practice incest and the similarly promiscuous gods, human beings uniquely regulate sexuality and reproduction through marriage. In addition, the Wife, as I shall call her, constitutes the perfect counter to Prometheus' gift of fire, for like fire, she dries a man out (cf. *Works and Days* 705) and consumes the fruits of his labors; and like fire she must constantly be fed and tended while wasting her husband's substance. Yet, seduced by her beauty and lured by her lies, men eternally reenact the folly of Epimetheus and embrace the beautiful evil; too late they realize what they have done, but then the disaster is irremediable (*amechanos*). In the *Works and Days*, the woman, there named Pandora, is linked to a mysterious jar whose lid she raises, thereby allowing human ills to escape and bringing an abrupt and permanent end to human happiness. At the last moment, however, she replaces the cover and – in accordance with Zeus's plans – leaves Hope imprisoned under the lip of the jar.

As the scholia attest, the controversy concerning the meaning of Hope and her abiding "under the lips" of the jar is an old one. West summarizes the problem:

Hesiod clearly thinks of the ills as what came out of the jar: formerly men were free of them, now they are everywhere; and they are contrasted with Hope which stayed inside. How is it that they are among men because they came out, while Hope is among men because it was kept in? What was Hope doing in the jar anyway, if it was a jar of ills? . . . It is of course illogical to make the same jar serve both purposes at once.[7]

Stated in these terms, the problem seems insoluble. But if one realizes that the jar itself is a doublet of Pandora, attractive on the outside, but a bane within, then Hope can likewise be understood to be as ambiguous as Pandora herself.[8] Her seductive attraction befuddles the mind and promises bliss while her deceptive inner nature contains a bitchy mind, lies, wheedling words, and a thievish character (67, 78). With a similar ambiguity, Hope promises and seduces, but all too rarely delivers. In an absolute sense, then, Hope is an evil, deluding us into cultivating illusions: hence it rightfully belongs in the jar, but in relation to mankind its character is more complex.

Before mentioning his gift of fire to mankind, the Prometheus of the *Prometheus Bound* recounts how he prevented men from foreseeing their own death by implanting blind hopes in them (*PV* 248–50). Such hopes, equivalent to ignorance of the hour of one's own death, are an essential precondition for all human activity:[9] only human beings have hope. The brutes, without consciousness or *nous*, lack it. The gods, on the other hand, do not need it since they possess sure knowledge and, in any case, as immortals they are exempt from anticipating their death. Thus Hope, the ultimate *kalon kakon*, characterizes the human condition and once again situates us between the ignorance of the beasts and the certain knowledge of the gods, between forethought and hind-thought, between Prometheus and Epimetheus. Hesiod further clarifies the character of Elpis by having Zeus remove the voices of all the devastating diseases that escape from the jar through his devising. They come unannounced and thus allow us to hope for tomorrow. Hope is the necessary illusion that informs human life and makes it bearable.

Zeus's supreme move wins the match with Prometheus and simultaneously checkmates mankind, permanently unable to escape its human

---

[7] West (1978) 169–70. Leinecks (1984) offers an overview of older scholarship.
[8] Cf. Benardete (1967) 154–56.   [9] Achilles constitutes the exception that proves the rule.

condition, a condition founded on the institutions of sacrifice, agriculture, and marriage, and predicated on Hope.

This summary only sketches the richness of Vernant's interpretation. What has perhaps not received sufficient consideration, however, is the differences between the two versions of the myth as recounted in the *Theogony* and the *Works and Days*, not only in their narrative strategies, but also within their wider contexts.[10] It would by no means be surprising to discover that the Olympian perspective on the human condition differs from the human one since, as we have seen, the two accounts of the origin of human beings in the two poems are surely heterogeneous if not contradictory. And we might well expect the gods to view the process of their separation from mankind, which is the focus of the Prometheus myth, and the resultant condition of mankind from an angle divergent from our own.

In the *Works and Days* Hesiod tells the story of Prometheus to Perses to convince him of the necessity of work, "for the gods have hidden from men their livelihood" (*bios*) (42–46). There is no mention of Prometheus' trick involving the division of the sacrifice or of Zeus's choice between the two portions proffered by the Titan. The narrative in the *Works and Days* begins from Zeus's hiding of fire and remains centered on Zeus's actions and their painful consequences for human life.

If the first act of the drama of Prometheus, the sacrifice trick, is omitted in the *Works and Days*, that omission means that the poem in some sense *presupposes* the separation of gods and men, symbolized by the sacrifice. At the beginning of the *Works and Days*, then, that separation has already taken place. Hesiod has thus truncated the beginning of the story, but, conversely, he extends the final section by elaborating on the story of Pandora: the account of the *pithos*, the escape of the evils that beset human beings in accordance with Zeus's plan, and Hope's place on the lips of the jar. The story told in the *Works and Days* is explicitly predicated on an earlier state when men lived without evils or suffering and diseases (90–92): a kind of golden age that Hesiod goes on to describe in the immediate sequel (109–19). But, as we have already seen, there is no place for a golden age enjoyed by mankind in the *Theogony*; human history begins from the Giants, who spring fully armed from the blood of Uranus. As a result, in the *Theogony* the change in the status of mankind and its separation from the gods precipitated by the duel of wits between Prometheus and Zeus cannot be

---

[10] Cf. Vernant (1974) 185: "Les deux versions peuvent donc être traitées comme des éléments qui s'ajustent pour former un ensemble." Rudhardt (1981a) also tends to homogenize the two versions. But Judet de La Combe (1996) and Judet de La Combe and Lernould (1996) make important contributions in this direction.

understood simply as the consequence of mankind's fall from a previous paradisiacal state.

In the *Works and Days*, Hesiod concludes his narration by remarking: "Hence there is no way to escape the mind of Zeus" (οὕτως οὔ τί πη ἔστι Διὸς νόον ἐξαλέασθαι, 105). Here the poet clearly refers to human beings, henceforth the victims of countless evils, diseases that prey on them day and night, and every kind of misery that comes upon them silently and without warning, since Zeus "deprived them of their voices" (100–04).[11] The *Theogony*'s version concludes with almost the same phrase: "Thus it is not possible to escape the mind of Zeus nor to by-pass it" (ὣς οὐκ ἔστι Διὸς κλέψαι νόον οὐδὲ παρελθεῖν, 613). The similarity of the words should not obscure the important difference in their referents. In the *Theogony*, they are aimed at Prometheus, who could not escape the punishment meted out by Zeus. That punishment, recounted at both the beginning and the end of the narrative, sets the framework within the coordinates of the enmity between Prometheus and Zeus; tellingly, the *Works and Days* omits all mention of Prometheus' fate, and focuses on the human lot. These contrasts draw attention to the very different perspectives of the two versions.

At the center of the narrative as it is recounted in the *Theogony*, mankind, always marginal in the poem, is almost completely absent; the rivalry between Prometheus and Zeus occupies center stage. An understanding of its significance requires us to take account of the wider context as well as the placement and framing of the myth and its function within the architecture of the poem. First of all, the genealogical line of the sons of Iapetus is not in its expected position.[12] When Hesiod lists the Titan children of Uranus and Gaia, Iapetus is born before Cronus (134–38); accordingly, the offspring of Iapetus should be enumerated *before* the offspring of Cronus, the last son of Uranus. But Hesiod defers the catalogue of the sons of Iapetus (507ff.) and inserts it *after* the birth of Zeus, the youngest of the Cronides (457), but *before* Zeus's final defeat of the Titans and his accession

---

[11] Verdenius (1971) 7 believes that line 105 "obviously refers to Prometheus."

[12] Cf. Meyer (1887) 37; and Robert (1905) 166. West's (1966) 305 explanation is unconvincing: "Iapetus' family occupies the last place in the Titan group, because of the length of the mythical digression to which it leads . . . and because the myth cannot well be told before the birth of Zeus, who is involved in it." Zeus, of course, is involved in the "Hymn to Hecate," before his birth. Lauriola (1995) reviews earlier opinions concerning the anomalous placement of the Iapetids and concludes that the Prometheus episode, and hence the insertion of the Iapetid line, forms a climax after the proleptic episodes of Styx and Hecate. She too seems to locate the Hecate passage in a time prior to Prometheus, in which Zeus plays the role of "dominatore e ordinatore del mondo divino" (91). But the description of mankind contained in the Hecate episode is clearly post-Promethean. Although recognizing that Cronus and Zeus are the youngest sons, she does not realize the implications of positioning the offspring of Iapetus last.

to supremacy. In delaying the line of Iapetus, Hesiod manages to reverse the expected genealogical order and, in a way, makes the Iapetids appear to be the younger sons of the family of Cronus. The significance of this genealogical sleight-of-hand derives from the repeated pattern of the succession myth, where it is always the youngest son who deposes his father. And significantly Prometheus is the only figure who shares the epithet *ankulometis* ("of crooked-devisings") with his uncle Cronus.

Secondly, the genealogy of the Iapetids is immediately preceded by the story of the liberation by Zeus of the Cyclopes, who, in gratitude, gave him thunder and lightning "relying on which, he reigns over gods and men" (501–06). Immediately after the Prometheus episode, Hesiod narrates the parallel account of the unbinding of the Hundred-Handers (617–63).[13] In contrast to the punishment and binding of Prometheus, these two actions of unbinding prefigure Zeus's victory in the Titanomachy. Moreover, they share a common feature: a benefaction on the part of Zeus (his liberation of those previously imprisoned) elicits, so to speak, a counter-gift which ensures his final and permanent victory. These are, as Brown has aptly put it, "political deals" whereby "Zeus secures the instruments of organized violence which are characteristic of political power: an armament industry (the Cyclopes), and a mercenary army (the Hundred-Arms)."[14] One may compare the account of Styx, to whom Zeus promised honor (*time*), while she, in return, gave Zeus the gift of her children, Violence, Power, Zeal, and Victory, who never depart from Zeus's side and hence guarantee the eternal duration of his regime (383–403).

The framing of the story of Prometheus by the episodes of the Cyclopes and the Hundred-Handers must not be considered fortuitous. Rather, it offers a key to a problem that most scholars either suppress or ignore, although it is clearly of critical importance: the question of Prometheus' motivation.[15] Why did he take up the cause of mankind? Whence comes this philanthropy? Later traditions explain the Titan's humanism by the fact that he created men.[16] Thus, his philanthropy can be understood as the partiality of the creator for his creatures. But in the *Theogony*, the only creature created by the gods is Woman.

---

[13] Schmid (1988b) 137.   [14] Brown (1953) 20.

[15] Arrighetti (1998) 347 suggests that the problems involving Prometheus' favorable attitude toward mankind and his hostility to Zeus "rimangono ribelli ad ogni tentativo di spiegazione."

[16] Robert (1905) 362–65 attributes this version to Protagoras. Heitsch (1963) 425 believes Hesiod omitted Prometheus' creation of mankind, and that the story as presented only makes sense if it is presupposed. Cf. Blumenberg (1985) 299–327, who offers a provocative discussion of this aspect of the myth. In the *Prometheus Bound*, Prometheus pities mankind for its helplessness.

The Titan's motivation remains obscure. But we may recall that the first men in the *Theogony* resemble the race of bronze in the *Works and Days*, who resemble the horrendous Hundred-Handers, and the Giants, *Gegenes*, endowed with enormous physical force, armed and ready for combat from the moment of their birth. Here one can perhaps discern a motive for the partiality shown by Prometheus. In preparation for the Titanomachy, Zeus allies himself with the Cyclopes and the Hundred-Handers by giving them the gift of liberty. Through this act, Zeus gains their gratitude; they in turn help Zeus against his enemies and make possible his complete victory. The story of Prometheus is thus framed between two incidents that emphasize the principles of reciprocity and the importance of political alliances. The narrative itself repeatedly involves gifts and counter-gifts.

In the first move of what resembles a chess match – or perhaps a poker game – between Zeus and Prometheus, the Titan attempts to make a gift to mankind, a gift with particular resonance for an audience versed in the rules of Greek culinary etiquette. The setting is clearly a communal feast shared by gods and men, a δαίς, whose very name derives from the act of division or apportionment; hence the formulaic expression, δαὶς ἐΐση, referring to a fair or equitable distribution. As a social institution, the δαὶς ἐΐση involves two distinct kinds of apportionment: the first is a division into strictly equal parts (*moirai*) that affirms the communal bonds and mutual obligations of *philia* for all those admitted to participate in it; the second constitutes the portion of honor, the *geras*, assigned in recognition of particular excellence or esteem.[17] With his division of the meats, Prometheus honors men by giving them all the edible parts of the ox. By this very act, he deprives the gods of that part of the δαὶς ἐΐση that legitimately belongs to them and inverts the proper hierarchy of gods and men. That Prometheus, apparently on behalf of mankind, issued the invitation and played host only aggravates the breach of propriety. The equitable feast has now become *inequitable*. Moreover, the extraordinary privilege (*geras*) accorded to mankind by Prometheus presupposes a reciprocal counter-gift on the part of men: presumably, their support of Prometheus in the contest between the Titan and Zeus. Through the use of the word δασσάμενος applied to Prometheus' action in dividing up the ox, the text of the *Theogony* offers a hint of his longer-range intentions. Prometheus' literal division of the portions alludes to Zeus's supreme function as apportioner in the final distribution of honors that inaugurates his reign:

---

[17] Cf. Saïd (1979) 17–23; also Judet de La Combe (1996) 273.

δή ῥα τότ' ὤτρυνον βασιλευέμεν ἠδὲ ἀνάσσειν
Γαίης φραδμοσύνῃσιν Ὀλύμπιον εὐρύοπα Ζῆν
ἀθανάτων· ὁ δὲ τοῖσιν' ἐὺ διεδάσσατο τιμάς.

Then indeed [the gods] urged Olympian wide-seeing Zeus,
On the advice of Gaia, to be king and rule
Over the immortals; and he divided up their honors well.

(883–85)

By taking over the function of distribution, Prometheus reveals his ambition
to be the supreme god and to usurp Zeus's power and status. Zeus clearly
understands the significance of Prometheus' act when with heavy irony he
addresses him:

Ἰαπετιονίδη, πάντων ἀριδείκετ' ἀνάκτων,
ὦ πέπον, ὡς ἑτεροζήλως διεδάσσαο μοίρας.

Son of Iapetus, exalted among all lords,
My good man, how unfairly have you divided the portions!

(543–44)

With his foresight, Zeus is, of course, able to counter Prometheus' ruse.
The Olympian's first move is to deprive men of fire, the cooking fire, which
reduces them to the level of beasts. Zeus's action is described in enigmatic
lines that are usually translated as follows:

ἐκ τούτου δὴ ἔπειτα χόλου μεμνημένος αἰεὶ
οὐκ ἐδίδου μελίῃσι πυρὸς μένος ἀκαμάτοιο
θνητοῖς ἀνθρώποις οἳ ἐπὶ χθονὶ ναιετάουσιν.

From that time forward always remembering his anger,
He did not give the strength of tireless fire to the ash-trees
For mortal men who inhabit the earth.   (562–64)

West claims that "we may be fairly sure what Hesiod's audience would
understand by the phrase 'giving fire to the ash-trees'."[18] I am less certain,
since, as West himself admits, ash-trees do not have any special association
with fire in Greek lore nor do ash-trees elsewhere stand for trees in general.
Ash-tree nymphs, however, as the Scholia remark, are traditionally linked
with the origins of mankind, and they interpret μελίῃσι as μελιηγενής,
"born from ash-trees" or "from ash-tree nymphs." Moreover, on at least
two occasions in his poems, Hesiod himself alludes to this belief (*Theog.*
187; *W&D* 145). It seems, then, somewhat perverse to ignore the evidence of

[18] West (1966) 323.

a well-attested tradition in order to embrace one that is unattested. I suggest then that the true reading at line 563 might be μελίνοισι, which Hesiod intended to be an adjective modifying mortal men and meaning something like "sprung from the ash-tree nymphs" as the Scholiast claims.[19] We could then translate: "[Zeus] did not give to mortals, sprung from the ash-tree nymphs, the strength of tireless fire." Finally, the reminiscence here of the origin and nature of men as powerful and threatening to the gods at the very moment when Zeus's actions are about to change their lot forever would provide a special point to this pivotal moment in human history. However that may be, when Prometheus surreptitiously restores fire to men, Zeus responds with his trump card, the gift of Woman, or rather, the Wife, who establishes forever the status of mankind between god and beast through the human institution of marriage, and defines for all time the coordinates of the human condition.

Commentators have long debated whether the supreme god was not in fact genuinely deceived – at least in the beginning – by Prometheus, despite the assurances of Hesiod who emphasizes:

Ζεὺς δ' ἄφθιτα μήδεα εἰδὼς
γνῶ ῥ' οὐδ' ἠγνοίησε δόλον.

Zeus, who knows imperishable plans,
recognized the trick and did not ignore it.   (550–51)

Some have suspected the text, while others have tried to excuse Hesiod's somewhat inept naiveté, which attempts at all costs to justify the omniscience of Zeus.[20] West insists that Zeus was indeed completely taken in.

We must pause here to examine West's interpretation of the original distribution of the meat and the meaning of Prometheus' ruse as well as his proposed emendation to the text.[21] The MSS give τῷ μέν at line 538, which describes the portion of edible meats covered in a *gaster* of an ox; and τῷ δ' αὖτ' at line 540, which depicts the other portion containing cleverly

---

[19] The corrupt μελίοισι, not otherwise attested, is found in a group of manuscripts and may represent an intermediate stage. Cf. Wilamowitz (1928) 54. Masaracchia (1961) 231 supports μελίοισι because "Questa corrispondenza permette di identificare la generazione umana che visse al tempo di Promiteo e di Epimetei con l'età del bronzo." μέλινον occurs at *Odyssey* 17.339 (elsewhere in Homer, μείλινον). Stephanus' emendation, μελέοισι, "wretched" "miserable," was accepted by many earlier editors (e.g. Goettling [1843], Paley [1861], Welcker [1865], and Schoemann [1868]). But Muetzell (1833) 73–75 pointed out that μέλεος only means "idle," "useless" in early Epic.

[20] See, for example, Aly (1913) 330, who regards 551–52 as interpolated. Cf. von Fritz (1947) 253; and Solmsen (1949) 49: "Hesiod has worked his conception of the all-knowing Zeus into the story regardless of the improbable situation which he thus created."

[21] West (1966) ad loc.; and (1961) 137–38. Solmsen (1970) and Marg (1970) 231 adopt West's reading.

arranged bones packaged in shining fat. Many editors have adopted τοῖς, referring to human beings at line 538,[22] and retain τῷ at 540 as referring to Zeus. But, as West points out, if the appetizing portion were placed before him, Zeus would have no reason to complain about the unfairness of the distribution – as he immediately does in lines 543–44. As a result, West keeps τῷ at 538 but prints τοῖς at 540: Zeus has the apparently less attractive portion set before him and not unexpectedly complains. It is at this moment that Prometheus invites Zeus to choose whatever portion he wishes. As West says: "Prometheus' object in offering Zeus the choice is to induce him to take the bad share of his own accord, so that he has nobody but himself to blame. The beautiful subtlety with which he achieves this object seems to have escaped the critics."[23]

Subtle it is, but West has missed the forest for the trees and overlooked the larger context on which the whole narrative is predicated: the Titan's object is not merely to trick Zeus, but to reward mankind. He has stealthily attempted to allot the better portion to human beings by making it appear inferior. The first portion, then, must clearly be intended for human consumption – although it is unnecessary to alter the text. Guyet's τῇ μέν . . . τῇ δ' αὖτ' (on the one hand . . . on the other) seems temptingly non-committal,[24] but the received text can be retained ("for the one [men] . . . for the other [gods]. . . .").[25] West, however, recognized that Zeus would have no cause for complaint if the fat-covered share were placed before him, but this scenario presupposes what West in fact presupposes: that Zeus was taken in by the outward appearance of the two portions from the beginning. Nevertheless, West puts his finger on a crucial element in the narrative. When the portions are set out, Zeus complains not just of their disparity or inequality, but of the unfairness and partisan character of the distribution: ἑτερόζηλος, a rare word, is not simply equivalent to ἄνισος.[26] Significantly, the best parallel for its usage here also involves an unequal

---

[22] First suggested by Gerhard (1853); then adopted by Paley (1861), Schoemann (1868), and Rzach in his editio maior (Leipzig 1902). It is found in one MS, West's U, copied by Constantine Lascaris and probably a conjecture.

[23] West (1961) 138.   [24] Supported most recently by Kassel (1973) 99.

[25] Cf. Kohl (1970) 31–36; and, on different grounds, Latacz (1971); see also Pötscher (1994). Wirshbo (1982) 104 believes that Hesiod "need have had no specific referent in mind for each τῷ."

[26] Schmidt (1988b) 138–40 unconvincingly argues that Zeus is merely benevolently pointing out the inequality of the two shares to encourage Prometheus to make a more just distribution. Similarly Latacz (1971) 28, who speaks of a "scheinbar unkluge Teilung." Cf. also Kassel (1973) 99 and Wirshbo (1982) 109. Kohl (1970) 34 argues that Prometheus sets both portions before Zeus. Once again, this interpretation blunts the meaning of ἑτερόζηλος. See also the recent interpretation of Judet de La Combe (1996) 286: "La colère [of Zeus] vient donc de ce que le souverain ne peut ici jouer son rôle de garant du partage."

distribution; in commenting on *Iliad* 1.399–400, Eustathius explains why Poseidon joined both Hera and Athena in attempting to bind Zeus: ὁ δὲ Ποσειδῶν διὰ τὸ τῆς μερίδος ἑτερόζηλον. Ζεὺς μὲν γὰρ εἶχε τὰ περὶ οὐρανόν, Ποσειδῶν δὲ τὰ περὶ θάλασσαν ἔλαχεν ("Poseidon [was angry at Zeus] because of the unfairness of the division; for Zeus possessed the heavens, but Poseidon got the sea.") Poseidon was miffed not at the inequality of his share, but because he got the short end of the bargain. The term ἑτερόζηλος serves to reveal that Zeus was fully aware of what the gleaming fat portion before him contained.

It is only after Zeus remarks on the unfairness of the distribution that Prometheus proposes – with a confident smile – that Zeus himself choose between the two portions. Now it is at this very moment that the Hesiodic text explicitly states what West dismisses as special pleading: that "Zeus recognized and did not ignore" Prometheus' ruse (550–51). Hesiod's statement emphatically insists that Zeus was indeed able to penetrate the difference between the outward appearance and the contents of the two servings, and the narrative only makes sense if he does. That Zeus sees through Prometheus' deception and motivation is also evident from the phrase that follows:

> κακὰ δ' ἄσσετο θυμῷ
> θνητοῖς ἀνθρώποισι, τὰ καὶ τελέεσθαι ἔμελλε.

> He foresaw evil consequences in his heart
> For mortal men, which he himself was going to carry out.

> (551–52)

Zeus's X-ray vision not only penetrates the contents of the two shares of meat, but, far-sightedly, it also apprehends Prometheus' ultimate goal of favoring mankind. Moreover, the formula, ἄφθιτα μήδεα εἰδώς ("knowing imperishable thoughts"), repeated three times in this passage (545, 550, 561) and nowhere else in the *Theogony*, underlines Zeus's unerring insight and long-range planning. He proves himself more Promethean in his foresight than his rival.

Yet another decisive indication, whose significance has not been sufficiently appreciated, undermines an interpretation that claims that Prometheus actually succeeded in hoodwinking Zeus: the word κερτομέων in line 545. When Zeus points out the inequality of the portions, Hesiod tells us that he spoke κερτομέων. West's interpretation of the word, " 'carping', not in jest but in displeasure," will not stand up to scrutiny.[27]

---

[27] West (1966) 320. By ignoring the implications of Zeus's κερτομέων, which he renders as "höhnt" (28) and "spöttelte" (34), Latacz (1971) claims that leaving the choice to Zeus was an original part

The verb κερτομέω and its congeners have provoked considerable discussion. The verb does not mean "to mock" or "to reproach," as it is often translated, but rather "to provoke." κερτομέω involves a complex dynamic between a speaker and his addressee; in speech-act theory it signals an indirect but intentional perlocutionary act,[28] and means "to provoke or goad someone indirectly into doing something," "intentionally to elicit a response that one expects, anticipates, or desires." Some simple examples: if I ask someone, "Do you know where the post office is?", I want him to tell me the way to the post office; or if I say "You're standing on my foot," I intend my auditor to remove his foot from mine. The provocation signaled by *kertom-* words is intended to produce a certain reaction; it may, of course, succeed or fail if the addressee does not rise to the bait, or simply does not "get it."

Perhaps the most illuminating parallel for the dynamics of κερτομέω in the Prometheus episode comes from a passage in the fourth book of the *Iliad*.[29] At the end of the preceding book, Agamemnon had declared Menelaus the victor in his duel with Paris. Everything seems to be settled: the terms set down prior to the duel concerning the restitution of Helen and her goods are about to be fulfilled. The Greeks will return home and leave the Trojans in peace. The war is over – and so, for that matter, is the *Iliad*. But if the truce between the warring parties is not violated, Zeus's plan, announced in the fifth line of the poem, will not be accomplished. At that moment, Zeus proposes to the gods assembled on Olympus a reconciliation between Greeks and Trojans. But Homer tells us that Zeus speaks "obliquely with provocative words" (κερτομίοις ἐπέεσσι παραβλήδην, 4.6),[30] with words intended to provoke Hera, who will predictably and angrily reject her husband's proposal and bring about the violation of the truce and the continuation of the war. Zeus thus purposefully goads Hera into delivering her violent response. He can then appear to give in to his bloody-minded wife reluctantly, all the while, however, getting his own way. To summarize: κερτομέω thus means "to provoke someone into doing something," to elicit a response that one expects, anticipates, or desires, and sometimes to make

---

of Prometheus' plan. Kassel (1973) 99 speaks of Zeus's "Unmut," while Schmidt (1988b) 138 detects "ein freundliches, jedenfalls nicht bösartiges Sticheln." In *Works and Days* 788–89, Hesiod links κέρτομα βάζειν with ψεύδεά θ' αἱμιλίους τε λόγους κρυφίους τ' ὀαρισμούς. It belongs therefore to the vocabulary of deception rather than mockery or teasing.

[28] Cf. Austin (1975) 101–32; also Davis (1979); and Searle and Vanderveken (1985) 10–12.

[29] For a discussion of some other passages, see Clay (1999b).

[30] Cf. *H. Hermes* 55–56, where Hermes tries out his newly invented lyre and improvises a song, "just as young men at feasts παραιβόλα κερτομέουσιν." The youths' oblique provocations are meant to elicit improvised counter-provocations to produce a flyting contest.

someone give himself away. In fact, it is a subtle way of manipulating someone to do what you want him to do without explicitly saying so.

In the *Theogony*, then, by drawing attention to the inequality of the two portions and commenting on the unfairness of the distribution κερτομέων, Zeus intends to provoke Prometheus: more precisely, to provoke the Titan to invite Zeus to choose between the two portions. Had Zeus simply accepted the portion before him, he would indeed appear to have been tricked by Prometheus. Zeus precipitates the choice because he is fully aware of the contents of both portions, and he chooses consciously and with full knowledge. The white bones henceforth belong to the gods' portion, while the corruptible meat of the sacrifice that is constantly renewed to feed mankind is an emblem of their mortality.[31] The Olympian is not fooled; it is in that choice that man's doom is eternally sealed. But if the immediate outcome and its long-range consequences are not only foreseen, but also provoked by Zeus, what exactly did Zeus "of imperishable counsels" seek to accomplish? The conclusion seems inescapable: he planned for things to turn out exactly the way they actually did. The Olympian himself, then, fully intended to bring about the separation of gods and men that was the final consequence of the contest between Prometheus and Zeus. In this context, one must remember that the *Theogony* depicts human beings as closely related to gigantic warriors, creatures perhaps even capable of challenging Zeus himself. In that light, Zeus's imperishable counsels (ἄφθιτα μήδεα) can be understood as protecting the status of the gods by weakening his potential adversaries so that they can never again pose a serious threat to his regime.

Why Hesiod never mentions the Gigantomachy or Prometheus' role in the Titanomachy[32] has always been puzzling. The Gigantomachy, at least, is a widespread and popular theme in archaic Greek art, far more common than the Titanomachy, and becomes the emblem of the triumph of the forces of order over violence and disorder.[33] Strikingly, the depiction of the Giants in the early period shows them, not as brutal and snake-tailed primitives, but as fully armed hoplites, whom Hesiod perfectly describes as:

---

[31] Cf. Vernant (1979) 65–68, who stresses the correspondence between the white bones of the sacrifice and the white bones that remain after cremation.

[32] In *Prometheus Bound* 199ff., at least, Prometheus presents himself as a crucial player in that contest, first advising his fellow-Titans and then going over to Zeus's side, thereby ensuring his victory. There, of course, it is Prometheus who knows the secret of succession.

[33] Cf. Vian (1952). Rudhardt (1981b) 269 notes the absence of the Gigantomachy in the *Theogony*. However, it and the participation of Heracles is mentioned in fr. 43.65 M–W and seems to be alluded to at *Theog.* 954 as ὃς μέγα ἔργον ἐν ἀθανάτοισιν ἀνύσσας.

τεύχεσι λαμπομένους, δολίχ ᾽ἔγχεα χερσὶν ἔχοντας.

Shining in their armor, and holding long spears in their hands.

(*Theog.* 186)

The absence of allusions to the battle of the Giants and Olympians in the *Theogony* might perhaps be explained by the fact that chronologically it belongs to a later era in the mythical history of the gods – but so too does the Prometheus myth. The Gigantomachy represents a renewed threat to the hegemony of the Olympians after the consolidation of their power. Moreover, the defeat of the Giants requires the participation of the mortal hero, Heracles. It is plausible that Hesiod has replaced the Gigantomachy with the Prometheus episode, in which Heracles likewise plays a critical part. A hint at the rationale behind this narrative strategy is provided by a remarkable fragment of Callimachus:

> Μηκώνην μακάρων ἔδρανον αὖτις ἰδεῖν,
> ἧχι πάλους ἐβάλοντο, διεκρίναντο δὲ τιμάς
> πρῶτα Γιγαντείου δαίμονες ἐκ πολέμου.

(119 Pfeiffer)

> To behold again Mekone, seat of the blessed ones,
> Where the gods cast lots and distinguished their honors
> First, after the war of the Giants.

Callimachus here locates the final distribution of *timai* at Mekone, where Hesiod had situated the *krisis* between gods and men;[34] but instead of a war between the gods and the Giants, a *krisis* decided by force of arms, Hesiod recounts a *krisis* between gods and men decided by trickery or *metis*. In other words, the crisis at Mekone between Zeus and Prometheus, which determines forever the status of mankind as subordinate to the gods, replaces the traditional Gigantomachy. This replacement may explain the somewhat awkward reference to Herakles' killing of the eagle that Zeus sent to torment the Titan. In the Gigantomachy, Herakles traditionally played a decisive role: without his help, the Olympians would have been unable to defeat the Giants. Here, Zeus sets aside his anger to give his son glory and to show him respect in an extraordinary way.[35] Since, as we have seen, the theme of reciprocity both frames and permeates the Prometheus story,

---

[34] It is difficult to believe that so learned a poet as Callimachus might have confused the Titanomachy with the Gigantomachy, as others sometimes did.

[35] Cf. West (1966) 317 on ἁζόμενος: "It is not (otherwise) attested in early epic for a god's regard for a mortal."

the unusual honor Zeus grants to his son may repay his critical aid to the gods in the Gigantomachy.[36]

In this context, it may be useful to review the description of the various punishments of the other sons of Iapetus, which immediately precedes the Prometheus story (514–25).[37] In addition to the well-known punishment of Prometheus himself, it also describes how Atlas holds up the sky at the western rim of the earth, so that the heavens can never again fall upon the earth. Such an eventuality would undo the whole cosmogonic process, as once almost happened in the course of the Titanomachy (700–703). What is interesting for our purposes, however, is the first of the Iapetids mentioned, Menoitios, a rather obscure figure otherwise unknown, who is characterized as ὑπερκύδαντα and ὑβριστήν. Because of his ἀτασθαλίη and his ἠνορέη ὑπέροπλος, that is, his recklessness and excessive violence, Zeus punished him by striking him with his thunderbolt and sending him to Erebos. This punishment resembles the one meted out to Typhoeus but also corresponds to the lot of the Giants in traditional Gigantomachies; it is likewise reminiscent of the destruction visited on hybristic human beings who challenge the power of the gods, like Salmoneus, for example, who harbored the mad desire to imitate Zeus (fr. 30 M–W). Striking him with his thunderbolt, Zeus hurled him into the darkness of Tartarus. Thus the punishment of Menoitios follows the pattern of the mortal enemies of Zeus. One could say that in a sense Hesiod projects the fate of men/Giants onto the Iapetid line.

Hesiod deploys a similar strategy in describing the punishment of Prometheus, narrated before his crime. The Titan's liver, consumed all day by Zeus's eagle, grows back at night, so that Prometheus' torment, called a disease (νοῦσος) in 527, may be endless. (Similarly, the daily toil of the bees is consumed endlessly by the idle drones [cf. πρόπαν ἦμαρ, 525 and 596].) Thus, through a grim inversion, Prometheus, though a god, experiences the ceaseless renewal of hunger and the insatiable demands of the belly that constitute the human lot within his own immortal body: the eagle who is never sated and the liver that never remains whole.

There is an old controversy surrounding Prometheus' punishment, for in line 616 we learn that he is still bound, while line 528 asserts that Heracles

---

[36] Zeus's honoring of Heracles also points to a post-Promethean epoch when gods and men have become separated. See Chapter 7.

[37] Cf. Judet de La Combe (1996) 280: "par leurs actes et le sort que Zeus leur réserve, les fils dessinent les structures et les qualités du monde humain, du côté de la force pour Atlas et Ménoitios, et de l'esprit pour Prométhée et Epiméthée."

liberated him from his torments. But the contradiction, as West saw, is only apparent[38] – although he does not interpret its significance. In its context, Heracles' act looks forward to a time when the drastic consequences of Mecone, the separation of gods and men, are mitigated by the generation of the heroes whose genetic makeup unites the human and the divine. But like his Titan brethren, Prometheus, as an enemy of Zeus's order, must remain bound. Significantly, in the immediate sequel, the Olympian *unbinds* the Hundred-Handers so that they can assist him against the Titans. Prometheus' two punishments thus allude to a partial reconciliation with mankind on the part of Zeus, but also emphasize his unrelenting hostility against the enemies of his domination.

In keeping with its more human focus, the *Works and Days* recounts neither Prometheus' punishment nor his liberation by Heracles. The alleviation of Prometheus' punishment and its motivation through Zeus's desire to bestow honor upon his son points to the renewed closeness between gods and men. This new intimacy comes about through the generation of heroes. But the Prometheus story as recounted in the *Works and Days* has no room for the heroes: it presents only two phases of human history, an earlier period of happiness and a later one of tribulation. The heroic age, however, plays a crucial role in the myth of the races that focuses on the human need for justice. We may conclude that Hesiod's teaching concerning work and scarcity in the Prometheus myth is grimmer than his teaching concerning justice.

To summarize the results of our investigation thus far: the *Works and Days* and the *Theogony* offer differing versions of the origin of mankind and the human condition. In the former, we find a multiplicity of races created by the gods which progress from an idyllic golden age to the Iron Age in which we live. By the will of the gods, human beings have become increasingly distant from the gods, as if the gods in their blissful state needed the presence of inferior creatures to enjoy their superiority fully. At the beginning, men lived like the gods, but now only their representatives Aidos and Nemesis remain among them, goddesses whose departure is imminent if mankind continues to reject the imperatives of justice. The fate of human beings is in their own hands; nevertheless they remain subordinate to the gods, who retain the power to destroy the race.

In the *Theogony*, the origins of mankind arise from a cosmic accident; the primordial disposition of men is scarcely peaceful but, on the contrary,

---

[38] See West (1966) 313. Arrighetti (1998) 349 finds West's solution unconvincing; Solmsen (1970) brackets 526–34.

as menacing and violent as the brutal act that engendered them. The separation of gods and men there is a consequence of Zeus's Olympian politics to preserve and strengthen his divine supremacy. That separation, whose emblem is the sacrifice, reminds human beings of their inferiority each time they eat meat, and their subordination to, and dependence upon, the gods. It also entails the domestication of mankind through the institutions of marriage and agriculture that redirects the energy and innate violence of men to the necessities of daily existence.

The Prometheus narrative in the *Works and Days* differs from the story recounted in the *Theogony* not only in its immediate details but also in its divergent understanding of man's nature and his relation to the gods.[39] Not surprisingly, the interest in the intrigue between Zeus and Prometheus recedes as the focus shifts to the actions of Zeus and their impact on human life. Beginning from an explanatory γάρ, the narrative offers an elucidation of the human necessity for work:

> κρύψαντες γάρ ἔχουσι θεοὶ βίον ἀνθρώποισιν.

> For the gods hid and keep hidden livelihood from men.
>
> (42)

In what could constitute a paradigm of mythological aetiology, a past action by the gods (κρύψαντες), precipitates a fundamental change in the human condition that continues into the present (ἔχουσι). This general statement is then amplified by a contrafactual assertion:

> ῥηιδίως γάρ κεν καὶ ἐπ᾽ ἤματι ἐργάσσαιο,
> ὥστε σε κεἰς ἐνιαυτὸν ἔχειν καὶ ἀεργὸν ἐόντα·
> αἶψά κε πηδάλιον μὲν ὑπὲρ καπνοῦ καταθεῖο,
> ἔργα βοῶν δ᾽ ἀπόλοιτο καὶ ἡμιόνων ταλαεργῶν.

> [If they had not done so] you could easily have worked only for
>   a day
> So as to have enough for a year, even if you were lazy;
> Straightway, you could have stored the rudder over the fireplace,
> And there would have been no need for the work of oxen and
>   hard-working mules.   (43–46)[40]

---

[39] Cf. Calame (1996) 182–85 for some good observations.

[40] Note the repeated use of the root *erg-* in this passage: ἐργάσσαιο, ἀεργόν, ἔργα, ταλαεργῶν. The reference to sailing and agriculture looks ahead to the sections on these topics. These lines would seem to undermine Ballabriga's (1998) 318–21 argument that the pre-Promethean age involved a hard (gathering of wild fruits) as opposed to the soft primitivism (agricultural abundance) of the golden age.

Previously, there may have been some minimal work, but it must have been quick and easy. At any rate, sailing and agriculture were formerly unnecessary.

Because the version of the story from the *Theogony* has infiltrated interpretive readings of the narrative in the *Works and Days*, its structure has not been properly understood. As Hesiod resumes the story, Zeus hid *bios*, which previously had been easily available, because of his anger at Prometheus' deception. That the action of hiding *bios* was earlier ascribed to a plurality of gods (cf. 42) points to the fact that Hesiod here equates Pandora, who is simultaneously Zeus's idea and produced by all the gods (hence her name), with the hiding of *bios*. As a result of Prometheus' deception, evidently (ἄρα), Zeus plotted dreadful sufferings for mankind.[41] It is critical to recognize that in this version Zeus's anger at Prometheus does not arise from the sacrifice trick, which is never mentioned – or even alluded to.[42] In fact, as the translation makes clear, lines 47–53 offer a typical example of ring composition, moving backwards in time to explain the source of Zeus's anger (50–52) and then returning to the narrative present with the reiteration of the point of departure (χολωσάμενος, 47, 53):

> ἀλλὰ Ζεὺς ἔκρυψε χολωσάμενος φρεσὶ ἧσιν,
> ὅττί μιν ἐξαπάτησε Προμηθεὺς ἀγκυλομήτης.
> τούνεκ' ἄρ' ἀνθρώποισιν ἐμήσατο κήδεα λυγρά·
> κρύψε δὲ πῦρ· τὸ μὲν αὖτις ἐὺς πάις Ἰαπετοῖο
> ἔκλεψ' ἀνθρώποισι Διὸς παρὰ μητιόεντος
> ἐν κοίλῳ νάρθηκι, λαθὼν Δία τερπικέραυνον.
> τὸν δὲ χολωσάμενος ...

> But Zeus hid it (*bios*), angered in his heart,
> Because crooked-devising Prometheus had deceived him;
> For this reason, evidently, he devised baneful woes for human beings:
> He had hidden fire; but the goodly son of Iapetus had stolen
> It back again for human beings from Zeus, full of devices,
> In a hollow reed, escaping the notice of Zeus who rejoices in thunder.
> Angered at him, Zeus ...   (47–53)

---

[41] See Bakker (1997)17–20 for the evidentiary force of ἄρα, which he defines as a marker "of *visual evidence in the here and now of the speaker*" (pp. 17–18); we know Zeus plotted sufferings for us because we are suffering them at present.

[42] Cf. the Scholia, with the exception of one that offers both explanations (48e Pertusi), which Pertusi believes to be later; and West (1978) on line 48: "The swindle alluded to is that over the division of meat." Cf. Verdenius (1962) 123; and Arrighetti (1998). But compare Neitzel (1976) 408–11; Krafft (1963) 98; and Broccia (1954) 118–25; and (1958) 296–99, who have read the passage correctly. For a defense of the usual reading, see Casanova (1979) 36–37. Despite assuming an allusion to the sacrifice trick, Verdenius (1985) 45 seems to recognize the sequence of actions here: "Hes. first states the final result (47 Ζεὺς ἔκρυψε) and the primary cause (48 ἐξαπάτησε Προμηθεύς) of the conflict, and then relates the details." The passage offers a perfect example of the distinction between augmented and unaugmented forms made by Bakker (1999b).

The story in the *Works and Days* begins from an action of Zeus, the hiding of fire, whose theft by Prometheus ultimately provokes the making of Pandora. In the absence of the sacrifice trick, the significance of fire changes from the cooking fire, which distinguishes men from beasts, to the fire of technology. That the first act in this version of the story is Zeus's removal of fire substantially shifts the center of narrative gravity from the confrontation between Prometheus and Zeus to the unilateral action of Zeus upon men.[43] As a sign of this shift, the *Theogony* presents a dialogue between the two antagonists concerning the division of meats (542–61), whereas Prometheus never speaks in the *Works and Days*, which records only the speech of Zeus announcing his revenge for the Titan's theft of fire (53–59). At this point, Zeus apparently chooses not to take fire back; men will retain fire, but Pandora, who is coeval with the hiding of *bios*, ensures their misery. In substituting Pandora for fire (ἀντὶ πυρός, 57), Zeus renders human technology, as attested by the arduous manufacture of the plow and wagon (420–36), a necessary evil, inextricably joined to the toil that now characterizes human life. Henceforth, the earth ceases from her earlier generous fertility; wives and children must be fed, and men must henceforth coax their sustenance from the earth through unrelenting labor. In perhaps the final irony, Pandora herself is the product of divine *techne*, made, not born, of earth, resembling both immortal goddesses and a respectable maiden, yet at the same time a seductive object of painful desire – and dressed to kill. Within, however, resides a shameless (bitchy) nature and, twice repeated, a thievish character. Not only that, but men will henceforth willingly embrace their fatal doom, recognizing only afterwards – like Epimetheus – the evil they have taken to their bosom. No wonder that Zeus laughs out loud.[44]

In neither the *Theogony* nor the *Works and Days* does the manufactured woman constitute the female principle *tout court*. In the former, the generative principle involving birth and fertility, represented by Gaia in all her boundless proliferation and procreative drive, has been active from the very beginning of the theogonic process. In the *Works and Days* Pandora's name ironically usurps and subverts the epithet of the all-giving Earth. Hesiod radically disassociates fertility, maternity, and nurture, which, after all, are the driving forces behind cosmogony, from both the Woman/Wife

---

[43] The common view that "in both texts . . . Prometheus, therefore, is the real cause of the disaster that befalls mankind" (Pucci [1977] 82–83) must thus be substantially modified.

[44] On Zeus's laughter, see the remarks of Neitzel (1976) 417: "Ich habe dieses Auflachen des Zeus immer als besonders schrecklich empfunden. . . . Wer dieses Lachen des Zeus einmal 'gehört' hat, wird es nie wieder vergessen." Neitzel's conclusion, however, that our misery is our own fault because we took Pandora in, misses the point.

and Pandora.[45] Neither one can simply be considered the Greek Eve, if we mean by that solely the female of the species.[46] Both are artificial creatures, made rather than born, and bring in their wake marriage, the family and its continuity, the human concern for generating and feeding legitimate children, hence also toil and the worries entailed by property and inheritance – in short, all the miseries of human existence.

The two accounts of the fabrication of the Woman/Wife in the *Theogony* and Pandora in the *Works and Days*, while complementary, display divergent narrative strategies.[47] In the first, only the divinities of craftmanship, Athena and Hephaestus, participate in her making, whereas a host of gods contribute in the latter undertaking so as to justify her bitterly ironic name, Pandora, "because all those who inhabit Olympian homes gave her as a gift, a bane to grain-eating males (ἀνδράσιν)" (81–82). Moreover, the nameless Woman/Wife is first described purely in terms of her appearance and repeatedly called a wonder to behold (575, 581, 584, 588), not only for men, but also for the immortal gods when she is displayed among them.[48] Bedecked like a bride, she wears on her head not only the bridal veil, but also garlands of flowers and an ornate golden crown (576–84).[49] This double headgear with its doubling of the natural and the artificial, of nature and culture, would seem to be a perfect emblem of the Woman/Wife herself and the marital institution she embodies. While her adornment and dressing occupy seven lines (571–77), Hesiod devotes an equal number of lines to describing her gold diadem, adorned with lifelike images of "terrible monsters that the earth and sea nurtured" (578–84), which again doubles the figure of Woman herself.[50] These lines send us back to the catalogue of

---

[45] Cf. Loraux (1978) esp. 50–51; Arthur (1982) 74–76; and the elegant exposition of Zeitlin (1996). Hofinger (1969) 205–17 argues that only the *Theogony's* Woman is the "first woman." Fränkel (1962) 129 n. 9 claims that Pandora is only the first of one kind of woman, a "Luxuswesen."

[46] Casanova (1979) 63–64 identifies her as the first human woman; cf. Guarducci (1926) 448 and Pucci (1977) 208, who point out that, prior to Pandora, there were only men.

[47] Again, too often the two are read together, which destroys the specificity of their respective narratives. A recent example: Becker (1993) compares the two descriptions in terms of their effect but perhaps does not sufficiently emphasize the more subjective mode used to describe Pandora. Cf. Calabrese de Feo (1995).

[48] Cf. Prier (1989) 94–97, who notes (p. 95) that "the purview of a *thauma idesthai* [lies] balanced between the place of the gods and that of men. It is a brightly wrought object surrounded by light, one that is quite clearly 'other' in origin." This statement could stand as a definition of the Woman herself.

[49] See *Iliad* 22.468–72 for the connection of Andromache's elaborate headgear and veil with her wedding day. West (1966) believes that 576–77 are interpolated, while Solmsen (1970) brackets 578–84. But Neitzel (1975) 22–28, who reviews the main objections, argues persuasively for the retention of the text. In Aristophanes' *Lysistrata* 602–04, the Proboulos is likewise decked out with *both* a garland of flowers and a tiara of the wife. Cf. Henderson (1987) ad loc.

[50] Note the verbal parallels between 571–77 and 578–84. Cf. Redfield (1993) 44.

monsters at lines 270–336 of the *Theogony*, creatures who constitute a self-enclosed genealogical line, a kind of anti-cosmos in which the evolutionary cosmological processes that function elsewhere in the poem do not operate. The fabricated Woman likewise defies categorization. In addition, the elaborate decoration of the diadem that crowns her in the *Theogony* offers a reminder of the inborn violence and the potential for disorder inherent in the men/Giants, who through the invention of Woman, the *kalon kakon*, are henceforth domesticated and subservient to the power of Zeus. Any *eris* primordial man might have directed toward the gods must now be channeled into the daily struggle for survival.

The wondrous exterior of this ancestress, or better, prototype, of female women/wives[51] is counterbalanced by the simile of the bees and drones which depicts her inner nature, invisible to the naked eye. She only *appears* as a likeness of a respectable virgin; her hidden character surfaces in a very different likeness drawn from the animal sphere; she resembles the drones, who consume the fruits of another's labor and gather it up into their belly, while the busy bees toil from morning till night. The Woman is a semblance of a semblance, whose fair exterior stands in complete opposition to the bitter facts of her true nature. Furthermore, the inversion of genders in the simile where the female bees represent males and the masculine drones the "cursed race of female women" points to the gulf between the animal and the human.[52]

The dilemma that follows is exclusively a human dilemma and Zeus's *coup de grâce*. The trap so carefully laid now clangs shut: if a man manages to escape marriage, he will indeed have enough to eat, but he will have no one to look after him in his old age and, since he remains childless, distant relatives will divide his inheritance. If, however, he should marry and have the luck to find a good wife, even so misery will continually battle with good; but should he chance upon a bad one, then boundless and unremitting misery will fill his days (603–12). This description of the painful predicament to which all men are doomed seems to be viewed through the eyes (or as the narratologists would say, focalized) of the human male and thus momentarily abandons the divine perspective that dominates the *Theogony*. It is as if mankind, up to now silent victims of the divine

[51] See Loraux (1978) 43–52. Loraux, 49, notes that the Woman is "un être tout d'extériorité." "[L]a première femme *est* sa parure, elle n'a pas de corps."

[52] Cf. Loraux (1978) 47; Zeitlin (1996) 69–70; Redfield (1993) 49. Note also the frequent reference to the Woman/Wife in the neuter. A signal of the difference of perspective between the *Theogony* and the *W&D* is that the latter likens the lazy man to the drones who consume the toil of the bees (303–6). Cf. Aristotle, *De Gen. Animal.* 759b1–761a2, who argues against the view that the bees are female and the drones male.

conflict, breaks in – through the voice of Hesiod – to bemoan its inescapable fate.

The Scylla and Charybdis of the human dilemma are predicated on mortality and the institution of the family founded on marriage. That impasse has rightly been likened to the two jars of Zeus in the *Iliad* from which he apportions human destiny, the one full of evils, the other, of good things (24.525–33).[53] No man can hope to receive a lot of unalloyed good; at best, he may hope to encounter some good amid the inevitable evils. One wonders if the analogy between this passage and the Iliadic parable may not have inspired Hesiod to develop the image of the *pithos* when he returned to this theme in his later composition.

In keeping with the *Theogony*'s insistent emphasis throughout the Prometheus story on the deceptive contrast between outer appearance and inner reality, inner and outer are starkly juxtaposed in the description of Hesiod's Woman/Wife. There is as little similarity between the beautiful semblance of the Woman and the simile of the drones as between the life-sustaining meat and the white bones of Prometheus' initial deception. The fabrication of Pandora of the *Works and Days*, on the other hand, involves a more complex and intricate mixture of visible and invisible characteristics, which from the outset emphasizes not merely her beauty, but her deceptive and seductive nature.[54] Right from the beginning, Zeus orders Hephaestus to place within her "the voice and strength of a human being" (61–62), and he concludes by commanding Hermes to set inside her "the mind of a bitch and the character of a swindler" (67). Furthermore, Aphrodite is to pour over her *charis* and the wondrous abstractions "painful longing and limb-devouring cares" (65–66).[55] These are not physical characteristics, but the subjective reactions to physical characteristics. Their presence in the description of Pandora demonstrates the subjective human viewpoint or focalization of the narrative. For the desires she provokes and the limbs she will devour are those of the human male.

In the execution of the orders,[56] Pandora's physical adornment (70–76) is capped by her seductive character and voice:

[53] Cf. Redfield (1993) 49. The connection is already made in the Scholia ad loc.

[54] Cf. West (1978) 158: "in the *Theogony* she is made like a dummy, here attention is given to her animation and character." Zeitlin (1996) 67–70 rightly notes the emphasis on the Woman of the *Theogony* in economic terms, as consumer, whereas Pandora's seductiveness is foremost.

[55] Verdenius (1985) 52 defends γυιοκόρους as opposed to γυιοβόρους, but the meaning is the same. He also notes the possible Hesiodic etymologizing of μελεδώνας from αἱ τὰ μέλη ἔδουσαι φροντίδες (*Etymologicum Magnum*).

[56] On the old controversy concerning the discrepancies between Zeus's orders and their execution, see West (1978) 161; Pucci (1977) 96–101; and Calabrese de Feo (1995) 109–21, who not only sees the divergences as the movement between abstract and concrete (p. 113), but also remarks that the orders

ἐν δ' ἄρα οἱ στήθεσσι διάκτορος Ἀργεϊφόντης
ψεύδεά θ' αἱμυλίους τε λόγους καὶ ἐπίκλοπον ἦθος
τεῦξε Διὸς βουλῇσι βαρυκτύπου· ἐν δ' ἄρα φωνήν
θῆκε θεῶν κῆρυξ . . .

In her breast [Hermes], the guide, slayer of Argus,
Fashioned lies, wheedling words and the character of a swindler
In accordance with the plans of deep-thundering Zeus;
And within her breast the herald of the gods placed a voice . . .

(77–80)

The difference in these two descriptions is subtle but meaningful. In the *Theogony*, the anonymous Woman/Wife is depicted as a statue, a work of art; tellingly, she has no voice and thus no interior from which her voice can emanate.[57] In fact she is sister to Hephaestus' golden robot maidens (*Iliad* 18.418), likewise products of divine art: "Golden women, resembling living young girls." In keeping with the human perspective of the *Works and Days*, Hesiod gives us a more subjective view of Pandora, not as a robot, but as a beautiful and enticing living woman, whose looks and voice have a devastating effect upon men. Her speech above all constitutes the vehicle of seduction and deception.[58] And, unlike the *Theogony's* anonymous generic prototype, she is endowed with a name to complete her as an individual. As the *Odyssey* tells us:

οὐ μὲν γάρ τις πάμπαν ἀνώνυμός ἐστ' ἀνθρώπων,
οὐ κακὸς οὐδὲ μὲν ἐσθλός, ἐπὴν τὰ πρῶτα γένηται,
ἀλλ' ἐπὶ πᾶσι τίθενται, ἐπεί κε τέκωσι, τοκῆες.

No human being is completely nameless
Neither a base nor a noble one, once he is born,
But to all human beings parents, once they give birth to them,
    assign a name.   (*Od.* 8.552–54)

To be sure, that name is as ambiguous as she is: promising all, but in reality all-consuming. In the *Theogony*, however, the anonymity of the Woman/Wife stands out conspicuously in a composition that is almost

are given from Zeus's perspective, while their execution is described from the perspective of men. For Zeus's ὡς ἔφατο (69) with indirect discourse, see *H. Dem.* 316 and 448. It suggests his distance from the action.

On the contradiction between lines 63–64, where Athena is ordered to teach Pandora weaving, and line 72 where the goddess merely dresses and adorns her, I am inclined to accept the arguments of Neitzel (1975) 28–32, who reads ἔργα διασκῆσαι rather than ἔργα διδασκῆσαι in line 64. To have Athena instruct Pandora in the useful art of weaving undercuts her description as a *kalon kakon*.

[57] Hesiod draws our attention to this absence by describing the monsters on her diadem as ζωοῖσιν ἐοικότα φωνήεσσιν (*Theog.* 584).

[58] Cf. *Theogony* 205, 224, 229.

completely given over to names and naming. If naming is a means of classification, then within the context of the *Theogony*, the Woman is, literally, unclassifiable. The closest parallel again links her to the monsters, those creatures that likewise defy classification. Her nearest counterpart, in fact, is the final member of the monster catalogue, a nameless serpent (334).

As her double, Pandora's *pithos* possesses the same seductive but deceptive promise she herself embodies. Made of the same materials as she, the receptacle of foodstuffs, *bios* itself, the jar promises to sustain life, but within contains only life-destroying ills of every kind. For the race of gold, the earth bore fruit generously and αὐτομάτη (118); here it is the diseases who bring suffering day and night that are αὐτόματοι (103). Hope which remains within, under the lips (ὑπὸ χείλεσιν, 97), corresponds to Pandora's seductive voice which utters lies, and wheedling words, and reveals her swindling character.[59] Zeus's silencing of the countless evils the flesh is heir to (104) constitutes the exact counterpart of Pandora's replacing the cover of the jar "by the plans of aegis-bearing Zeus, the cloud-gatherer" (99). For Hope would be unnecessary if human miseries announced their arrival; on the other hand, human life would be unbearable if we had precise knowledge of the hour and manner of our death.

Plato defines hope as δόξα μελόντων, "opinion about future events," that comprehends both fear of future pain and confidence in future happiness.[60] But whether expectation of good or of evil, Hope belongs to the realm of *doxa* rather than sure knowledge, of seeming rather than being. Even though he has himself foretold it, Hesiod still *hopes* that Zeus will not destroy mankind (273).[61] Like all humans, Hesiod remains, in the final analysis, a thrall to Hope and ignorant of Zeus's plans. Mortality can only be endured in the presence of Hope.

The *pithos* enters the story abruptly; Hesiod does not explain where it comes from, and perhaps we should not ask.[62] Nevertheless, some scholars assume that the jar was already in the house, presumably, of Epimetheus, and that Pandora's removing the lid was motivated "out of curiosity or believing it held something beneficial to herself."[63] The latter is contradicted

[59] Cf. Penelope's ploy: πάντας μὲν ἔλπει, καί ὑπίσχεται ἀνδρὶ ἑκάστῳ | ἀγγελίας προϊεῖσα, νόος δέ οἱ ἄλλα μενοινᾷ (*Odyssey* 2.91–92).

[60] *Laws* 644c.   [61] Cf. Theognis 1135–36.

[62] The scholiasts already do (94a (Pertusi) and use it to prove that Hesiod is later than Homer, since he adapted his *pithos* from him.

[63] West (1978) 168, who, although he believes that Pandora brought the jar along with her, refers to Psyche's box and the bag of the winds in the *Odyssey*. Neitzel is more consequent in believing that the domestic jar contained foodstuffs, i.e. good things, which Pandora squandered. But this leaves the source of the "countless banes" (μυρία λυγρά, 100) unleashed upon human life obscure.

by the text that expressly says, "the woman . . . planned evil woes for human beings" (95). She thus consciously makes Zeus's project for mankind (cf. 49) her own and likewise replaces the lid in accordance with Zeus's plans (99). And if, as we have just learned, men previously lived remote from evils, harsh toil, and painful diseases (91–92), they may well have had as little need for jars to store the sustenance that then existed in abundance as for plow and sails; those necessities arise from the scarcity that Pandora brings with her. I suggest, then, that the jar and the "gifts" of Zeus to mankind it contained accompanied Pandora as a part of her dowry.[64] Perhaps the human dilemma outlined in the *Theogony*, which parallels the Iliadic fable of the *pithoi* of Zeus, inspired the story. In that case, one might suppose that the jar contained the human ills generated by Night and Eris in the *Theogony*. Indeed, the "countless woes that wander among men" that Pandora let loose upon humanity resemble the lethal offspring of Night. It is as if Zeus had packed them all off to exert their evil influence on mankind, thus leaving the gods, "who live easy," in untroubled bliss. Eris, at least, "the son of Cronus set in the roots of the earth" (18–19);[65] and Nemesis surely does still dwell among men though her departure may be imminent. The sending of Pandora and her jar would then constitute part of Zeus's final dispensation, simultaneously ridding Olympus of noxious forces and foisting them off on mankind.[66]

In the preceding analysis, I have consciously kept the two versions of the Prometheus story separate in order to avoid homogenizing them. My examination has attempted to highlight their differences in order to expose the divergent perspectives of the two accounts. A comparison of both with the myth of the five races only emphasizes their incommensurability. While the myth of the races demonstrates many of the same concerns as the Prometheus stories, it deploys them differently. The bliss of the golden race gives way to the silver where reproduction and the family become possible. The bronze race, for all its violence, possesses technology, especially the craft of metallurgy, with its intimate connection to fire, while the heroes,

---

Cf. Miralles (1991) 42–45; Goettling (1843) 170 suggests that Prometheus gathered all the evils and put them in Epimetheus' house, "ut homines liberi essent a malis." But why in Epimetheus' house? Not a very safe place. Cf. also McLaughlin (1981). Zeitlin (1996) 64–66, however, has it right.

[64] Note ἔδωκαν (92), which continues the ironic implications of Pandora's name.

[65] The *Iliad* offers a parallel to such a dispatching of evil forces when Agamemnon recounts how Zeus hurled Ate out of Olympus, and she "quickly came upon the works of men" (*Il.* 19.131).

[66] Between the Pandora story and the description of the Iron Age, Hesiod accommodates almost all the dread offspring of Night in some form: e.g. Μῶμος and Ὀιζύς (*Theog.* 214), μέμφονται (*W&D* 186), ὀιζύος (*W&D* 177).

better than us, are nonetheless obliged to work the earth and sail the seas. Thus work, fire, and marriage likewise form the coordinates of the myth of the races. But the Prometheus narratives cannot be grafted on to the succession of human races in any simple way.[67] Both versions involve only two stages in the history of mankind: a before and an after. In the *Theogony*, before the intervention of Prometheus, human beings, as we have seen, resembled the bronze men. They had fire, which they used for warfare, and armor that made them a threat to the gods. Prometheus' attempt to usurp Zeus's power through an alliance with these powerful men prompted Zeus to deprive them of fire and thereby to neutralize any threat they might pose. Although Prometheus succeeds in stealing fire back again, Zeus's creation of the Woman/Wife permanently weakens men by forcing them to toil ceaselessly to feed wife and children.

The *Works and Days* likewise allows for only two stages of mankind in its version of the Prometheus story: a golden age before and a post-Promethean age of suffering and toil after. There, Zeus's hostility to mankind manifests itself in his unilateral removal of fire. In compensation for Prometheus' counter-theft, Zeus orders the fabrication of Pandora and sends her off with the *pithos* of ills, thus not only ensuring human misery, but also the gods' eternal carefree bliss.

The two Prometheus narratives in Hesiod's poems both present mankind's evolution to its permanent condition poised problematically between god and beast. Different as these two accounts are, they nevertheless share an important feature: both insist that the history of the human species represents a decline in relation to an earlier state, whether a blissful existence in a golden age, now lost, or a state of immense physical force, now enfeebled. In both the *Theogony* and the *Works and Days*, the progress of human history thus entails the loss either of physical power or of a primordial happiness. In the former, the rivalry between Prometheus and Zeus has as its final consequence the distancing of men and gods by deflecting human energy to the struggle for survival. As Zeitlin notes, man "burdened by these limitations [needing children because of aging and mortality] . . . through woman, can never successfully challenge the rule of Zeus who has now earned his title as 'father of gods and men'."[68] In the *Works and Days*, Zeus is portrayed as the direct instigator of the deterioration of the human lot by introducing scarcity and its attendant ills. In the first case, human

---

[67] Bianchi (1963) 148–52 tries unsuccessfully to harmonize the Prometheus narrative with the myth of the races. Cf. Rudhardt (1981b) 272–77 and his conclusion: "Chacun à sa manière, ils [the two myths] énoncent ainsi des messages très voisins, sans être synonymes" (277).

[68] Zeitlin (1996) 84.

beings appear as a threat to divine supremacy, while the second suggests an inherent hostility of the gods toward mankind.

The central theme of the *Theogony* is the genesis and evolution of the gods and the teleological succession of the three generations of the gods that culminates in the stable organization of the cosmos. The evolution of the cosmos, expressed in terms of divine genealogy, presents a development toward the differentiation of the gods and of natural phenomena leading to increasing order. The positive direction of this development is manifest right from the beginning when, for example, black Night and dark Erebos bring forth Brightness (Aither) and Day (124–25). The successive differentiation and articulation of natural phenomena is also revealed in the genealogy of Theia, an obscure deity, perhaps a Hesiodic invention, whose name means something like "Visibility." This goddess gives birth to Helios, the Sun, Selene, the Moon, and Eos, the Dawn – all well-known visible phenomena of our world. At the end of the development outlined in the poem, the cosmos is ordered and the sovereignty of Zeus brings it to a state of permanent stability.

The contrast between this cosmic and divine evolution with the development of humanity is striking.[69] For mankind, succession and evolution for the most part follow a negative direction, one that would naturally lead to its annihilation at the end of the race of iron. The sole means of braking this decline lies, as Hesiod warns, in the practice of justice. Nevertheless, the human condition cannot be fundamentally altered; work, marriage, and sacrifice remain its distinctive hallmarks. Even if it is possible to avoid the final catastrophe, mankind can never escape its permanent condition or recover its primordial happiness.

The tension, if not opposition, between the destiny of the gods and the fate of mankind is expressed emblematically in the passage of the *Theogony* that describes the consequences of the defeat of Typhoeus, last threat and last adversary of Zeus before his accession to power. For the Olympians, Typhoeus' defeat signals the triumph of order and the permanence of Zeus's reign. But for mankind, this emblem of the hegemony of the "father of gods and men" has a very different significance; from Typhoeus, Hesiod tells us, come the winds – not the good winds that benefit men but the storms and tempests "that destroy the ships on the sea and the works of men on the earth," that is, the cultivated fields human beings must tend

---

[69] Cf. von Fritz (1947) 248: "the question remains how Zeus, who represents a more perfect, a better, a more intelligent, and a juster order, can have been the god under whose rule the human race deteriorated from the bliss and justice of the golden age to the wickedness and misery of the iron age."

to feed themselves (869–80). The winds themselves are as invisible as the evils liberated from Pandora's jar. Thus the moment of final and definitive victory for the gods is, from the human perspective at least, a moment of failure, if not catastrophe. For mankind, destined by the gods to cultivate the earth and to sail the seas to gain his livelihood, Zeus's triumph over his last enemy brings about a new and inescapable evil, only adding to the fragility and misery of the human condition.[70] In short, what is good for the gods is by no means necessarily good for mankind.

The two versions of the Prometheus myth offer a vivid demonstration of the differences in the outlook of the two compositions: in the *Theogony*, mankind is viewed externally, politically, one could say, from the perspective of the gods as potential enemies of Zeus's order; men are caught up in the intrigues of the succession myth; and their power, like that of the Titans, must finally be broken, tamed, and domesticated to ensure the stability of Zeus's reign. The *Works and Days*, however, presents mankind from an internal subjective human standpoint: the gods, who have deprived mankind of an earlier bliss, have filled human life with misery. In both versions, Zeus's ultimate weapon is the plastic woman, fabricated to render the human lot inescapable. The Woman/Wife is intended to weaken mankind and make it subject to the gods; in the second, Pandora completes the process of the demise of human happiness while at the same time bestowing upon men the seductive illusion of hope. Only from combining both perspectives does the full pathos of the human condition emerge.

---

[70] Cf. Blaise (1992) 369–70.

CHAPTER 6

Perspectives on gods and men

The preceding discussions of human origins and the human condition as inscribed in the two versions of the Prometheus story have demonstrated how the two Hesiodic poems simultaneously oppose, complement, and mutually illuminate each other. A similar strategy underpins the present chapter, which examines the role of human beings in the *Theogony* and the role of the gods in the *Works and Days*. Here we are dealing not with explanatory accounts of origins, but with the present relations of gods and men that inform the consequences of those originary events. Once again, Hesiod insists that we combine these two perspectives in order to grasp his cosmos.

MEN IN THE *THEOGONY*

Human beings are mentioned sporadically throughout the text of the *Theogony*,[1] for the most part merely in passing references such as the formula describing Zeus as "father of gods and men." In addition, right from the beginning, Hesiod mentions Eros' power over both gods and mortals; and, as we have seen, many of the descendants of Night are singled out as having a special – usually negative – impact on the lives of human beings. The winds that blast the sea and destroy the fields, which arise from Typhoeus' defeat, likewise constitute a "bane to mankind" (872–80). Despite the relative scarcity of such explicit references, it is nevertheless appropriate to claim that "Hesiod's plan covers not only the divine and the physical cosmos, but also the human cosmos".[2] With the exception of the Prometheus episode, where mankind constitutes the mute victim of the contest between the Titan and Zeus, human beings are most actively present in the so-called "Hymn to Hecate." In fact, it is only in this section of the poem that men

---

[1] Cf. Arrighetti (1998) 299–301.

[2] Brown (1953) 10 refers not only to the Hecate and Prometheus episodes, but also to the genealogies of Night and Pontos, as well as to the description of Tartarus.

appear as active agents engaged in a wide range of human endeavors.[3] If, as we claimed, the *Theogony* offers an Olympian perspective on the cosmos, then the Hecate passage provides a unique opportunity to examine the divine viewpoint on human life in our age of iron.

Unfortunately, the section devoted to Hecate has long been mired in controversy. Because of its length and apparent lack of integration into its context, but above all because of the peculiar terms of praise reserved for the goddess, older scholars often dismissed the entire passage as an intrusion into the Hesiodic text.[4] Unitarians, however, found reasons to defend the lines,[5] and, at present, the passage stands unbracketed in most modern editions.[6] But even if the authenticity of the lines is acknowledged, many questions remain. Why does Hesiod devote so much space to a deity who has only a minor place in the Greek pantheon?

There has been a great deal of speculation concerning the origins of this goddess and the relation of her cult to Hesiod and his family.[7] But much of the discussion has been tangential to an understanding of her role in Hesiod's theogonic poem.[8] Interpretations of Hesiod's Hecate generally share a common assumption: her place in the poem is motivated by the poet's beliefs or private devotion, his wish to honor a local deity or to identify himself with a social class. Yet all these reasons for Hecate's inclusion are extraneous to the structure and context of the *Theogony*, and all have recourse to the personal quirks, beliefs, or circumstances of the

---

[3] Schoemann (1868) 183 grasps the unique character of the passage: "Es ist dieses Stück der Theogonie das einzige in seiner Art. Denn von dem, was die Götter für die Menschen thun, von ihrem Walten im Leben derselben, von den Gaben die sie gewähren oder versagen, kurz von Allem, um deswillen sie von den Menschen verehrt und angerufen werden, ist in keinem anderen Theil der Theogonie eigentlich die Rede."

[4] Most notably by Wilamowitz (1931) 172. Wilamowitz is followed by Nilsson (1969) 1.723. Condemnation is fairly universal among earlier editors. Cf. Gruppe (1841) 72; Schoemann (1868) 190, who, after many good observations, concludes that the passage is a later interpolation; Flach (1873) 81; Fick (1887) 17 ("Der Verfasser war ein Orphiker"); Jacoby (1930) 162–64; and Schwenn (1934) 100–05, who considers only nine verses genuine. See also Rzach (1912) 1189 *s.v.* "Hesiodos"; Sellschopp (1934) 52; Kirk (1962) 80 and 84–86.

[5] For instance, by Pfister(1928) 1–9; Friedländer (1931) 125–26; Solmsen (1949) 53, n. 169; and van Groningen (1958) 267–70.

[6] Mazon (1928); West (1966); Solmsen (1970); and Arrighetti (1998). Both Mazon and Solmsen bracket line 427, and Solmsen also considers 450–52 interpolated. For transpositions, see below, n. 17.

[7] For a summary, see Clay (1984) 28–30. This section is a version of that earlier article.

[8] The question of the relation between Hesiod's apparently 'universal' goddess and the Hecate of a later era, with her marked chthonic associations and her unappetizing connections with magic, corpses, the moon, crossroads, and dogs, belongs properly to historians of Greek religion and cannot be dealt with here. I would, however, suggest that the interpretation of Hesiod's Hecate presented here may have important points of contact with certain mediating aspects of the Hecate of the *Hymn to Demeter*. Moreover, some of her later associations with magic and crossroads may not be unrelated to the arbitrary willfulness Hesiod ascribes to her. See below, n. 33.

poet.[9] Of course, if Hecate is included only for personal reasons, we need not ask whether or how she is integrated into the theological argument of the poem or the cosmos Hesiod so carefully constructs for us. Far more fruitful are discussions that focus on what Hesiod actually says about this enigmatic divinity and her place in his poem.[10] The *Theogony* culminates in the triumph of Zeus and the establishment of the eternal Olympian order. The question abides whether Hecate, so elaborately praised, remains peripheral to that order. A fresh scrutiny of both the structure of the "Hymn to Hecate" and its pivotal position in the *Theogony* can simultaneously throw light on Hesiod's purpose as well as on the significance of the goddess in his theology.

As we saw in our preliminary survey of the *Theogony's* structure in Chapter 1, Hesiod positions his description of Hecate so as to set her in a special relation to Zeus, whose birth, which forms the central event of divine history, is narrated in the immediate sequel. By making the goddess the last divinity preceding the Olympian's birth, Hesiod allows Hecate to appear as the summation and embodiment of the entire cosmic process thus far and a powerful female heir of Gaia, Uranus, and Pontos. Thus, on the divine level, Hecate's relation to Zeus is relevant to the repeated patterns of the succession myth; by not uniting with this potentially dangerous goddess, Zeus takes a step to ensure the stability of his final dispensation. Moreover, by framing the account of Zeus's birth with both the Hecate and the Prometheus episode, Hesiod also links Hecate with Prometheus and thus foreshadows Zeus's final ordering of relations between men and gods.

A quick review of the passage will be helpful. Zeus, we are told, "honored Hecate above all and gave her splendid gifts, to have a share of the earth and sterile sea. And she also received a share of honor from the starry sky; and is very much honored by the immortal gods" (411–15). Later we learn that "of all those who were born from Earth and Sky and received honor, of all these, she keeps a share" (421–22). But it turns out that these universal privileges are not a new dispensation under the reign of Zeus, but in fact

---

[9] Perhaps the most extreme among these is Walcot (1958) 13–14, who after noting the coincidence of the name of Hesiod's brother and that of Hecate's father, concludes: "the story of Hecate had a very personal implication as far as Hesiod was concerned. Hesiod's respect for Hecate is of the same order virtually as his love of the Muses. Both provide a contrast with *his normal hatred of women*" (italics mine). Van Groningen (1958) 269 asserts that the *Theogony* was performed at a festival in honor of Hecate. Needless to say, no evidence exists for either view.

[10] For instance Griffith (1983) 37–65. See also the discussion of Marg (1970) 194–201; the analysis of Bollack (1971); the observations of Neitzel (1975) 84–117; the provocative remarks of Arthur (1982) 68–70, concerning the role of Hecate within the larger framework of male and female roles in the *Theogony*; Boedeker (1983), who views Hecate in Dumézilian terms; Rudhardt (1993) 204–13; and Zeitlin (1996) esp. 74–86.

belonged to Hecate originally: "Nor did the son of Cronus do her violence, or strip her of what she had received from the Titans, the earlier gods; but these she keeps, as, from the beginning, the distribution was accomplished" (423–25). Several features merit attention in these lines. First, it is clear that Hecate does not simply receive earth, sea, and sky as her sphere of influence. The Greek is quite precise: the goddess received a *moira*, a *share* of honor on earth, in the heavens, and in the sea. The notion of portion or share is emphatically repeated twice (413, 426). All talk of Hecate as a 'universal goddess' must therefore be carefully modified.[11] The second characteristic of Hecate's power, which Hesiod underlines by threefold repetition (ἔχειν 413, ἔχει 422, 425),[12] is the continuity of the goddess' share of *time*. She *keeps* the honor she originally had[13] and, in fact, "even got much more, because Zeus honors her" (428).

The story of Hecate's cousin Styx, told a few lines earlier (383–403), offers a revealing comparison. There, Hesiod describes the policy of Zeus on the eve of his battle with the Titans, when he promised that those who joined his side would be allowed to keep the honor they held previously; and whoever had been without honor or privilege under Cronus would receive both, as appropriate, ἦ θέμις ἐστίν. In an act that ensures Zeus's ultimate victory, Styx throws in her lot with Zeus, bringing along her appropriately named children, Kratos, Bie, Zelos, and Nike. In return, Zeus makes her "the great oath of the gods" and establishes her children as his constant companions. Styx's loyalty to Zeus was amply rewarded and, as keeper of the oath of the gods, she becomes in a sense the embodiment of that loyalty.

In addition to foreshadowing the final victory of Zeus, this little episode also points up a peculiar feature of the Hecate story. As West notes, unlike Styx, Hecate does not appear to render any special service to Zeus,[14] yet she not only retains her prerogatives from the old order, but also is accorded the additional title of *kourotrophos*. Indeed, the text emphasizes repeatedly

---

[11] Rohde (1898) 2.82, n. 3, who considers the entire passage an interpolation, calls Hecate a "Universalgöttin" and adds: "Das Ganze ist eine sonderbare Probe von der Ausweitung, die in einem lebhaft betriebenen Localcult eine einzelne Gottheit gewinnen konnte. Der Name dieses durch die ganze Welt herrschenden Dämons wird dabei (da eben Alles auf den Einen gehäuft ist) schliesslich gleichgiltig." I hope to show below that the latter statement is incorrect and that Hecate's name is not irrelevant. Friedländer (1931) 125 correctly explains the limitation of Hecate's powers: "Nicht Herrin des Alls ist sie, sondern überall hat sie 'Anteil' . . . Nirgends verdrängt Hekate die anderen Götter. Von einer Allgottheit vollends ist in diesem Bezirk religiösen Denkens nicht die Rede. Doch überall ist sie dabei." Cf. Kraus (1960) 62; and West's (1966) comments (281–82) at lines 413–14.

[12] Hesiod may well be punning on the similarity of sound between *echein* and Hecate.

[13] For ἐξ ἀρχῆς, see Classen (1996) 23–24.

[14] Cf. West (1966) 284 on 423–24; and Marquardt (1981) 247: "Zeus's reasons for honoring Hecate, which presumably go beyond affection or familial ties, are never mentioned by Hesiod."

that it is Zeus who honors *her* – and not the other way around. Zeus, in fact, almost seems to court Hecate's favor.[15] He must in some sense recognize the importance and utility of maintaining Hecate's functions and *timai* under his new regime. As her epithet *mounogenes* and her geneaology indicate, Hecate's status as an only daughter and *epikleros* gives her the right to transmit her powerful inheritance to any potential husband. Zeus, however, does not marry her; rather, he grants her a unique position within his regime that retains her privileges and exploits her powers but disarms any potential threat she might pose to his supremacy. Through the prerogative that he adds to Hecate's older privileges, the role of *kourotrophos*, a childless protector of the young, virgin and nurse, but never mother, Zeus appears to divert the great powers of the goddess away from the gods onto the world of men where her good will and support lead to success in all areas of human endeavor.[16]

The catalogue at 429–49 reveals both Hecate's functions and the extent of her powers over the lives of men, more specifically, males.[17] Yet the list makes equally clear that Hecate's wide-ranging powers are not independent of those of other divinities. In council, she grants pre-eminence, while in war she gives victory and glory "to whom she wills"; but Victory has taken up her abode with Zeus, who likewise has the power to grant *kudos*.[18] Hecate may sit by kings as they render judgments; yet we know from Hesiod's proem that kings are "from Zeus," and their successful judicial pronouncements depend on the honey of the Muses. Similarly, we are told that Hecate is beneficent when she stands by horsemen and those who

[15] Griffith (1983) plays down the important differences between Styx and Hecate; Hesiod does not tell us that the latter "chose to join Zeus and was duly rewarded" (p. 54). Rather, the text suggests Hecate's independent power. While Zeus co-opts Styx's children, Hecate, significantly, has none. Boedeker (1983) 90 notes: "We might conclude that Zeus needs her more than she needs him." Cf. Rudhardt (1993) 209; and Zeitlin (1996) 76, n. 44.

[16] As protector of the young, Hecate is later assimilated to Artemis, likewise a virgin goddess. Griffith (1983) 54 ignores the potential threat in Hecate's femaleness. Cf. Arthur (1982) 69–70. Zeitlin (1996) 77 emphasizes the role of Hecate as nurturer rather than mother.

[17] Cf. Zeitlin (1996) 75, n. 39. Note especially ἀνέρες in 432 and ἄνδρες in 435, but ἐπιχθονίων ἀνθρώπων in 416. All human beings may pray to her, but only males seem to benefit from her. Following Schoemann (1857c) 2.220–21, but not his edition of 1868, West transposes 434 before 430 despite the harsh change from singular to plural. This ignores the fact that 430–33 define the traditional twofold virtues of the epic hero, who excels both in speech and warfare. Cf. *Iliad* 9.443, cited by Schoemann. Kings rendering judgments, like the rest of the activities in Hesiod's catalogue (434–46), belong to peacetime. Cf. *Iliad* 16.387–88 and 18.497–506, cited by West. Horsemen, to be sure, belong to both peace and war, but there is no compelling reason to transpose 439. In their present context, they are related to horse racing. For a convincing defense of the paradosis, see Neitzel (1975) 89–103; and on different grounds Bravo (1985) 761–64.

[18] Cf. fr. 75.19–20 M–W, where Zeus and the other immortals are said to be able to grant *kudos*; also *Scut.* 339, where Athena νίκην ἀθανάτης χερσὶν καὶ κῦδος ἔχουσα.

compete in games: "and easily he carries off a fine prize, having won with strength and might, and he gives glory to his parents" (435–39). Once again, it is clear that Hecate is not being made into a goddess who presides over athletic competitions; as we know from countless tales of heroic contests, any god can intervene on behalf of his favorite. Yet Hesiod assures us that Hecate's support and good will are somehow crucial to winning. Exactly how becomes clearer in the following verses:

καὶ τοῖς, οἳ γλαυκὴν δυσπέμφελον ἐργάζονται,
εὔχονται δ' Ἑκάτῃ καὶ ἐρικτύπῳ Ἐννοσιγαίῳ,
ῥηιδίως ἄγρην κυδρὴ θεὸς ὤπασε πολλήν,
ῥεῖα δ' ἀφείλετο φαινομένην, ἐθέλουσά γε θυμῷ.

And for those who work the stormy sea,
And who pray to Hecate and to the Earthshaker,
Easily the splendid goddess grants a big catch,
And easily she takes it away, once it has appeared –
if indeed she so wills it.   (440–43)

Here, finally the operation of Hecate's extensive yet not fully independent powers becomes clearer. She grants success in fishing *if* she is invoked in conjunction with Poseidon and *if* she is willing. So too in conjunction with Hermes, Hecate can increase the flocks, and, *if* she wills it, she can make many from the few and, on the contrary, diminish the many (444–47).

Hesiod's catalogue of Hecate's powers, while not exhaustive, gives the impression of universality.[19] But it is also quite evident that these powers are not autonomous. Each area in which Hecate manifests her influence belongs either to a specific god (Poseidon, Hermes) or to a possible diversity of gods.[20] Yet in each sphere her good will forms an essential ingredient of success – just as its absence seems to lead to failure. Consequently, Hecate must not be regarded as simply beneficent or as a kindly *Helfergöttin*, for that aspect constitutes only half her power and neglects her darker side.[21] Bollack draws attention to her ambiguous nature: "Immoderate for good or

[19] Cf. Boedeker (1983) 79–80; and Friedländer (1931) 125.
[20] Cf. Schoemann (1857c) 225: "Mercurium deum pastoralem fuisse nemo ignorat. Atque sicut huius in hoc munere socia esse Hecate dicitur, et paullo ante in navigantium tutela Neptuni, sic etiam in ceteris, quae supra commemorata sunt, omnibus alii quidam dei nominari potuissent, quorum illa munerum societatem haberet."
[21] Arthur (1982) 69 considers Hecate as "the first of the major female figures in the poem who is presented in a wholly positive light" and speaks of "her beneficent character" (70). Marquardt (1981) 244 first claims that "expressions of Hecate's . . . benevolent nature form a recurring theme in the Hymn," but then more correctly asserts that "the unpredictability of Hecate's favor is a recurring theme in the Hymn" (247). Cf. Griffith (1983) 53.

ill, she operates with lighthearted caprice" and he defines her dominant trait as "the *constant presence of chance*."[22] In fact, she bears a striking resemblance to Pindar's σώτειρα Τύχα:

> Through you swift ships are guided on the sea
> And on land, darting wars
> And assemblies that pass decrees. The hopes of men are tossed,
>   often up and sometimes down again,
> Windy falsehoods, cutting through the seas.
> No man can discover a reliable sign
> From the gods concerning future action;
> Their minds are blind to what's to come;
> Many things befall men unexpectedly,
> Inverting their joy, but others,
> Who have encountered storms of distress, in a moment exchange
>   their woe for solid good.   (*Olympian* 12.3–12)

Like Pindar's *Tycha*, the essential character of Hecate, then, resides in her easy exercise of arbitrary power over success or failure in every human enterprise. But why should Hecate be the deity to incorporate this particular function?[23] The repeated emphasis throughout the passage on Hecate's will (ᾧ δ᾽ ἐθέλῃ, 429; ὃν κ᾽ ἐθέλῃσιν, 430; οἷς κ᾽ ἐθέλῃσι(ν), 432, 439; ἐθέλουσά γε θυμῷ, 443; θυμῷ γ᾽ ἐθέλουσα, 446) has led some scholars to postulate a Hesiodic etymology of her name as "the willing goddess".[24] This gloss is surely in keeping with Hesiod's intention, but the perspective is once again

---

[22] Bollack (1971) 115: "Unmässig im Guten wie im Bösen, wirkt die Göttin mit einer schwerelosen Leichtigkeit", "die *Allgegenwart des Zufalls*"; cf. Neitzel (1975) 108: "sie ist die Göttin der *Willkür des Zufalls*" (italics in original). Neitzel argues that Hecate is the embodiment of the irrational in human life. Schoemann (1868) 185 suggests that Hecate should be understood as a personification of "die göttliche Wirksamkeit": "Diese Wirksamkeit wohnt nun freilich allen Göttern bei, ist eine Eigenschaft von allen; das aber konnte den Dichter nicht hindern, sie doch auch als eigene göttliche Person aufzuführen."

[23] Griffith (1983) 53–54 offers three reasons: first, she is not part of the Olympian pantheon and hence does not interfere or threaten established spheres of activity; second, as a female she poses less of a threat to Zeus than a male divinity would; and, finally, she demonstrates Zeus's generosity toward at least some of the older gods.

[24] Walcot (1958) 11; and Neitzel (1975) 109. Cf. Hermann (1827) 185, and (1839) 306, who, deriving Hecate from ἑκών and ἕκητι, nicely renders her name as Volumnia. Fick (1894) 452 translates Hecate as "nach dem Willen." Cf. Prellwitz (1929) 147. Schoemann (1857c) 228–30 offers an alternative etymology connecting Hecate with ἑκάς; also Brugmann (1904/05). The modern consensus is that Ἑκάτη is the feminine of Ἕκατος, epithet of Apollo, and perhaps of Anatolian origin. Cf. Wilamowitz (1931) 117; and Kraus (1960) 14: "Dass Hekatos die männliche Form zu Hekate ist und dass beide aus der gleichen Wurzel, dem gleichen Vorstellungskreis entsprungen sind, ist sicher." Cf. Derossi (1975), who gives an overview of discussions and concludes that the name signifies the benign will of the goddess. What matters of course is not the 'scientific' etymology but Hesiod's interpretation of the goddess's name.

skewed by mistaking for good will what is Hecate's essential arbitrariness.[25] Hecate is not the "willing goddess," but the willful goddess, the one *by whose will* – ἕκατι – prayers are fulfilled and success granted. As such, Hecate offers a solution to a prickly and delicate problem posed by any theology: Why is it that the gods sometimes fulfill human prayers but at other times reject them? Or, Pindarically, why is there no reliable sign from the gods concerning future actions? For example, I can pray to Hermes to increase my flocks or to Zeus for victory. Both Hermes and Zeus surely have the requisite power to accomplish my wish; yet my prayer may or may not be answered. Something has intervened to bring about my success or failure. That something is, in fact, Hecate. It is her will – or caprice – which is impossible to foresee, that has intervened. If I have been successful, it is because of the propitious conjunction of Hecate and some other god; success comes *by the will* of Zeus, ἕκατι Διός, or another divinity, and Hecate has played her critical role as intermediary.

On the basis of this interpretation, it is possible now to understand the enigmatic statement, omitted in the discussion of the opening section of the passage:

> καὶ γὰρ νῦν, ὅτε πού τις ἐπιχθονίων ἀνθρώπων
> ἔρδων ἱερὰ καλὰ κατὰ νόμον ἱλάσκηται,
> κικλήσκει Ἑκάτην· πολλή τέ οἱ ἕσπετο τιμὴ
> ῥεῖα μάλ᾽, ᾧ πρόφρων γε θεὰ ὑποδέξεται εὐχάς . . .

> And thus even now, whenever someone of men on earth,
> Making fine sacrifices, appropriately propitiates [the gods],
> He calls on Hecate; and much honor follows him
> Most easily, the one, that is, whose prayers the goddess kindly receives.
>
> (*Theog.* 416–19)

These lines appear to introduce a ritual aetiology,[26] but go on to assert the bizarre notion that every act of sacrifice or propitiation involves an invocation to Hecate and that success depends on the goddess's kindly reception of the prayer. Yet no such custom ever existed among the Greeks. The few scholars who have confronted this oddity have suspected some ritual basis for Hesiod's curious assertion, but they do not elaborate.[27] There

---

[25] Schmid and Stählin (1929) 1.256, n. 7: "Sehr stark wird bei der Göttin . . . betont, dass sie nur hilft, wenn sie will." Cf. Marg (1970) 197–99. Marquardt (1981) 245 observes the parallel to αἴ κ᾽ ἐθέλω, as spoken by the hawk in the fable of the hawk and the nightingale (*W&D* 209), but insists nevertheless that "Hecate herself in no way resembles the hawk." Note also the Muses' εὖτ᾽ ἐθέλωμεν (*Theog.* 28).

[26] Cf. ἐκ τοῦ in *Theog.* 556 of the human practice of sacrifice instituted by Prometheus.

[27] For instance, Marquardt (1981) 244 comments on 416–18: "Hecate's presence in such prayers, especially if she is invoked with other gods, may reflect only ritual." Marg (1970) 200 appears to understand the mechanism: "bei jedem rechten Opfer wird in Wirklichkeit, auch ohne ausdrückliche Nennung des Namens, Hekate *mit* angerufen, als die große Potenz der Zuwendung."

is in fact some suggestive evidence for a custom that may have inspired Hesiod. When, on occasion, a series of offerings to various divinities was established, the goddess designated as *kourotrophos* was sometimes given the right of first sacrifice, the so-called *prothyma*.[28] The existence of such a custom would make sense of Hesiod's claim at the end of his praise of Hecate that Zeus added to her previous honors the role of *kourotrophos* (450). Be that as it may, Hesiod's peculiar statement supports our interpretation of the name and function of Hecate as the one *by whose will* prayers are accomplished and fulfilled.

The decisive proof of the correctness of such an understanding of Hecate's critical mediating role comes from the words of Hesiod himself in his opening invocation to the *Works and Days*. There he summons the Muses to hymn their father Zeus:

> ὅν τε διὰ βροτοὶ ἄνδρες ὁμῶς ἄφατοί τε φατοί τε,
> ῥητοί τ᾽ ἄρρητοί τε Διὸς μεγάλοιο ἕκητι.

> [Zeus] through whom mortal men are alike unmentioned
>   and mentioned,
> Famous and infamous, *by the will of* great Zeus.   (3–4)

The next two verses clearly echo the Hecate passage of the *Theogony*:

> ῥέα μὲν γὰρ βριάει, ῥέα δὲ βριάοντα χαλέπτει,
> ῥεῖα δ᾽ ἀρίζηλον μινύθει καὶ ἄδηλον ἀέξει . . .

> Easily he gives strength, and easily weakens the strong,
> Easily diminishes the proud and increases the humble . . .
>   (5–6)

The significance and importance of Hecate for the *Theogony* and for Hesiod's cosmos as a whole now begin to emerge. As in the case of several other deities, Hesiod develops Hecate's functions by etymologizing her name; thus he evolves the figure of Metis from the formulaic expression μητίετα Ζεύς and invents a new genealogy for Aphrodite from her epithet οὐρανία.[29] Similarly, Hesiod connects the name of Hecate to such common phrases as ἕκητι Διός and οὐκ ἀέκητι θεῶν.[30] But it must be admitted that such a verbal connection would have remained a minor curiosity, a clever

---

[28] See Price (1978) 10, 105, 108, 111, 123 (although Price may insist too much on identifying the *kourotrophos* with Ge). For the meaning of προθύω and πρόθυμα see Casabona (1966) 103–8, and Mikalson (1972). For the ancient literary and epigraphical evidence, see Clay (1984) 35, n. 34.

[29] On Uranian Aphrodite, see West (1966) 212.

[30] Cf. *Theog.* 529, *Iliad* 12.8, 15.720; *Odyssey* 1.79, 3.28, 4.504, 6.240, 12.290, 20.42, 24.444; *Hymn Ven.* 147. The best parallel perhaps occurs at *Od.* 15.319–20, where the disguised Odysseus boasts of his skill at tending fires and serving Ἑρμείαο ἕκητι διακτόρου, ὅς ῥά τε πάντων | ἀνθρώπων ἔργοισι χάριν καὶ κῦδος ὀπάζει.

conceit and nothing more, if Hesiod had not recognized its theological utility.

The lengthy treatment accorded to Hecate at a pivotal moment in the *Theogony* attests not merely to a personal whim of Hesiod's, but to the poet's understanding of her critical mediating function. Hecate mediates not only between the old and the new order, the Titans and the Olympians: her powers bridge the three spheres of the *cosmos*, and she forms the crucial intermediary between gods and men.[31] The logic of the placement of the Hecate episode now becomes apparent. It stands directly before the focal event of divine and cosmic history, the birth of Zeus, and forms the necessary complement to the story of Prometheus, which follows. In the Prometheus myth, Hesiod offers an account of the origins of the great schism separating gods and men and what will henceforth be the eternal condition of mankind. Thereafter, all communication between men and gods requires the mediation of sacrifice and prayer.

In a bold *hysteron proteron*, Hesiod explains how the mediation inaugurated by Prometheus' deception operates in the post-Promethean age and how Hecate's intervention bridges the distance established by Zeus between mankind and the gods.[32] If in the Prometheus episode human beings are the passive victims of a divine comedy played out at their expense, in the passage devoted to Hecate, by contrast, men are not only more prominently present than elsewhere in the *Theogony*; they are also depicted as actively and busily involved in all spheres of human affairs. But, above all, they are men 'like us' who pray and sacrifice to the gods κατὰ νόμον. "And so, even now, whenever someone of earthly men prays or makes sacrifice, he invokes Hecate," by whose will success is granted or denied. Absorbed and consolidated into the Olympian pantheon and taking her place in Zeus's cosmos as an essential element of the post-Promethean order, Hecate thus forms the middle term of Hesiod's theodicy and fully deserves her place in the *Theogony*.[33]

---

[31] Although etymologizing her name as "Fernwirker," Klaußen (1835) 452–58 already understood her theological function as intermediary.

[32] Cf. Griffith (1983) 53: "the Hecate episode . . . shows how Hesiod's theology actually works for mankind." Cf. Rudhardt (1993) and Zeitlin (1996) 76: "As an intermediary in human affairs between gods and men, honored by all alike, Hekate may be said to neutralize or at least mitigate in advance the negative effects for mortals of Prometheus' guileful mediation."

[33] In the *Hymn to Demeter*, the goddess likewise fulfills the role of intermediary as she accompanies Persephone between the upper and nether regions. For Hecate's later connection with gates as Prothyraia, see Kraus (1960); also Johnston (1989) for the goddess' role as an intermediary in later literature. Rudhardt (1993) 212–13 emphasizes that Hecate, insofar as she exerts her power over individuals rather than possessing a defined sphere of influence as the other gods do, has an affinity with magic, which, of course, is the preserve of the later Hecate attested in cult.

The catalogue of human activities contained in the Hecate passage merits further attention insofar as it suggests a "gods' eye view" of human existence. It begins ἐν ἀγορῇ (430);[34] then devotes three lines to men engaged in warfare (431–33); one line, to kings in their judicial capacity (ἔν τε δίκῃ), followed by four describing success in athletic competitions and one for horsemen (435–39). Fishermen and herdsmen, each occupying four lines, conclude the list (440–47).[35]

Perhaps the most striking feature of the catalogue is the place assigned to war and that imitation of warfare, athletic competitions. These two spheres of activity would appear to be features of the aristocratic or heroic life as opposed to the lives of the peasant farmer Hesiod describes in the *Works and Days*.[36] Moreover, the word *kudos*, "heroic repute" or "glory," occurs only here in the *Theogony*. Hecate grants *kudos* to those who are successful in war and in athletic games (433, 438). In the *Works and Days*, however, *kudos* also appears only once but in an ironic context: "excellence and glory are the companions of wealth" (πλούτῳ δ' ἀρετὴ καὶ κῦδος ὀπηδεῖ, 313).[37] Indeed, from the perspective of the *Works and Days*, the goal of human life is neither heroism nor glory, but the drabber ends of work and justice.

Equally remarkable is the absence of agriculture, since for Hesiod it constitutes the characteristic activity of the human race.[38] Just as Hesiod ascribes a successful catch and the multiplication of flocks to the conjunction of Hecate's benevolence with that of Poseidon and Hermes respectively, he surely could have included a bountiful harvest dependent upon the collaboration of Hecate and Demeter or Zeus. The inclusion of fishing and herding and the omission of farming remain puzzling. In the *Works and Days*, fishing is never mentioned even in connection with sailing, which is there viewed as ancillary to the business of farming; while herding receives short shrift, despite the fact that Hesiod represents himself as a shepherd when he encountered the Muses at Helicon. Both activities would appear

---

[34] See above, n. 17, on West's transposition.

[35] For Boedeker (1983) fishing and herding represent the third Indo-European function after sovereignty and warfare.

[36] Neitzel (1975) 100–102 argues that the mention of horsemen here refers to chariot racing, an aristocratic pastime. Fränkel (1962) 145, n. 30 notes that the description of public life in the Hecate episode is "Homeric," but he does not think the passage genuine.

[37] Perses' κυδαίνων of the kings (*W&D* 38) is likewise ironic.

[38] Cf. Boedeker (1983) 85. Also Bravo (1985) 764–65, who rightly rejects the possibility that for the Greeks agriculture was less risky than fishing and herding, but then concludes: "le silence d'Hésiode au sujet de l'agriculture dans ce passage de la *Théogonie* témoigne qu'il ne s'intéressait pas spécialement à cet aspect de la vie humaine," but later changed his mind when he came to compose the *W&D*. On the shield of Achilles, the gods are visible only in the city at war, and are absent from both the peaceful city and the various agricultural scenes.

to be either inferior, or subordinate, to agriculture and hence of a lower order.

If, as I suggested, the *Theogony* offers an Olympian perspective on human life, then it would appear that what interests the gods is not the daily life of the average man who gains his livelihood by working the land – precisely the farmer of the *Works and Days* – but instead great men, such as heroes, kings and warriors to whom the gods grant *kudos*, but also, perhaps more suprisingly, those of lower status. The gods concern themselves less with the middle, the run-of-the-mill. That this middle, which is bracketed in the *Theogony*, should be the focus of the *Works and Days*, once again suggests that the two poems must be read together and form complementary perspectives on Hesiod's cosmos.

GODS IN THE *WORKS AND DAYS*

To complement our examination of human beings in the *Theogony*, we must examine the role of the gods in the *Works and Days*. The argument of the *Works and Days* can be traced by mapping the changing faces of Zeus in the course of the poem. If the *Theogony* represented a collaboration of Hesiod and the Muses, the *Works and Days* offers a partnership between Hesiod and Zeus in which Hesiod sets out to expound the *noos* of Zeus. After a brief invocation, the Muses take, as it were, a back seat to Zeus, who from the beginning occupies the central role. The poet requires the Muses' assistance only in the section on sailing; the *etetuma* he expounds are those things he knows from lived experience, matters for which he does not need the Muses' help. He is, after all, the *panaristos* who "can understand all things on his own" (293).

As we have seen, after the Muses extol Zeus's power over human beings, Hesiod requests in the proem that the Olympian make use of that power to watch and listen and straighten their (crooked) *themistes* by means of justice.[39] What the poet does not pray for is that the just be rewarded; his is a punitive prayer. Moreover, his request appears aimed at the kings, for it is they who dispense decrees.[40] Lines 9 and 10 thus express a division of labor: Zeus is to watch and punish the unjust kings while Hesiod will instruct Perses in the ways of the world.

---

[39] Cf. Rousseau (1996) 106–109, whose interpretation I follow. He likewise points out that "le principe qui gouverne l'action des dieux ne se manifeste, négativement, que par le châtiment dont il accable l'injuste et l'oppresseur" (106). Cf. Wilamowitz (1928) 42–43: "An Zeus wird die Allmacht gepriesen, nicht die Gerechtigkeit. Wenn er gebeten wird, für diese zu sorgen, dann ist zugestanden, daß er das nicht immer tut."

[40] Cf. Pucci (1996) 202–3.

In any case, Hesiod immediately begins his instruction of Perses concerning the *etetuma* with three myths: that is, stories that take place in the remote past in which gods are active agents, but whose consequences shape the world, as we know it. In all three, as we have seen, Zeus plays a critical role. It was he who set Eris in the roots of the earth, simultaneously exiling her from Olympus and transforming her into a potentially positive force among mankind.[41] The other two *logoi* studied earlier offered a complex picture. In the Prometheus story, Zeus appears less than beneficent, rendering human life – previously carefree – painful through work, scarcity, and disease, yet salvaging it through the sweet illusion of Hope. The myth of the races likewise revealed how the gods deprived human beings of a primordial felicity and an earlier intimacy with the divine. While distancing themselves from mankind, the gods gave men the ability to procreate without divine intervention, thereby granting human beings a certain degree of independence from the gods. But that independence was restricted by the human consciousness of their inferiority vis-à-vis the gods. For a time, Zeus brought the gods again closer to mankind by permitting the mingling of the two races; and through the gift of justice, he made it possible for human beings to live and work together in communities. When the gods again withdrew from human intimacy, justice was left behind, but on its own justice revealed its weakness in regulating human conduct. Such is the world in which mankind finds itself and with which it must come to terms.

The accounts of the two Erides, Prometheus, and the five races are complementary and share a common motif: what is beautiful or attractive turns out to be bad or at least ambiguous, while the apparently ugly may hide something beneficial. Thus Eris, bad enough to be kicked out of heaven, can take on a positive aspect when Zeus places her in the roots of the earth. The competition she institutes among human beings and the passions she inspires are in themselves neither beautiful nor noble;[42] they could well lead to the kind of mutual destruction that precipitated the demise of the Bronze men. If I envy my neighbor, become enraged, and begrudge him his success, I may try to steal or plunder his property instead

---

[41] Zeus's tossing Ate out of heaven and exiling her among the ἔργ' ἀνθρώπων in *Iliad* 19.126–31 offers a nice parallel. Davies (1995) 1–4 emphasizes the Hesiodic character of the parable.

[42] Cf. the Scholia at 25–26: τὸ κοτέειν καὶ τὸ φθονεῖν κακά ἐστι καὶ ἐκείνης [the bad Eris] οἰκεῖα καὶ οὐ τῆς ἀμείνονος. Cf. Fuss (1910) 28–29, who takes lines 25–26 to refer to the bad Eris: "Nur dem Landmann ist die gute Eris . . . gnädig, in allen andern Berufen dagegen waltet die schlechte Eris." Blümer (2001) 2, 42–49, simply ejects lines 25–26 from the text. Which removes the problem. On the ambiguity of even the good Eris, see Gagarin (1990) esp. p. 175: "there is no clear distinction between the positive inspiration to work and the negative begrudging of another's success." Also Nagler (1992) 87–93.

of working, or perhaps even do away with him. Eris must be tempered to become productive, and what tempers her is work and justice.

In accounting for the scarcity and harshness of human life, the Prometheus story describes how labor, specifically the necessity of working to produce food, became the compulsory condition of humanity. An ugly necessity, alien to the gods who "live easy," but, like Eris, in its mortal guise, labor also benefits and sustains mankind. Fire, Pandora, and Hope, all at first glance attractive and desirable, turn out to be *kala kaka*, both a curse and a blessing. The competitive Eris is finally channeled by Zeus's justice, which on the grossest level denies mankind the right to acquire the food they need by eating each other, but also rejects stealing, lying, cheating, and the abuse of the obligations of reciprocity toward family, friends, and strangers. In severely limiting the human means for acquiring a livelihood, Justice (who did not exist in the golden age of abundance, but entered the world only in the age of heroes) like Eris wears a double face: an avenging divinity who observes and punishes, and a lovely goddess who dispenses blessing on the community that honors her.

One could say that the poem that follows constitutes an elaboration of these three myths: Hesiod's primary task is to strengthen Justice, so easily traduced and assaulted, by linking her tightly to Zeus's power to reward and, more importantly, to punish through the agency of Hope, who embraces both fear of punishment and hope for reward. Second, Hesiod teaches and encourages the kind of work decreed by Zeus and, finally, healthy rather than destructive competition. If getting more is a human imperative, but justice dictates that such acquisition can only be accomplished without doing violence to others, then productive work – and that means fundamentally agriculture – is the only human option. Perses has rejected these imperatives: instead of tilling his fields, he has spent his time quarreling, talking, and cheating; inevitably, hunger and poverty will follow. Likewise, Perses' desire for getting more without toil leads to his stealing and cheating others – not we note by force, but by speech through legal disputes and flattery of those who do have power, the kings. Thus Perses has not only practiced injustice toward his fellow man; he has also corrupted his betters whose job it is to dispense justice and to speak straight.

What is striking, especially for students of Greek polytheism, is the very attenuated position of the other gods of the pantheon in Hesiod's poem, especially in contrast to the *Theogony*. If in the earlier poem Hesiod attempts a systemization of the whole pantheon, in the latter composition he severely limits the interventions of gods other than Zeus. Outside of the Pandora story, Athena is mentioned only once in the body of the poem, as are Apollo, Dionysus, Poseidon, and Hephaestus. Even the name of Demeter occurs only seven times, of which four are found in the formula, "the [holy] grain of Demeter" – surprising in view of the poem's subject-matter. Zeus, on the other hand, is named explicitly more than forty times. This does not necessarily mean that Hesiod is moving in the direction of monotheism, but rather that justice and work, the central themes of the *Works and Days*, belong primarily to Zeus's domain, for it is he who has decreed them as the condition of human life. Moreover, the pervasive presence of Zeus paradoxically serves to underline the distance between human beings and the gods in Hesiod's age of iron.[43] Even in the Homeric epics, Zeus intervenes in the activities of the heroes only indirectly through messengers, omens, and signs. Likewise, in the *Hymn to Demeter*, the king of the gods is presented only in indirect discourse, which suggests his distance from the action. Whereas the *Theogony* exploited Hecate as the crucial intermediary between gods and mortals, within the framework of the *Works and Days*, her functions are taken over by Zeus; in other words, we move from the goddess Hecate to Διὸς μεγάλοιο ἕκητι (4). This distinction is important: it means that from the human perspective the mediating role of Hecate disappears; Zeus and Zeus alone controls the fate of mankind.

With the gradual withdrawal of the gods that characterizes the race of iron, Hesiod shows how Zeus exercises control over human life through his emissaries, especially Justice and her companions. Aidos, the sense of shame that prevents men from committing transgressions, and Nemesis, who punishes them, fill the void along with Zeus's 30,000 guardians. Some of these divinities are new; while implacable Nemesis was one of Night's children, neither the birth of Aidos nor Elpis was recorded in the *Theogony*. Apparently, they have no influence in the divine sphere: the gods have no need of shame or hope, which characterize human life. Indeed, the departure of Aidos and Nemesis will signal the final stage of the iron race, when Zeus will destroy mankind. Finally, at a certain moment, Hesiod invites us to participate in the birth of a new goddess: Pheme, Reputation or, perhaps, Gossip.

Many of these divinized forces have appeared in the *Theogony* among the children of Night or of her daughter, Eris. In the final organization of the cosmos, Zeus relegated some of those offspring to the depths of Tartarus. But Zeus may perhaps have sent others, henceforth banished from the

---

[43] Arrighetti (1998) 401 elegantly sums up the character of the *W&D*: "Da una parte dunque una maggiore dipendenza degli uomini dagli dèi, dall'altra una distinzione sempre piu precisa dei due mondi."

blissful existence of the gods, to dwell among mankind, the same evils that constituted the contents of the jar that accompanied Pandora. Exiled forever from Olympus, they now dwell permanently among us. But because of the ambiguous character and status of mankind, these same forces, although fundamentally negative, at least from the divine perspective, sometimes reveal a double nature; that which is purely negative from the point of view of the gods may in fact have a positive influence on human life. Herein may lie the origin of what has been called Hesiod's *Begriffsspaltung*, the doubling or splitting of concepts such as Eris.[44] Such doubling is not limited to Eris alone, but also occurs in the case of other entities such as Hope, Nemesis, Horkos, and Aidos.

Throughout the great protreptic to justice, Zeus and his helpers appear as watchers and avengers of iniquity. Both the just and the unjust city are under his direct control, as the repeated phrase τεκμαίρεται εὐρύοπα Ζεύς (229, 239) implies. War, which earlier was a harsh human necessity (14), has become an instrument of Zeus's punishment (229). As we might expect, Zeus's avenging ministers are most emphatically invoked in the threats addressed to the kings (248–69). The immortals are near and observe when men pronounce crooked judgments: the 30,000 invisible guardians of Zeus patrol every corner of the earth; and Zeus's daughter, Dike herself, denounces human injustice to her father, so that the entire population must pay for the crimes of their kings. Finally the all-seeing eye of Zeus observes directly what kind of justice the city contains.

Throughout this section of the poem, Zeus and his representatives have played a dominant role. Dike and Zeus have become inseparable, or, rather, Zeus has become the enforcer of her decrees. He has hearkened to the poet's pious prayer of the poem's opening. Zeus, whose power rather than justice was praised in the proem, has in the course of Hesiod's protreptic been converted – along with the kings and Perses – into her champion.[45] The role of Zeus will palpably diminish in the rest of the poem at the same time that the poem's field of vision will narrow to the *oikos* and the farms of Perses and his neighbors. This should not surprise us, since the Olympian shows greater interest in the kings and the affairs of the community; neither the *polis* nor justice is ever mentioned again in the poem. Moreover, the character of Zeus's interventions will also change once his association with *dike* is loosened, but at first the change appears gradual.

---

[44] See especially Martinazzoli (1946); and Livrea (1967).

[45] Cf. Lamberton (1988) 94–95: "The deliberate association of Zeus with dike in the *Works and Days* . . . is just the opposite of the redemption of mankind by Zeus through dike. Rather, it is the redemption of the Zeus of tradition, through dike, by poetry . . ."

Zeus and the three daughters Themis bears to him, Eunomia, Dike, and Eirene (*Theog.* 901–02) are, so to speak, the patron saints of the first half of the *Works and Days*. But these same figures, now under their collective name as Horai, play a similar role in the next section of the poem, the Calendar. In etymologizing their names, Hesiod had explained their functions: αἵ τ' ἔργ' ὡρεύουσι καταθνητοῖσι βροτοῖσι (*Theog.* 903). Hence they are the divinities who *delimit* and make seasonable the works of mortal men. Work that previously had been imposed upon mankind as an inescapable evil now appears as a sure path to wealth; moreover, if done correctly, it will make a man dear to the gods (300, 309). Zeus's active participation in the so-called Farmers' Almanac diminishes because the cycle of the seasons, the Horai, functions on its own, without the need for direct divine intervention. In addition, there are useful astronomical signs and other indications that signal the timing of agricultural chores. Nevertheless, Zeus plays a role to which Hesiod alludes but whose importance he downplays, a role that cannot be foreseen with the same certainty as the regularity of the cycle of the seasons: the weather. As every farmer knows, the weather is critical, but unpredictable. You can do everything right and at the proper time, but too much or too little rain can render all your efforts vain. In this section of the poem, Zeus becomes the god of rain (416, 488, 626, 676). For reasons which are not difficult to figure out, Hesiod says little about the uncertainty to which all agriculture is inevitably prone.

Up to this point, Hesiod has managed to convince his brother that the only just path to success and wealth is farming. He does not reveal to Perses – or at least he does not reveal right away – that neither the practice of justice nor correct working habits always lead to prosperity. After all, in the *Theogony*, Ploutos is identified as:

> . . . ὃς εἶσ' ἐπὶ γῆν τε καὶ εὐρέα νῶτα θαλάσσης
> πᾶσαν· τῷ δὲ τυχόντι καὶ οὗ κ' ἐς χεῖρας ἵκηται,
> τὸν δὴ ἀφνειὸν ἔθηκε, πολὺν δέ οἱ ὤπασεν ὄλβον.
>
> . . . he who goes on the earth and the broad back of every sea;
> And he makes the one he happens upon and into whose hands
>   he comes –
> That man he makes very rich and grants him prosperity.
> (*Theog.* 972–74)

There Wealth appeared, not as the sure consequence of steadfast labor, but as a result of luck. There are no guarantees. Hesiod is fully aware of the uncertainty that surrounds any human enterprise; otherwise, men would have no need of hope. In this part of the *Works and Days*, the name of that uncertainty is Zeus. After plowing and sowing, the farmer should, according to Hesiod, pray to Zeus Chthonios and to Demeter for a good harvest (465–66); and he predicts success "if the Olympian himself grants a good outcome (*telos esthlon*, 474). But a few lines later, Hesiod announces:

ἄλλοτε δ' ἀλλοῖος Ζηνὸς νόος αἰγιόχοιο,
ἀργαλέος δ' ἄνδρεσσι καταθνητοῖσι νοῆσαι.

At times, the mind of Zeus who holds the aegis is variable and changeful,
Hard it is for mortal men to figure it out.   (483–84)

Yet here the example that Hesiod gives of the impenetrability of Zeus's intentions features not an unforeseen disaster, but an unexpected success: if you plow late, you may nevertheless still have a bountiful harvest *if* Zeus rains just the right amount on the third day (485–90). To keep Perses on the hard, steep, sweat-soaked path to *arete*, Hesiod bends the truth ever so slightly.

Because seafaring is far more dangerous and unpredictable than agriculture, Hesiod advises against it. If, however, Perses insists, Hesiod will indicate the best time for navigation:

οὔτε κε νῆα
καυάξαις οὔτ' ἄνδρας ἀποφθείσειε θάλασσα,
εἰ δὴ μὴ πρόφρων γε Ποσειδάων ἐνοσίχθων
ἢ Ζεὺς ἀθανάτων βασιλεὺς ἐθέλησιν ὀλέσσαι·
ἐν τοῖς γὰρ τέλος ἐστὶν ὁμῶς ἀγαθῶν τε κακῶν τε.

. . . then you won't
Wreck your ship and the sea may not destroy your crew,
If indeed graciously the earth-shaker Poseidon
Or Zeus, king of the immortals, should not will their destruction;
For in them is the outcome of good and evil alike.   (665–69)

Little by little, the earlier guarantees and promises give way to growing uncertainty. And the gods, especially Zeus, contribute to it. Tellingly, in the later sections of the poem, Zeus, who had previously been said to grant prosperity (ὄλβον, 281, 379), is now named as the source of poverty. Of his father Hesiod tells us that he left Kyme:

οὐκ ἄφενος φεύγων οὐδὲ πλοῦτόν τε καὶ ὄλβον,
ἀλλὰ κακὴν πενίην, τὴν Ζεὺς ἄνδρεσσι δίδωσιν.

. . . not running away from wealth and riches,
But from wretched poverty, which Zeus gives to men.
                                              (637–38)

Soon after, Hesiod seems to contradict all his earlier teaching:

μηδέ ποτ' οὐλομένην πενίην θυμοφθόρον ἀνδρὶ
τέτλαθ' ὀνειδίζειν, μακάρων δόσιν αἰὲν ἐόντων.

Don't ever dare to blame a man for cursed soul-destroying poverty,
A gift of the blessed ones who live forever.   (717–18)

Earlier, Hesiod had relentlessly hammered away at Perses, had in fact abused him and insisted that only he himself was responsible for his own poverty; and he had also reassured his brother that working in the appropriate way would indeed lead to success and divine favor.[46] Now a harder truth emerges: failure too and poverty are gifts from the gods.

After the advice about sailing and marriage, an apparently even riskier activity, the *gnomai* take on a darker coloring[47] that emerges most clearly in the religious prohibitions. Previously, Hesiod had listed some clearly defined evil acts (328–32) that Zeus will punish: "in the end Zeus will give requital for unjust acts" (ἐς δὲ τελευτήν | ἔργων ἀντ' ἀδίκων χαλεπὴν ἐπέθηκεν ἀμοιβήν (333–34). He had also recommended sacrificing to the gods to the best of one's ability (κὰδ δύναμιν, 336) so that they may be propitious and you may buy someone else's land rather than he, yours (336–41). Here Hesiod held out certain punishment for injustice and potential rewards for piety. But toward the end of the poem, he instructs:

μηδέ ποτ' ἐξ ἠοῦς Διὶ λείβειν αἴθοπα οἶνον
χερσὶν ἀνίπτοισιν μηδ' ἄλλοις ἀθανάτοισιν·
οὐ γὰρ τοί γε κλύουσιν, ἀποπτύουσι δέ τ' ἀράς.

Do not pour shining wine to Zeus at dawn
With unwashed hands, nor to the other gods;
For they won't hearken to you, but will spit out your prayers.
                                                      (724–26)

Here there are no rewards, only vague threats of unspecified punishment (741, 745, 749, 750, 752, 754–56, 758–9). Moreover, human beings are viewed as unclean and polluted producers of excreta – urine, feces, fingernail clippings, semen, and even bath water polluted by a woman's use. Zeus is only mentioned once (724); otherwise, only nameless gods and the "blessed ones" (*makares*) to whom the nights belong (730). The "godlike man who has good sense" is no longer the man who tills the soil and practices justice, but now the one who hides his nakedness and urinates sitting down (731).

---

[46] For the disappearance of Perses from the last 200 lines of the poem, see Clay (1993b) 32–33.
[47] Heath (1985) 252–53

We seem to find ourselves in a universe where justice and labor will not suffice to ensure prosperity. Significantly, words for wealth (*ploutos, aphenos*) disappear after line 637. Every human action is fraught with danger and nameless dread; any wrong move will cause catastrophe. Mankind seems more distant from the gods than ever, although their punitive powers are all the more pervasive.

In addition to his vulnerability to divine displeasure, man must also face another threat from a closer source:

> δεινὴν δὲ βροτῶν ὑπαλεύεο φήμην·
> φήμη γάρ τε κακὴ πέλεται, κούφη μὲν ἀεῖραι
> ῥεῖα μάλ᾽, ἀργαλέη δὲ φέρειν, χαλεπὴ δ᾽ ἀποθέσθαι.
> φήμη δ᾽ οὔ τις πάμπαν ἀπόλλυται, ἥντινα πολλοὶ
> λαοὶ φημίξουσι· θεός νύ τίς ἐστι καὶ αὐτή.

> Avoid the dread talk of men;
> For talk is bad, nimble, and easily rises up,
> But painful to bear and hard to get rid of.
> Never does it perish altogether whenever
> Many people spread it; so now she too is a god.
>
>   (760–64)

Like other divinities, this new goddess is generated and then becomes deathless. But, unlike the other gods whom Hesiod describes, she is born from the mouths of men. In fact she is the negative counterpart of undying *kleos*, the reward for heroic striving: *kleos* is to be heard about; *pheme*, to be talked about.[48] The substitution of *pheme* for *kleos* again reminds us that Hesiod is depicting a decidedly post-heroic world. At any rate, at the end of the *Works and Days*, Gossip or Bad Repute, borne aloft by the mouths of men, returns us to the poem's opening.[49] There it was through Zeus's agency that men became spoken of or unspoken: ἄφατοί τε φατοί τε. Zeus is no longer required, and our earlier interpretation – that to be φατοί was a positive quality – seems mistaken. Now it turns out that to be spoken of means to be infamous or notorious: perhaps it is best to be passed over in silence.

The increasing unpredictability of human life continues into the "Days," which I believe to be authentic because they seem to complete the program Hesiod announced in the proem: to tell Perses *etetuma*, things the way they really are. Eris, who at the beginning of the poem was split into a positive

---

[48] Cf. Bakker (2002) 140–42. I prefer to read δεινήν at line 760 rather than δειλήν, printed by West (1978), since Pheme ends up being a goddess to be feared.

[49] For this reason, Wilamowitz (1928) 129 argued that the poem ended at line 764, with the new divinity Pheme balancing the good Eris of line 11.

and a negative force, now returns with a vengeance in the guise she wore in the *Theogony* as the mother of her last born, baneful Oath (*W&D* 804; cf. *Theog.* 231). Twice Hesiod tells us that the days are "from Zeus" (765, 769). If we accept the text as it has come down to us and calculate the days about which Hesiod has something to say, we find that, out of the thirty days of the month, ten days remain.[50] These ten days are *metadoupoi* and *akerioi* (823), days about which nothing is known for good or ill. One-third of human life is thus unknown and unknowable. That seems about right or, as Hesiod would say, *etetumon*.

The results of our two-pronged investigation have revealed a significant gap between the theology of the *Work and Days* and the anthropology of the *Theogony*. The latter suggests that the gods interest themselves in the great or the humble rather than the middling. The inscrutable mediation of Hecate provides a theodicy whereby Olympus appears to be absolved of responsibility for human weal and woe. The theological teaching of the *Works and Days* is both more complex and shifting in the course of the poem. For human beings, Zeus takes the place of Hecate and indeed of the whole pantheon. The certainty of his capacity to reward, but, more especially, to punish the wicked, an ability that again touches the great more directly than the multitude, who nevertheless suffer indirectly, diminishes as the poem progresses. Zeus gives way to nameless gods and inscrutable powers, and the human condition is viewed as naked and vulnerable. It is no exaggeration to say that the order of the cosmos appears more beautiful from Olympus than on earth.

---

[50] Cf. Benardete (1967) 169–70. David Mankin has worked out the details of this important observation. West (1978) claims only eight days are unaccounted for.

CHAPTER 7

Hybrids

πολλὰ μὲν ἀμφιπρόσωπα καὶ ἀμφίστερνα φύεσθαι,
βουγενῆ ἀνδρόπρωιρα, τὰ δ᾽ ἔμπαλιν ἐξανατέλλειν
ἀνδροφυῆ βούκρανα, μεμειγμένα τῆι μὲν ἀπ᾽ ἀνδρῶν
τῆι δὲ γυναικοφυῆ σκιεροῖς ἠσκημένα γυίοις.

Many creatures came forth with double faces and double chests,
Cows with human heads, and others on the contrary developed
Human form with ox-heads, hybrids,
Furnished with shadowy members, some from males, others with
  female natures.   Empedocles, fr. 61 DK

The divine and the human constitute the poles of Hesiod's cosmos. The
Theogony presents the gods as a product of a genealogical evolution and
successive individuation that ultimately achieves a stable *telos* under the
tutelage of Zeus. While taking into account the evolution of mankind
to its present state, the *Works and Days* emphasizes the *hic et nunc* of the
human condition. With violent battles, revolutions, and brutal wiles behind
them, the gods' unchanging present stands in sharp contrast to the ever-
increasing human subjection to the circles of time. The order of the cosmos
emerges both in its coming-to-be and in its achieved form as a system of
classification, of categories and hierarchies. Hesiod offers us an insight into
the character of that system by his presentation of two types of hybrids
who violate those boundaries: the monsters and the heroes. Moreover,
these two categories of mixed beings represent two different cosmogonic
moments: the monsters arise early in the cosmogonic process and represent
a kind of wild efflorescence whose continuation might imperil the final
stability of the cosmos. The heroes, on the other hand, come into being
at a later stage, after Zeus accedes to the kingship over the gods and after
the Promethean settlement separating gods and men. While the monsters
come into being spontaneously in their exuberant disorder, the heroes are
the products of a distinctive divine intervention that momentarily blurs

the boundaries between gods and men. Yet for all their differences, these two hybrid species are linked insofar as the heroes are the instruments of the monsters' destruction.

In his catalogue of monstrous beings (*Theog.* 270–336), Hesiod brings together creatures of diverse origins, from diverse traditions, and unites them into a family. One could argue that these creatures were too well known from Greek art and legend to be omitted, so that Hesiod felt obliged to accommodate them somewhere in his poem.[1] Yet such a presumed obligation to include some mention of the monsters accounts neither for their lengthy treatment nor for their place within the genealogical scheme of the *Theogony* as a whole.[2]

By definition, the monstrous is the anomalous, that which does not fit into usual classifications or transgresses normal limits, and hence may be considered dangerous.[3] A detailed examination of Hesiod's catalogue of monsters will reveal that not only do its individual members violate the classificatory system of the *Theogony*, but that the catalogue as a whole subverts the process of individuation and articulation that underlies the Hesiodic scheme of evolution.

Generally speaking, Greek monsters are hybrid creatures that unite normally disparate elements, for example, the human and the bestial, or combine distinct species.[4] Frequently, too, they involve a multiplication of human or animal features or, conversely, a subtraction and isolation of features that usually occur in pairs. The monstrous creatures found outside the monster catalogue proper, the Hundred-handers, Typhoeus, and the Cyclopes, display these characteristics. They all diverge from an implied canonical form that is simultaneously theo- and anthropomorphic. Thus the Cyclopes are described as:

---

[1] Cf. Schoemann (1857) 179; and also (1868) 152. It is worth noting that the proliferation of monsters in the art of the Orientalizing period may be contemporaneous with Hesiod. Hesiod's list, however, is not complete. The Centaurs, for instance, are not included.

[2] West's statement (1966) 244 that the monsters "are put among the descendants of Pontos not because they have any connexion with the sea, but because they could not be put among the descendants of Uranus" simply sidesteps the question.

[3] Cf. Douglas (1966) esp. 122 and 160.

[4] Cf. Plato, *Resp.* 9.12 (588c), where Socrates describes the monstrous creatures of old legends as ξυμπεφυκυῖαι ἰδέαι πολλαὶ εἰς ἓν γενέσθαι.

οἱ δ' ἤτοι τὰ μὲν ἄλλα θεοῖς ἐναλίγκιοι ἦσαν,
μοῦνος δ' ὀφθαλμὸς μέσσῳ ἐνέκειτο μετώπῳ.

In other respects they were indeed like the gods,
But a sole eye was set in the middle of their forehead.

(142–43)

Similarly, Echidna:

οὐδὲν ἐοικὸς
θνητοῖς ἀνθρώποις οὐδ' ἀθανάτοισι θεοῖσι.

. . . in no way resembling
Either mortal men or the immortal gods.

(295–96)[5]

Occasionally also, as we shall see, the monsters incorporate contradictory elements that violate fundamental categories, for instance, mortal/immortal, young/old, and male/female.[6] Thus examining Hesiod's monsters can shed useful light on the underlying categories that inform the *Theogony*.

For the most part, scholars have neglected these issues. If they discuss the passage at all, they tend to focus narrowly on the admittedly difficult problem of the referents of the pronouns in lines 295, 319, and 326.[7] Yet I would argue that the catalogue as a whole represents an important phase in the evolution of the cosmos and that it can teach us a great deal about the articulation of Hesiod's cosmogonic thought. But first the catalogue of monsters must be situated within the overall architecture of the *Theogony*.

After the primordial principles (Gaia, Uranus, etc.), the cosmos takes on its recognizable configuration in the generation of the Titans; but only in the following generation, that of the Olympians, does it acquire its final organization under the rule of Zeus. This genealogical evolution can be seen as a process of successive separation, differentiation, and hierarchization.

---

[5] Cf. *H. Apoll.* 351–52 of Typhaon: ἡ [Hera] δ' ἔτεκ' οὔτε θεοῖς ἐναλίγκιον οὔτε βροτοῖσι | δεινόν τ' ἀργαλέον τε Τυφάονα πῆμα βροτοῖσιν or, more correctly, πῆμα θεοῖσι. Cf. Clay (1989) 71, n. 167.

[6] This is *mutatis mutandis* true for the monsters in the *Odyssey* who inhabit the fabulous edges of the world, but the coordinates are different: agriculture and sacrifice, family and social organization, alternately sub- and super-human, and thus moving to a definition of the properly human. See Vidal-Naquet (1991).

[7] See, for instance, Abramowicz (1940–46); Lemke (1968); Siegmann (1969); and Schwabl (1969); see also the discussion of Hamilton (1989) 89–92. Both Hamilton, 29–32, and Bonnafé (1984) 205–7, attempt to situate the catalogue of monsters more broadly within the framework of the *Theogony* as a whole. Bonnafé emphasizes their chthonic character, inherited from the ancestral mother of the whole family, Gaia, while Hamilton underlines the importance of the heroes and mankind in the passage. Despite valuable observations, Hamilton's overall view of the *Theogony*'s architecture and the place of the monster catalogue within it raises more questions than it solves. For instance, he acknowledges (24) that his insistence that the catalogue belongs to his category of narrative digressions is problematic, yet his schema demands such a classification.

At the same time, however, this process is radically teleological in that it culminates in Zeus's kingship. As a result, Hesiod frequently collapses chronology, most blatantly perhaps in the Prometheus story, where Zeus plays a central role, although his birth has not yet taken place. Elsewhere, too, allusions to the final and permanent ordering of the cosmos under Zeus anachronistically intrude on descriptions of earlier phases of cosmic evolution, thus giving the *Theogony* as a whole a double perspective in which being and becoming are intertwined.[8]

Such a double vision likewise informs the catalogue of monsters. While their births occur at a relatively early phase of cosmic evolution (and hence toward the beginning of the poem), Hesiod also relates how six of them are dispatched by heroes, who belong to a much later stage of cosmic history, postdating Zeus's accession to power. Those monsters that survive are all given both a place and a function in Zeus's dispensation. This pattern again parallels the treatment of the monsters outside the catalogue proper, the Cyclopes, the Hundred-Handers, and Typhoeus. All are children of Gaia, πελώρια, like their mother; their excessive power inspires fear, especially in those who rule. Zeus's thunderbolt neutralizes the would-be usurper Typhoeus, but the king of the gods manages to harness the monstrous might of the others and incorporates them into his new order; the Cyclopes produce the weapons that allow Zeus to win and maintain power, while the Hundred-Handers are assigned the guardianship of the defeated Titans.

Among the descendants of Phorkys and Keto, the female, the chthonic, and the bestial predominate. In the first generation, only their last-born is male.[9] Moreover, the family is characterized by a promiscuous conflation of the distinguishing features of the divine, the bestial, and the human. The Graiai, like their mother Keto καλλιπάρηοι (270; cf. 238), are nevertheless ἐκ γενετῆς πολιάς, gray like their father, the Sea, whence the name that gods and men assign to them. Curiously, Hesiod ignores their most notorious characteristic, their sharing of an eye and a tooth, but emphasizes rather their paradoxical combination of youth and age.[10] Living at the most remote edge of the world, in the nocturnal far West, the Gorgons embody yet another fundamental dichotomy; for while two of the sisters are immortal, Medusa is singled out as mortal.[11] Her union with the Olympian Poseidon in a soft meadow amid spring flowers calls to mind the beginning of

---

[8] Cf. Philippson (1936) esp. 18–20.

[9] This remains true no matter how one interprets the genealogical ambiguities in the text.

[10] Cf. Goettling (1843) at 280: "Nam summae apud Graecos debilitatis atque sterilitatis notio est nasci cum canis capillis." Cf. *W&D* 181 and the description of the final decadence of the Iron Age.

[11] For further contradictions in the figure of the Gorgon, see Vernant (1991) esp. 113.

countless legendary genealogies, much like those contained in the *Catalogue of Women*. But here the conventional idyllic scene masks the incongruous and the grotesque. In fact, the monstrous maid will herself be dispatched by one of those heroic offspring of divine/human unions. It is as if, with the mating of Medusa and Poseidon, a first attempt to create demigods had failed; her line will die out at the hands of the heroes.

When Perseus decapitates Medusa, Chrysaor and Pegasus are produced from her severed neck. This mode of birth, violent and unnatural, resembles both Cronus' castration of Uranus and Zeus's birthing of Athena, yet significantly deviates from both. If Uranus' unmanning allowed the cosmos to come into being and the birth of Athena from Zeus's head guarantees its final ordering and permanent stability, Medusa's bizarre delivery has no such cosmic consequences. It is merely an unnatural sideshow. Then, too, she herself dies at the moment of giving birth. Pegasus takes after his immortal equine father and is ultimately integrated into Zeus's realm, bringing the thunderbolts, emblems of his invincible power, to the king of the Olympians. Evidently mortal like his mother, Chrysaor's birth conforms more closely to that of a divinity in his "leaping forth," ἐξέθορε (281).[12] In turn Chrysaor forms an exogamous union with the Oceanid, Kallirhoe, to produce the triple-headed Geryon who will be slain by Zeus's son, Heracles.

While Geryon is a well-established figure in Greek myth, Chrysaor remains a shadowy presence. Yet Hesiod mentions him again at the end of the *Theogony* (line 979) in the catalogue of goddesses who united with mortals.[13] In fact, he appears largely to be a linking figure, Medusa's son and Geryon's father, yet he himself does not seem particularly monstrous. His one distinctive feature, according to Hesiod's etymologizing of his name, is his golden sword with which, apparently, he is born.[14] This armed birth again reminds of Athena, but perhaps it is likewise evocative of the Giants who were engendered, along with the Erinyes and the Melian nymphs, from the bloody drops of Uranus' severed member (lines 183–87). These Giants, as I have argued, in union with the Meliai, are the ancestors of the human race. If this is so, one could suggest that Chrysaor, mighty and armed like the Giants, and who also unites with a nymph, the Oceanid Kallirhoe, represents an alternative progenitor to an alternative race of mortals. That

---

[12] Cf. *H. Apoll.* 119: ἐκ δ' ἔθορε πρὸ φόως δέ (Apollo); and *H. Hermes* 20: ὃς καὶ ἐπεὶ δὴ μητρὸς ἀπ' ἀθανάτων θόρε γυίων (Hermes).

[13] Doubts have been raised on the genuineness of 979–83. Cf. West (1966) ad loc.

[14] Note that χρυσάορος is an epithet of divinity, usually Apollo (*Il.* 5.509; 15.256; *W&D* 771; *H. Apoll.* 123, 392, 395; *H. Art. [xxvii]* 3), but also of Demeter (*H. Dem.* 4).

race, however, is short-lived. At line 981 Geryon is described as βροτῶν κάρτιστον ἁπάντων. In this context, one may recall the newly-found fragments of Stesichorus' *Geryoneis*, where, before facing Heracles in combat, Geryon muses at length over the question of his mortality:[15] does he take after his goddess mother or his mortal father? His encounter with Heracles will reveal his destiny. Geryon's dilemma is that of every offspring of a divine/human union. Of course, we know he will die at the hands of Heracles, another product of such a union, but one sanctioned by Zeus himself. What I am suggesting is that the hybrid Geryon along with his hybrid ancestry parallels the mixed breed of heroes. But while Geryon and his kin are doomed to destruction, the similarly mixed race of heroes not only thrives, but also becomes the instrument of the annihilation of the monstrous brood.

Next in the catalogue comes Echidna, who, while emphatically divine (θείην, 297; ἀθάνατος . . . καὶ ἀγήραος ἤματα πάντα, 305), resembles "neither mortal men nor the immortal gods" (295–96). Half lovely maiden and half huge snake, she unites the anthropomorphic and the bestial. Moreover, although apparently female, she nevertheless incorporates both male and female elements.[16] Like her mother Keto, Echidna is καλλιπάρῃος (298, cf. 238), but she also takes after her grandmother Γαῖα πελώρη (cf. πέλωρον, 299). That the crucial events in Echidna's biography all occur in subterranean settings may be due to Hesiod's etymologizing of her mother Keto's name from "hollow" or "cavern".[17] Born in a cave, she mates under the earth with Typho, and finally, by divine dispensation, she is assigned a cavernous abode "far from gods and men".[18] Her reported[19] union with Typho occurs ἐν φιλότητι, and in fact he seems an altogether suitable consort, sprung as he is from the mating of Tartarus and πελώρη Gaia, likewise ἐν φιλότητι (822).[20] For his hundred snakeheads

---

[15] Frs. S 10 and 11 (Davies [1991] 155–56).

[16] The gender of ὄφις is, of course, masculine, but Hesiod could have used the feminine δράκαινα. Cf. *H. Apoll.* 300.

[17] For the possible (false) etymological play on κῆτος, "cavern" (cf. epic κητώεσσα), see Chantraine (1968) 1.528.

[18] Lines 304–5 have wrongly been athetized or condemned as variants. Cf. West (1966) ad loc. West's proposal, to take οἳ in line 301 to refer to Keto, does not solve the problem. But if one recognizes that the tense of ἔρυτ' in line 304 is imperfect, it becomes clear that Echidna mated with Typho εἰν 'Αρίμοισιν, but then returned to her birth place as her permanent home by the gods' dispensation.

[19] This use of the indeterminate φασι (306) is unique in the *Theogony*. It may indicate that even the Muses cannot vouch for this monstrous union; or perhaps it represents the tales that human beings tell. Cf. Wilamowitz (1959) 359. It may also point to the apparent contradiction between these lines and 821–36, where Zeus presumably blasts Typhoeus almost immediately after his birth. When would there be time for this monstrous mating?

[20] Cf. Apollodorus 2.1.2, where Echidna too is a daughter of Tartarus and Gaia.

appropriately complement Echidna's snaky half, while his multiple voices unite the divine and the bestial (825–35). Not surprisingly, their children embody features of both parents and share their epithets: κρατερόφρον' Echidna produces κρατερόφρονα τέκνα (297; cf. 308); Cerberus is ἀμή-χανος and ὠμηστής like his mother (310–11; cf. 295, 300); Hydra λυγρ' εἰδυῖαν takes after λυγρή Echidna (313; cf. 304). But the canine traits of Orthos and Cerberus as well as the polycephaly of the latter and his sister Hydra seem to be inherited from their father.[21] Cerberus will later receive a place and function in the organization of Tartarus, ensuring that the dead cannot escape from the underworld (769–73) and thus enforcing the iron curtain between gods and mortals. Heracles dispatches the two remaining siblings, Orthos, along with his master (293), and the Lernean Hydra.

The Hydra introduces something new into the catalogue. Hitherto, the monsters had been confined either under the earth or located at its extreme boundaries.[22] To destroy Medusa and Geryon (and his dog), the heroes Perseus and Heracles were required to journey thither. But with the Hydra, the monstrous erupts into the inhabited world, posing a threat to human beings. Iolaos, Heracles' nephew and sidekick, may perhaps be considered a representative of the human race here.[23] The collocation of Διὸς υἱός and Amphitryoniades to describe the Hydra's destroyer Heracles makes explicit the paradoxical nature of the heroes, themselves mixed creatures, and in some sense as anomalous as the beasts they slay. Moreover, the creature from the Lernean lagoon unleashes a larger divine drama embracing Hera, Zeus, his daughter Athena, as well as his son Heracles. Hesiod here alludes to a conflict within the Olympian order and the challenge to Zeus's domination posed by his wife Hera, who nurtures monsters to counter Zeus's heroic line. Toward the end of the *Theogony*, where these incidents belong chronologically, they are more or less suppressed. Once Typhoeus is dispatched, Zeus appears to have no further serious opponents. Intrafamilial Olympian tensions are, as it were, deflected onto conflicts between the heroes and the monsters.[24]

---

[21] Apollodorus 2.5.10 assigns two heads to Orthos.

[22] See Ballabriga (1986) 114–16, for the geographical distribution of the monster clan.

[23] He is, of course, the son of Iphikles, Heracles' mortal brother by Amphitryo and is the first fully human being named in the *Theogony*.

[24] For the parallels between Zeus/Typhoeus and Heracles/Hydra, see Hamilton (1989) 29–30 and his conclusion (32): "The close connection between Keto's monstrous brood and Typhoeus suggests the diminution of both the gods' enemies and of Zeus's role in the conflict. Zeus's power is still absolute but he works through agents, his children Athena and Heracles, and the results are much more satisfactory for mankind." Cf. Bonnafé (1984) 209.

The next creature to be described in the catalogue is the Chimaera.[25] This fantastical fire-breathing monster not only has three heads, but those heads derive from three different species, lion, she-goat, and snake; yet the middle female element seems to dominate and gives the creature her name, a name that is nothing but the common noun to designate a year-old she-goat. There is an almost comic incongruity in the combination of a fierce lion and huge serpent with a young female goat – hardly a terrifying beast and more appropriate as a sacrificial victim.[26] It is, then, perhaps no accident that the appellation comes to designate "an unreal creature of the imagination, a mere wild fancy; an unfounded conception".[27] Here, in a grand confrontation of *Mischwesen*, the offspring of Medusa and Poseidon, Pegasus, the only "good" monster, teams up with the hero Bellerophon, whose father is likewise reputed to be Poseidon, to annihilate the Chimaera. Curiouser and curiouser.

Now a she-monster, whose identity is subject to dispute, unites endogamously with the dreadful hound Orthos to produce the Phix, i.e. the Sphinx, and the Nemean lion. As the Sphinx is generally imagined as a combination of woman and lion, these offspring share leonine features, and, like the Hydra, they are situated within the world of men, Thebes in the one case, and Nemea in the other. About the Sphinx and her destiny we learn little, but Hesiod gives a fuller account of the beast of Nemea. Explicitly identified here as the wife of Zeus, Hera nursed the lion (as she did the Hydra) and κατένασσε, "settled," "established," him on the slopes of Nemea. Elsewhere in Hesiod, only Zeus and Cronus are subjects of κατεναίω,[28] and the verb appears to designate the ruler of the gods in his capacity as organizer of the cosmos. Here, on the other hand, Hera usurps and perverts her husband's role by establishing the lion at Nemea to be a bane for mankind.

---

[25] Marg (1970) 165 cites Wilamowitz' judgment ("Hesiods schlechtester Hexameter") but suggests that the verse is intentionally as monstrous as the creature it describes. Cf. Solomon (1985). Lines 323–24 are usually thought to be interpolated from the *Iliad*. Cf. West (1966) 256. Marg (1970) 166, however, believes they are conscious citations of the *Iliad*. They may, however, simply be traditional.

[26] Cf., for example, Aeschylus, *Agamemnon* 232, where Iphigeneia is likened to a sacrificial she-goat; Xenophon, *Hell*. 4.2.20; *An*. 3.2.12; and Plutarch, *Lyc*. 22.2.7. West (1966) 255 calls the Chimaera "the oddest and least satisfying of the mythical monsters." Marg (1970) 166 comments: "Es ist etwas gespielt mit dem Verhältnis des Ziege genannten Untiers insgesamt und des Ziegenteils." I cannot resist quoting Nietzsche's definition of Socrates: πρόσθε Πλάτων ὄπισθέν τε Πλάτων μέσση τε χίμαιρα (*Beyond Good and Evil* 190).

[27] The *OED s.v.* cites the first English occurrence of this usage from 1587. It can be traced back at least as far as Lucretius 2.705.

[28] At *Theogony* 620, Cronus "settles" the Hundred-Handers under the earth, while at *W&D* 168 Zeus "settles" the heroes on the blessed isles.

ἔνθ' ἄρ' ὅ γ' οἰκείων ἐλεφαίρετο φῦλ' ἀνθρώπων,
κοιρανέων Τρητοῖο Νεμείης ἠδ' Ἀπέσαντος.

And making his home there, he trapped the tribes of men,
As he ruled over Tretian Nemea and Apesas.   (330–31)

In an inversion of the natural hierarchy of men and beasts, the lion
rules over his surroundings[29] and ἐλεφαίρετο the tribes of men who inhabit them. According to LSJ, this rare verb of unknown etymology means
"to destroy" only in this passage, whereas it means "to deceive" in its two
Homeric occurrences.[30] These differing definitions clearly arise from the
fact that, while gods and dreams may deceive men, animals normally do not.
But this may be precisely the point of Hesiod's usage or, rather, misusage,
and it may give us a clue to the word's basic meaning. For if the Nemean
lion's behavior presents an inversion of the proper relations between men
and beasts through his "ruling over" men, so too may the ascription of
ἐλεφαίρετο to him. I suggest that ἐλεφαίρομαι means "to trap" and that it
may be drawn from the terminology of the hunt. Such an interpretation
would be appropriate to all three occurrences of the word and simultaneously emphasize the monstrousness of the lion, who, under Hera's tutelage,
both co-opts and inverts a properly human activity. In overcoming the
lion, whose pelt becomes his iconographic emblem, Heracles restores the
appropriate hierarchical order whereby men rule over beasts and not vice
versa.

While Medusa and the Chimaera perish at the hands of the heroes Perseus
and Bellerophon, Heracles remains the monster-slayer par excellence. In
fact, each sequence of monstrous births culminates in an exploit of Heracles:
lines 270–94 (Geryon and Orthos); lines 295–318 (the Hydra); and lines
319–32 (the Nemean lion).[31] Six of the monsters, then, perish at the hands
of the heroes. One might well wonder why one breed of *Mischwesen* is
honored and exalted while the other is either consigned to the depths or
ends of the earth or else annihilated by the heroes. The heroes of course
arrive on the cosmic scene much later than the monsters. But more than
mere chronology seems to be operative here. Or, rather, chronology cannot

---

[29] For the meaning of κοιρανέω, see Benveniste (1969) 1.113–14. His conclusion: "*koiraneîn* est le fait
du potentat local, excerçant son autorité sur les gens de sa maisonnée plutôt que sur une armée
entière." To take οἰκείων as a present participle, as West (1966) 257 does, rather than as a genitive
plural, strengthens the case, since wild beasts do not normally live in houses.

[30] *Il.* 23.388 and *Od.* 19.565. Cf. Chantraine (1968–80) and Voigt (1984) fasc. 11, *s.v.* Russo (1992) at
Od. 19.565 suggests the definition "Can cause harm." Similarly, Amory (1966) 22–24 proposes "to
damage." The Hesiodic Scholia at 330 (p. 64 Di Gregorio) gloss ἐλεφαίρετο as ἔβλαπτεν in Hesiod
but as παρελογίζετο in the *Iliad*.

[31] Cf. Thalmann (1984) 25; and Hamilton (1989) 92.

simply be regarded as temporal in the *Theogony.* Both monsters and heroes belong to the past, but to different phases of the past. The unions of gods and mortals that give rise to the race of heroes occur during the reign of Zeus and are sanctioned by him. The existence of the heroes thus presupposes a clear distinction and separation of gods and men as opposed to the promiscuous unions of Keto's brood. This means, in turn, that the heroes can only arise after the duel of wits between Zeus and Prometheus, a confrontation whose consequence is precisely that separation ("At Mecone . . ."). The monsters, on the other hand, arise at a much earlier phase of cosmic evolution, before those boundaries demarcating gods, men, and beasts are clearly defined and enforced.

At this point, we must raise the thorny question of the referents of the pronouns at lines 319 and 326.[32] Who is the mother of the Chimaera? Does she have a father? And, finally, who mates with Orthos to produce the Sphinx and the lion of Nemea? The literature both ancient and modern offers almost every possible solution to these questions, and consensus remains as chimerical as the creature herself.[33] Various critics have nominated Keto, Echidna, and the Hydra for the position of Chimaera's mother (line 319), while in line 326 the Chimaera herself is added to the list of possible candidates to be the mother of the Phix and the lion of Nemea.[34] Paradoxically, what is striking about all the proposed solutions is their persuasiveness: in each case they depend on reasonable assumptions and normative rules. For instance, it is argued that Echidna cannot be the mother of the Sphinx and the Nemean lion because mother–son incest no longer occurs at this

---

[32] There is a similar difficulty at 295, where ἥ designates the mother of Echidna. Here, however, the modern scholarly consensus (West [1966] 249; Abramowicz [1940–46] 171; Lemke [1968] 48–49; Siegmann [1969] 756; Wilamowitz [1959] 3: 259; and Hamilton [1989] 89) assigns the role to Keto, with the exception of Schwabl [1969] 174–76, who insists that the reference must be to Kallirhoe. Cf. Welcker (1865) 125.

[33] The lack of genealogical clarity within this brief passage has no parallel in the *Theogony,* although Jacoby (1930) 9 suggested a similar ambiguity at line 411 concerning the mother of Hecate, but the parallel is unconvincing. Inevitably, some scholars have taken refuge in the explanation of interpolations or successive expansions of an original Hesiodic catalogue. Cf. Jacoby (1930) 8–19; and Meyer (1887) 16–20. Yet it is difficult to understand why an interpolator would fail to integrate his additions into the existing genealogies and thereby introduce not one but two significant obscurities within seven lines. Amputating the text merely sidesteps the problem.

[34] At 319, the mother of the Chimaera is identified as Echidna by Wilamowitz (1959) 3.260; Marg (1970) 165; Schwabl (1969) 177–78; cf. Apollodorus 2.3.1 (citing Hesiod as his authority); Hydra, by West (1966) 254–55; Abramowicz (1940–46) 167; and Keto, by Siegmann (1969) 756; Lemke (1968) 52; and Hamilton (1989) 91–92. At 326, the mother of the Phix and the Nemean lion is identified as Echidna by Wilamowitz (1959) 3.260; Marg (1970) 167; and Schwabl (1969) 183; cf. Apollodorus 3.5.8; Chimaera: Abramowicz (1940–46) 167; Siegmann (1969) 756; West (1966) 256; Hamilton (1989) 91; cf. Scholia at 326 (p. 62 Di Gregorio). Only Lemke (1968) 53 nominates Keto. For a summary of earlier opinions, see Abramowicz (1940–46) 167.

point in the *Theogony*.[35] Similarly, the Hydra cannot be the sole parent of the Chimaera, because parthenogenesis characterizes only the earliest phases of cosmogony.[36] But all these arguments rest on the unspoken assumption that the generation of monsters follows the patterns and norms laid out elsewhere in the *Theogony* and presupposed by its whole genealogical schema: that is, that the evolution of the cosmos progresses from a relative lack of definition and differentiation to a successively higher level of differentiation and definition. It is, however, by no means clear whether, in the case of the monsters, such an assumption is warranted or whether the catalogue as a whole in fact presents such a progression.

A significant indication to the contrary occurs at the very end of the catalogue. The last-mentioned member of the clan, the last-born and only son of Phorkys and Keto, the snake who guards the golden apples, is no better defined than his brethren. In fact, even less so, for the "mark of the serpent" generically characterizes the entire monster brood.[37] Moreover, in striking contrast to the first-born of Keto and Phorkys, the Graiai and the Gorgons, who are assigned not only collective but also individual names, the apple-guarding serpent does not even possess a name.[38] Nor, for that matter does the lion of Nemea. By sandwiching the catalogue of monsters between two catalogues that are almost exclusively composed of names, that of the Nereids (243–63) and of the Oceanids (349–61),[39] and commenting on the difficulty of knowing the names of all the rivers (τῶν ὄνομ᾽ ἀργαλέον πάντων βροτὸν ἄνδρα ἐνισπεῖν, | οἱ δὲ ἕκαστοι ἴσασιν, ὅσοι περιναιετάουσι, 369–70), Hesiod draws attention to the importance of naming for his theogonic enterprise.

To name a thing is to assign to it an individual identity and to give it a place in the cosmic hierarchy.[40] Not only the nameless serpent with whom the catalogue of monsters culminates, but also the impossibility of ascertaining the precise parentage of some of its members, suggest that the

---

[35] E.g. Welcker (1865) 159 and Abramowicz (1940–46) 169–70. But cf. Wilamowitz (1959) 3.260, n. 1 and West (1966) 256.

[36] See Lemke (1968) 50 and Siegmann (1969) 756. But compare Abramowicz (1940–46) 170.

[37] Cf. Bonnafé (1984) 206–7, who notes that the serpentine form may be derived from their ancestral chthonic mother, Gaia.

[38] In later sources, the serpent is named Ladon. On the lack of a name, cf. Muetzell (1833) 463: "Etenim unum hoc est ex perpaucis exemplum, ubi commemoratur sine nomine soboles: id quod et ab consilio genealogici carminis et ab Theogoniae tenore sane quam multum discedit." Marg (1970) 169 aptly notes: "Hesiod hätte ihr gut einen Namen geben können, wenn sie wirklich noch keinen hatte, aber er wollte es nicht." Note also, by contrast, the explicit etymologizing of Chrysaor and Pegasus earlier in the catalogue.

[39] For an attempt to interpret the names in both catalogues, see Deichgräber (1965) 17–30.

[40] On the importance of naming, see Vernant (1986) 43–44; and Philippson (1936) 9–10.

cosmic process of individuation does not fully operate within this tribe. The jarring combinations of features that characterize Hesiod's monsters resemble the products of Empedocles' era of promiscuous Philia, when all sorts of bizarre hybrids arise. In Hesiod, these creatures are negative exemplars, failed experiments in the course of cosmic evolution. The whole family is confined temporally, to a specific epoch; spatially, to the ends of the earth; and genealogically, to endogamous unions, so that it does not interfere with the final and ordered arrangement of the cosmos. It gives us a glimpse of what an unregulated cosmos might look like. It is not accidental that the cacophonous flame-spewing Typhoeus, who represents a kind of throwback to such disordered creatures, constitutes Zeus's last adversary.

HEROES

The monsters point to an early cosmogonic phase when the categories and hierarchies that will govern the final ordering of the cosmos are still fluid. Significantly, it has been impossible to discuss the monster catalogue without simultaneously mentioning the monster-slaying heroes who rid the earth of these hybrid creatures, often with divine aid. According to Proclus, the demigods constitute τὸ σύμμικτον ἔκ τε θεῶν καὶ ἀνθρώπων, "that which is a mixture from gods and men".[41] The heroes too are hybrids, albeit of a very different sort. As such, they not only appear in the *Theogony*, but form part of human history and hence also play a critical role in the *Works and Days*. As we have seen in the myth of the races, the heroes are the race that immediately preceded ours. Their disappearance was a gradual process; after launching the great heroic expeditions against Thebes and Troy they died off or were transported to the Isles of the Blest. But the monster-slayers seem to belong to an earlier generation, perhaps closer to the men of bronze. Like the monsters that survived, the hybrid heroes that did not perish continue to exist only at the ends of the earth, where they are rendered innocuous. At the same time the gods distanced themselves from mortals and no longer generated more demigods. We who belong to the race of iron still maintain a tenuous if distant relation to the heroes.

Chronologically, the heroes constitute a bridge between the *Theogony* and the *Works and Days*. In the latter, the heroes are the "previous race" (προτέρη γενεή) and linked to the wars at Thebes and Troy, whereas they come into being at the very end of the *Theogony* and are especially

---

[41] Pertusi (1955) 64 ad *W&D* 159–60.

characterized as monster-slayers. Heracles, whom we may consider the paradigmatic hero, occurs three times in the poem. In the monster catalogue, he is mentioned proleptically as the slayer of Geryon, Orthos, the Hydra, and the Nemean lion, but the Prometheus story makes clear that he belongs to the post-Promethean age. For, to honor his son, Zeus allows him to achieve *kleos* by killing yet another beast, the eagle that gnaws on the Titan's liver (*Theog.* 526–32). Finally, Heracles' birth and subsequent apotheosis are recounted at the conclusion of the poem (*Theog.* 943–44; 950–55). The heroes can thus be situated between the two compositions not only chronologically, but also physiologically since the union of gods and mortals generates them. Only after the separation of gods and men brought about by the actions of Prometheus can the temporary reconciliation that produces the demigods take place.

Where the *Theogony* ended has long been subject to debate.[42] As it stands now, the close of the poem comprises three distinct sections. The marriages of Zeus are followed by an apparently heterogeneous group of other divine unions (930–62) before a new subject is introduced: a catalogue of goddesses who bore children to mortal men (963–1020). A two-line invocation to the Muses (1021–22) introducing the so-called *Catalogue of Women* or *Ehoiai* forms a bridge linking the two compositions. Even if we concede that individual lines and items in these genealogies may be interpolations, nevertheless, a general scheme seems to emerge. To understand it, we must keep in mind the dynamics of the succession myth and Zeus's need to forestall its recrudescence if his regime is to be eternal.

As we have seen, Zeus's first union with Metis prevents the birth of a male heir capable of succeeding his father. By swallowing the pregnant goddess, the Olympian not only precludes the generation of his successor: he simultaneously incorporates the provident cunning that can anticipate any potential threats to his rule. The product of their union, Athena, aligns herself with her father. Zeus's *metis* emerges most clearly in his subsequent conduct of marital politics and alliances. The antagonism between Zeus and Hera, his last and legitimate wife – and sister – surfaces in her giving birth by parthenogenesis to Hephaestus. By postponing Athena's birth for 23 lines, Hesiod manages to bring together and juxtapose these two offspring, both produced in anomalous ways. In particular, Hephaestus' birth by parthenogenesis forcefully reminds us of the formidable fecundity

---

[42] West (1966) 398–99 summarizes older scholarship and himself opts for line 900 although he thinks lines 901–29 contain Hesiodic elements. Taking issue with West, Northrup (1983) argues for 955 (although he regards 930–37 as interpolated) and the apotheosis of Heracles. See also Arrighetti (1998) 368–71, who rejects the arguments against Hesiodic authorship of the *Theogony*'s end.

of the female and the familiar pattern of conflict between husband and wife played out by means of the generation of children.

The subsequent catalogue of marriages (930–61) serves to resolve that antagonism by proxy and effects the reconciliation of Zeus and Hera through the harmonious unions of their offspring.[43] Thus Zeus's son, Heracles, is ultimately united with Hera's daughter, Hebe. Likewise, Ares, the first legitimate male offspring of Zeus and Hera, and hence a possible source of future instability, in union with primordial Aphrodite (who now becomes Zeus's daughter-in-law and hence part of his domain), begets not only Fear and Terror that accord with his martial nature, but also their opposite number, Harmony. In turn her daughter Semele unites with Zeus to produce Dionysus; and both Heracles and Dionysus become immortal. Hephaestus is brought into the Olympian fold through his marriage to one of the Graces, who simultaneously, one supposes, brings grace, if not to his body, then at least to the products of his skill. At Zeus's behest, Athena, Zeus's daughter, and Hera's son, Hephaestus, will join in fashioning the female Woman.[44] Like the marriage of Heracles and Hebe, the collaboration of these two divine artisans may be viewed as an emblem of the harmonious reconciliation of their parents. Such concord between Hera and Zeus guarantees the lasting stability of the newly established world order.

It is significant that the final resolution of these tensions – with their cosmic implications – between the king of the gods and his potentially disruptive wife are projected onto and played out in the human realm. The monster catalogue shows Hera exploiting her female capabilities by nursing the Lernian Hydra and the Nemean lion to vent her anger at Heracles and indirectly upon his father Zeus. Heracles, in turn, does away with these creatures and frees men from their power. The monster-slaying heroes thus appear as the final manifestation of the cosmic antagonism between male and female; they also constitute the means to its resolution.[45]

In our text, a brief invocation precedes a short catalogue of goddesses who slept with mortals and produced offspring. The whole section has

---

[43] Cf. Bonnafé (1985) 87–92. The marriages of Poseidon and Amphitrite and Zeus and Maia seem to have a different function. The latter represents Zeus's reconciliation with the Titans, since Maia is daughter of Atlas; but the former, whose union produces the "dread god" Triton, points rather to Poseidon's connection to the monstrous Pontids. He is now relegated to his own submarine sphere. I believe that this section ended with the marriage of Heracles and Hebe and that 956–62 may have been added, perhaps by Hesiod, but at any rate by the same poet who added 1011–18. See n. 47 below.

[44] Cf. Bonnafé (1985) 90, who notes the use of *charis* and *charizomenos* in the description of the Woman's manufacture (*Theog.* 583, 580).

[45] Note that most monsters are female. Compare the female serpent in the *Hymn to Apollo*, also nursed by Hera.

been viewed as an afterthought, inserted into the *Theogony* by the *Catalogue* poet or someone else who realized that this category of mixed marriages had been overlooked. Nevertheless, it might be worth considering whether the enumeration of unions of female divinities with human males might provide a suitable conclusion to the *Theogony*. The list appears to cover the heroic period in a wide geographical sweep within a generally chronological order; and it alludes to many of the major heroic cycles:[46] the Theban traditions and the labors of Heracles, the Argonautica, the Trojan War, and the post-Odyssean adventures of Odysseus.[47] I would be inclined to mark its end with the birth of Aeneas, who, according to the tradition of the *Homeric Hymn to Aphrodite*, was the last product of a divine/human union.[48]

Again, the dynamics of the succession myth may justify the inclusion of the unions between goddesses and mortal men in the manuscript tradition of our *Theogony*, while those involving male gods with mortal women are dealt with separately. Because of their seductiveness, their generative powers, and the maternal affection they have for their children, female divinities continue to be destabilizing forces, even in Zeus's cosmos. As the stories of Thetis and Achilles and Aphrodite and Aeneas attest, all unions of goddesses with mortals are potentially threatening to Olympian stability and serenity. Moreover, the understandable desire on the part of these female divinities to render their consorts or offspring immortal causes no end of trouble.[49] In the *Odyssey*, Calypso bitterly complains of the gods' hostility to such unions (*Od.* 5.118–29). Her outburst demonstrates that, from the perspective of the *Odyssey*, the possibility of such intimacies belongs to a bygone era. In presenting a telescopic version of the heroic age and hinting at the causes for its demise, Hesiod's final catalogue manages to provide a meaningful and satisfying end to the *Theogony*.

The discovery of a more extensive proem to the *Catalogue* in a papyrus published in 1956[50] revived the old question of the relation of the

---

[46] Cf. Jacoby (1930) 31 and 33.

[47] Malkin (1998) 180–90 effectively refutes the historical arguments for the lateness of lines 1011–18 put forward by West. Malkin also makes a more general case against the notion of Hesiod's parochial outlook. Lines 992–1002 and 1011–18 are prepared for in lines 956–62. That sequence has the apparent aim of incorporating the eastern and western boundaries of the Greek mythological tradition.

[48] Cf. Clay (1989) 160–70.

[49] The previous section (930–62) contains three explicit instances of apotheosis (Semele, Ariadne, and Heracles). In the list of goddesses, the closest we come is Aphrodite's abduction of Phaethon, who becomes a δαίμονα δῖον, although the catastrophic apotheosis of Tithonos could have been mentioned. If, as I believe, the list ends at line 1010, then the last two goddesses, Thetis and Aphrodite, would be unwilling participants in their respective unions with mortals.

[50] P. Oxy. 2354 first published in Lobel (1956) 1–3 = *Catalogue* fr. 1 (M–W).

Ehoiai to the rest of the Hesiodic corpus. While the authenticity of the *Catalogue* and its attribution to Hesiod were widely accepted in antiquity, modern philologists have reached no consensus on its genuineness or its date; indeed, at present agreement seems even more remote than formerly. As so often in such controversies, supposedly "objective" criteria – linguistic, stylistic, and historical evidence – have been invoked to argue both for and against Hesiodic authorship.[51] But these too have changed as our knowledge of archaic Greece has evolved and expanded. More recently, Dräger, on historical grounds, and Arrighetti, on literary ones, have argued for genuineness.[52] Stylistic arguments are, as we all know, notoriously subjective: if the *Theogony* and the *Works and Days* were not traditionally ascribed to one author, would most scholars have assigned them to a single poet?[53]

Often the rejection of Hesiodic authorship for the *Catalogue* derives from an unspoken premise: if Hesiod's poetry constitutes an implicit polemic against heroic epic, then we should not assign to Hesiod a composition dealing with the heroic tradition, far less one that attempts to give an exhaustive account of the heroic age from beginning to end. But such an antagonism to heroic epic is a scholarly invention, arising, as I have argued, from a misinterpretation of the *Theogony*'s proem. The Muses' words to Hesiod are taken to mean that Homeric epic is false, while Hesiod's own poetry is maintained to be true. It is on the basis – often enough not explicitly stated – of this supposed hostility to heroic epic that Hesiodic authorship of the *Ehoiai* is rejected. With its genealogical structure and

---

[51] An astounding distance of almost 175 years separates recent attempts to date the poem. If nothing else, such a gap vividly demonstrates our ignorance. Schwartz (1960) 498 suggests a date for its completion between 506 and 476; West (1985) esp. 127–36 puts forth a range between 520 and 580 and believes that the "*Catalogue* poet naturally knew the *Theogony* well, and the *Works and Days* too" (128). West also finds that the "Ehoiai were not flotsam but organic, immovable parts of the whole" (122). Cf. Merkelbach (1968), who does not commit himself on the question of authorship, but also views the work as a unified whole. Janko (1982) dates the *Theogony* to 680 and the *Catalogue* slightly earlier on the basis of linguistic and dictional criteria, and suggests that its style "is that of a composer with less range but some fluency in the diction, and otherwise very like Hesiod" (p. 86). His suggestion raises the intriguing possibility that the *Theogony* and the *Works and Days* were composed as complements to the *Catalogue*, rather than vice versa. In the footsteps of Wilamowitz (1905) 124, Stiewe (1963) 24–29, who dates it in the sixth century because of its pessimistic tone, and Schwartz (1960) 485 suggest a progressive accretion of materials.

[52] Dräger (1997) defends the Hesiodic authorship of both the end of the *Theogony* and the authenticity of the *Catalogue*; Arrighetti (1998) 445–47 draws attention to the weakness of the arguments against authenticity; and Casanova (1979) argues that both the plan and fundamental structure of the work is Hesiodic.

[53] Cf. Marg (1970) 8: "Wüßten wir nicht sicher, daß Theogonie wie Erga Hesiod gehören, wären wir von Stil und Anlage her versucht, die beiden Gedichte verschiedenen Autoren zuzuweisen. Das mag vorsichtig machen für die Echtheitsfrage der 'Frauenkataloge'."

emphasis on the female, the *Catalogue of Women*, which Rutherford argues belongs to a traditional genre of hexameter verse, constitutes a perfect complement to heroic epic with its narrative form and concentration on the male.[54]

Throughout this study, I have argued that the *Theogony* and the *Works and Days* must be interpreted together, each complementing the other, in order to form a unified whole embracing the divine and human cosmos. Whether Hesiodic or not, the *Catalogue of Women* seems to provide a suitable supplement to both compositions by offering a heroic perspective, intermediate between the divine and the human, both chronologically and conceptually. We must not, however, expect a simple correlation between these divergent frameworks. As I have argued, the gods' vision of the cosmos does not correspond to the human viewpoint; and likewise, from the vantage of mankind, the gods look very different. That tension, I would maintain, constitutes the core of the Hesiodic vision.

Thus it should not surprise us that the portrait of the heroic age presented in the *Catalogue* does not jibe in all respects with the accounts of the demigods in the *Theogony* or the *Works and Days*.[55] For example, the proem of the *Catalogue* offers a picture of the heroes that brings them closer in some respects to the race of gold. To be sure, neither the golden race nor the heroes of the *Catalogue* are exempt from mortality. These heroes may sit alongside the gods and feast with them, but they also sail on ships and engage in warfare; and unlike the golden race of the *Works and Days*, some die of old age, others are long-lived, and yet others die in their youth.[56] As distinct from the golden race who live *like* the gods, the heroes of the

---

[54] Rutherford (2000) convincingly explores both the generic character and the "archeology" of the Hesiodic *Catalogue*. See also the remarks of Fowler (1998) esp. 15–16. Kakrides (1972) argued that the integration and cataloguing of the various strands of the heroic traditions into one master genealogy must have taken place in Ionia.

[55] As we have seen, even the two contiguous accounts of the early history of mankind in the *Works and Days* (Prometheus and the Myth of the Races) do not simply correspond in a mechanical way.

[56] My interpretation of the fragmentary lines 8–13 generally follows that of Stiewe (1962) 297–99. West (1961) 133, however, believes that the heroes were not subject to old age and thus that "the heroic age is not distinguished from the golden age of the *Erga*." In fact, West sets the heroes of the *Catalogue* in a time "before the separation at Mekone" (133), and his supplements to the proem's lines 8–14 (p. 141) make those two epochs indistinguishable. But I think a Greek would be surprised to learn that the heroes never aged or sailed on ships. West's interpretation of the proem also permeates his view of fr. 204. See nn. 63 and 75. He is now followed by Koenen (1994). Schmitt (1975) successfully challenges West's interpretation. Schmitt, however, holds that lines 8–13 contrast the life-span of the heroes to human beings of the present, whereas I would argue that the conditions of the heroes' existence resemble our own in everything but their intimacy with the gods. Most recently Cerutti (1998) has argued in detail that the thesis of West and Koenen cannot be maintained.

Catalogue share both bed and board *with* the gods.[57] Moreover, since the *Catalogue*'s declared subject is the unions of gods with mortal women and their engendering of the heroes, it seems likely that its presentation of womankind would differ and in fact be more positive than that of either Pandora or the Woman/Wife. The heroines at least were desirable in the eyes of the gods and bore them splendid children.[58] The proem concludes with a list of divinities that begot children with mortal women. Although the list is lacunose, the order of names seems to correspond to the gods enumerated in lines 930–61 of the *Theogony*.[59] If, as I believe, such a correspondence does not merely constitute a mechanical imitation, it would then appear to confirm the continuity of Zeus's marital politics into the heroic age.

At any rate, the *Catalogue* apparently began from the familiar threesome, Prometheus, his brother Epimetheus, and the fabricated woman Pandora (frs. 2, 4, and 5 M–W). Their prominent position in the composition suggests a conscious attempt to link the *Catalogue* to the two other Hesiodic compositions. All three Hesiodic poems would then contain a variant of the Prometheus myth, in each case adjusted to fit the context in which it is embedded. But in the *Ehoiai*, the story offers yet another account of human origins that diverges from both those found in the other Hesiodic compositions. Apparently, the focus of this version was the story of Deucalion, the son of Prometheus, and Pyrrha, the daughter of Epimetheus and Pandora. After the destruction of mankind – whether through flood or some other catastrophe[60] – Deucalion and Pyrrha, the last remaining mortals on earth, repopulated the earth by throwing stones that gave rise to human beings. In addition, Pyrrha unites not only with Deucalion, but also with Zeus to produce the ancestors of the Greek tribes. This history of the human race thus implies a double origin: one half-divine, a hybrid of Olympian and Titanic, a heroic strand, sprung from Pyrrha and Deucalion

---

[57] Cf. Cerutti (1998) 129–38, who also points out that the golden race is said to live during the reign of Cronus, whereas the heroes are firmly situated in the reign of Zeus. One might remember again that women did not exist in the golden age.

[58] Cf. Dio 2.14, and Arrighetti's ([1998] 452–67) defense of Hesiod against the charge of misogyny. Odysseus rehearses the *Odyssey*'s Catalogue of Women (*Od.* 11.235–329), which closely resembles the Hesiodic *Catalogue*, in order to win over the good will of the Phaeacian queen.

[59] Cf. Treu (1957) 173, n. 8. But Treu wrongly believed that the *Catalogue* was organized according to this list of divinities.

[60] West (1985) 55–56 believes that the flood did not occur in the *Catalogue*, but is a later importation from the East. Merkelbach (1968) 144, however, assumes it does. The Scholia at *W&D* 157–58 suggest that the flood destroyed Hesiod's third race. In any case, Pyrrha and Deucalion seem to represent some sort of a new beginning. Cf. Stiewe (1963) 7, n. 2: "Die Verbindung von Göttern und Menschen hat in den Frauenkatalogen nicht nur ein Ende, sondern auch einen Anfang."

and constantly reinforced through human–divine unions; and a second strand, sprung from the earth and the rocks thrown by the first couple.

So much seems to be clear, but the sparse fragments and the contradictory testimonia render detailed reconstruction of the myth and the early genealogy of mankind difficult.[61] Yet certain general features can safely be posited. Like both the *Works and Days* and the *Theogony*, the *Catalogue* suggests that the heroic epoch is post-Promethean.[62] But the evolutionary model of mankind's history it implies diverges from both poems. The demigods are apparently preceded by an age in which the gods maintained more distant relations with human beings; the heroic age in turn is followed by our own era, when the gods again remove themselves from intimate commerce with humanity. In the *Catalogue*, the heroic age thus stands as an exceptional and ephemeral epoch of human proximity to the divine against a backdrop of more "normal" alienation from the gods. The passing of these half human / half divine hybrids therefore reinstates the status quo ante, ὡς τὸ πάρος περ.[63]

Both the beginning and the end of the race of the demigods are marked off by cataclysmic events: at the beginning, perhaps the flood; at its end, the Trojan War.[64] Spanning the heroic age, the *Catalogue* may also have documented a gradual distancing of gods and men during its course.[65] The composition ended with the war between the Greeks and the Trojans that traditionally signaled the demise of the heroic age. A good many fragments, apparently from earlier parts of the *Catalogue*, allude to incidents that formed part of that conflict. It would then be plausible that the War itself did not form part of the narrative, but that the various genealogical strands

---

[61] For some attempts, see West (1985) 50–53; Casanova (1979); Merkelbach (1968) 145; and Dräger (1997) 33–42.

[62] Cerutti (1998) 140–43 argues that the heroes of the *Catalogue* cannot be equated with the human beings before Mekone (because she follows West in believing that the demigods were not subject to old age), but she does not seem to acknowledge that the heroes arise subsequently in Zeus's reign. Later (176), however, she recognizes that the period covered in the *Catalogue* represents "una parentesi chiusa tra due situazioni di separazione."

[63] Fr. 204.102 M–W. West (1985) 119 understands the phrase to mean that the sons of the gods would "live apart in the paradise conditions they had enjoyed in the beginning." Cf. Koenen (1994) 29–30. Stiewe's (1963) interpretation of the fragment for the most part elaborates the observations of Wilamowitz in the *editio princeps* (Schubart and Wilamowitz [1907]).

[64] Scodel (1982) suggests that *Iliad* 12.3–35 may connect the Trojan War and the destruction of the Achaean wall with the Near Eastern Flood myth. Koenen (1994) surveys Oriental parallels. Note, however, that in both Homer and Hesiod, not all the heroes perish. However wretched our age of iron, we are still their heirs.

[65] See Davies (1992) 82–135 for this important point. She believes that the *Catalogue* was intended to fill in the gap between the *Theogony* and the Homeric poems. Within the Hesiodic cosmos, however, I would argue for a transition to the *Works and Days*.

concluded with the heroes that fought around Troy.[66] If so, the *Catalogue* would point to that culminating event of the heroic age and its aftermath. Be that as it may, the *Cypria*, an epic poem, now lost, but of which we have a summary and a few extant fragments, recounted the beginning of that war: there, Zeus is said to plan the Trojan conflict in order to lighten the burden of the earth which is weighed down by human over-population.[67] The instruments of Zeus's plan are Achilles and, above all, Helen.[68]

The *Catalogue* seems to allude to this motif in the enigmatic fragment 204 M – W, which is usually assigned to the end of the work. It enumerates a lengthy catalogue of the suitors of Helen – which resembles the list of warriors prominent in the *Iliad* – and their oath to punish anyone who carries her off (41–90).[69] After Menelaos' winning suit and the birth of their daughter Hermione, we suddenly shift to a divisive conflict among the gods brought about by an ominous plan devised by Zeus.[70] The plan that the Olympian was about to contrive would, we are told, be pleasing neither to gods nor to men. He was eager to "render invisible the numerous race of mortal men," προφασιν μὲν ὀλέσθαι | ψυχὰς ἡμιθέων "with the *prophasis* of destroying the lives of the demigods (99–100)." In early Greek poetry, the term *hemitheoi* always seems to convey not only their hybrid nature, but also a distancing perspective on the heroes that assigns them to a bygone era. The word thus suggests a retrospective vision, looking back at the legendary past from the vantage of the present.[71] Zeus's disclosure of his intention to destroy the heroes would inevitably unleash strife among the gods.[72] As the *Iliad* repeatedly demonstrates, the gods do indeed resent

---

[66] Cf., for instance, frs. 23, 35.10, 136, 141.14–32, 165.14–25, 176.5–7, 195, 212b M–W. The *Catalogue* would thus be a "prequel" to the Epic Cycle.

[67] *Cypria* fr. 1. Cf. Euripides, *Electra* 1282–83; *Helen* 36–41; and *Orestes* 1639–42 and the discussion of Jouan (1966) 39–54. Now also Burgess (2001) 132–71.

[68] Cf. Mayer (1996), who sees both Achilles and Helen as Zeus's instruments for bringing *eris* to mankind. This is interesting in the light of Hesiod's teaching about Eris in the *Works and Days*. Note also that in *Cypria* fr. 1, Zeus is said to "hurl the great *eris* of the Trojan War" (ῥιπίσσας πολέμου μεγάλην ἔριν Ἰλιακοῖο, 5) just as he "hurled" Ate from the starry heaven (ἔρριψεν) in *Iliad* 19.130.

[69] With of course the exception of Achilles mentioned at the end of the list (87–89), who was too young to participate. Cf. West (1985) 114–21. Heiliger (1983) doubts that the fragment comes from the end of the *Catalogue* and believes that lines 95ff. have nothing to do with what precedes.

[70] The *eris* dividing the gods could be either the cause or effect of Zeus's plan (cf. Marg [1970] 516), but I think the explanatory γάρ suggests the latter.

[71] Cf. *Il.* 12.23; *Works and Days* 159–60 (ἀνδρῶν ἡρώων θεῖον γένος, οἳ καλέονται | ἡμίθεοι, προτέρη γενεὴ κατ' ἀπείρονα γαῖαν, "the divine race of hero men who are called demigods, the previous race on the boundless earth") implies that they are called *hemitheoi* by those who aren't. Cf. Clay (1996). Similarly, the repeated τότε ("then," line 3 and 6) in the *Catalogue's* proem emphasizes the distance between "then" and "now."

[72] There is no need to see a specific allusion to the Judgment of Paris and the ensuing rivalry between the three goddesses.

the destruction of their children and grandchildren; on the other hand, some divinities applaud the notion of distancing themselves from excessive involvement with ephemeral mortals, not only on account of the pain, but also because of the menace such closeness can produce.[73] But, as the *Iliad* likewise reveals, the conflicts among the gods and their interventions on behalf of their favorites, both Greek and Trojan, materially contribute to a prolongation of the War and thus to greater loss of human life on both sides.[74]

From this perspective, we can perhaps better understand the significance of the difficult term that I left untranslated above, *prophasis*, which can mean a true motive or cause as well as a false one or a pretext.[75] In declaring his intention to annihilate the semi-divine heroes, Zeus precipitates internecine quarrels among the gods, quarrels whose final consequences entail not only the disappearance of the heroes and the restoration of the status quo that obtained before gods slept with mortals, ὡς τὸ πάρος περ,[76] but also, as a by-product of that plan, the decimation of the human race.[77]

The overpopulation motif, which introduced the *Cypria*, surfaces in the phrase, γένος . . . πολλόν in verses 98–99 (with πολλόν in an emphatic position at the beginning of the line), suggesting an excessive number. That motif has, to be sure, Near Eastern parallels, but it has always struck me

---

[73] Cf. for instance, *Iliad* 15.113–41 for Ares' reaction to news of the death of his son Askalaphos; Zeus's sorrow at the death of Sarpedon (*Iliad* 16.433–61); and Apollo's refusal to fight with Poseidon "for the sake of wretched mortals, who, while they eat the fruit of the fields, flourish luxuriantly like leaves, but then perish and die" (*Iliad* 21. 463–66). For the menace from human hybris, see *Iliad* 5.438–44; and Salmoneus in *Catalogue* fr. 30.1–23 M–W.

[74] Cf. Clay (1999a).

[75] On *prophasis* in general, see Rawlings (1975); and Heubeck (1980), who point out that a *prophasis* may be true or false. West (1961) 130–36 (followed by Koenen [1994] 28–29) believes Zeus's *prophasis* is a *false* pretense and that the Olympian intends to preserve the heroes on the Isles of the Blest, there to live happily ever after. Cf. Arrighetti (1998) 476. But as Koenen 27, n. 62, admits, "the island is not even mentioned in the *Catalogue*." Furthermore, this hypothesis is immediately contradicted in lines 118–19, where the heads of the ἀνδρῶν ἡρώων are going not to Elysium but to Hades. τέκνα θεῶν (101) could indeed refer to either the gods themselves or the heroes (cf. Stiewe [1963] 6, n. 2 and Marg [1970] 516). But μάκαρες in the next line is far more likely to refer to the gods (as it in fact does in line 117). Furthermore, οἱ μέν creates the expectation of a corresponding οἱ δέ. Cf. Stiewe (1963) 6, n. 2. Marg (1970) 516 suggests that πρόφασις refers to a nearer or more immediate goal rather than simply a false or pretended one. Moreover, the μέν in line 99 suggests a δέ that will follow. Stiewe p. 8 believes that the awkwardness in the passage arises because the poet tried to combine the *Cypria* motif and the Ages myth from the *Works and Days*.

[76] As everyone admits, ὡς τὸ πάρος περ here at the end of the poem alludes to its beginning and links the beginning and end of the heroic age. If, however, the poem began with the generation of the heroes, it must end with their demise, not, I think, with their translation to the Blessed Isles. Davies (1992) 131–33 gives an overview of the alternative interpretations proposed.

[77] I have argued for the coincidence of the *Heldendämmerung* with the over-population motif in the plan of Zeus that informs the *Iliad* in Clay (1999a).

as somewhat anomalous in the Greek context.[78] Yet if it was not simply mechanically adopted but, as I believe, integrated into its new environment, the surplus population motif forms a continuum with the cosmogonic background and the dynamics of the succession myth set in motion in the *Theogony*. There, the generation of the heroes formed part of Zeus's policy of stabilizing his sovereignty. At the very beginning of the *Theogony*, the procreative energies embodied by Gaia in her drive toward change and proliferation allowed the cosmos to unfold and to take on its present form. But, as the succession myth repeatedly reveals, this female drive toward expansion and proliferation inevitably menaces the stability of any regime if left unchecked by the male. Yet, as both Uranus and Cronus learned, if reined in violently, it provokes an equally violent reaction on the part of the female, Gaia or her double Rheia, that precipitates revolution and the overthrow of the old order.

By deflecting the erotic interest of the gods onto mortals, Zeus brings stability to Olympus. At least for a while. Thus, as we have seen, at the end of the *Theogony*, the potentially destabilizing conflicts between Hera and Zeus are played out and ultimately reconciled through their heroic offspring, perhaps ending with Heracles' apotheosis. In the long term, however, Zeus's policy apparently meets with such success that Earth herself becomes oppressed by the sheer weight of mankind. At the outset, the cosmos came into being when Gaia became oppressed by the burden of her children within; so now, in a parallel fashion, the *external* pressure of human population weighs her down. Its removal will inaugurate our age of iron, the final phase of cosmogony. And, as in each of the previous phases, Gaia is the motivating force that precipitates cosmic change. Thus, the overpopulation motif reveals its full significance in a cosmogonic framework. In making Gaia's cause his own, Zeus's strategy relieves Earth of her excessive burden; simultaneously, it distances the gods from their mortal offspring as the gods gradually withdraw from their commerce with men. Henceforth, the inequality of status between immortal gods and mortal men cannot be bridged and remains eternally fixed.[79] Cerutti has aptly called the two prongs of Zeus's plan "ecological hygiene" and "theological hygiene".[80] Zeus's house-cleaning, then, has both a cosmological and a theological

---

[78] Cf. Koenen (1994) 27: "Attribution of the first of these motives [i.e. to reduce surplus population on earth] to a god is less appropriate for the rather sparsely settled lands of the Greeks and far more at home in the densely populated areas of Mesopotamia and Egypt."

[79] Cf. Nagy (1979) 220: "besides entailing the death of heroes in the Trojan War . . . the Will of Zeus also entails *the permanent separation of gods and men* (emphasis in original).

[80] Cerutti (1998) 166; but she does not recognize the cosmogonic pattern in the overpopulation motif.

component and encompasses far more than the slaughter of the heroes indicated by his *prophasis*; it inaugurates our era by reducing the excessive population of the earth and brings the cosmogonic process, a process that began from Gaia's primal efflorescence, to a close; at the same time, it renders permanent the gulf separating the eternal gods from ephemeral mortals.

It is difficult to ascertain exactly what happens in the tantalizingly fragmentary lines 105–23 that follow; none of the various reconstructions proposed is completely persuasive. Without rehearsing them all, I will merely put forth some suggestions and a possible interpretation, all the while acknowledging that they are necessarily speculative. We seem to return to the main narrative, perhaps to Aulis where the Greek expedition has gathered.[81] Those taking part in the expedition have in a sense already been enumerated, since the warriors who participate on the Greek side are identical to the suitors of Helen who had taken an oath to defend her. Someone, whom I believe to be Calchas, pronounces a prophecy, for it is he who knows [what was and] "is and what things were going to happen" (113, cf. *Iliad* 1.70), as well as what the mind of Zeus devises and exalts (114–15).[82] There is some sort of warning: no one should set sail (110–11), perhaps before the sacrifice of Iphigeneia (mentioned in the *Catalogue* as Iphimede in fr. 23.17–24 M–W). The one who is "mightiest in strength" (line 111) might be Achilles, whom Calchas is supposed to have sent for, since he knew that Achilles' presence was an essential condition for the taking of Troy.[83] Lines 118–19 parallel the opening of *Iliad*; but we need not posit a direct allusion or imitation, for they seem to have a traditional connection to the Trojan War and with Zeus's plans (cf., for example, *Iliad* 11.55). But neither the prophet nor someone else, perhaps Agamemnon, understood the full import of Zeus's plan, but instead he rejoiced,[84] not comprehending its dire consequences.

---

[81] Cf. Stiewe (1963) 10.

[82] Cerutti (1998) 147 and West (1961) 119 follow Wilamowitz (in Schubart and Wilamowitz [1907] 42–43) in making the subject Apollo. Stiewe (1963) 10–12 suggests Agamemnon, who also misunderstands Zeus's prophecy at the beginning of *Iliad* 2.

[83] Cf. Apollodorus 3.13.8. Apollodorus frequently uses the *Catalogue* as his source. If β]ίηφι is the correct supplement at line 111, then it cannot refer to Agamemnon, as Stiewe (1963) claims. But it would fit nicely with the notice of Achilles' absence among the suitors of Helen in lines 87–92. In the opening of the *Cypria*, the birth of *both* Helen and Achilles are essential to the fulfillment of Zeus's plan.

[84] The motif of the misunderstood prophecy is, of course, a common one; but Agamemnon's failure to understand its full import is reminiscent of his role in *Odyssey* 8.73–82, where he apparently misunderstands a prophecy delivered by Apollo at Delphi before the beginning of the Trojan War. He is likewise deluded by the Dream sent by Zeus in *Iliad* 2. In addition, book 1 of the *Iliad* alludes to a tension between Agamemnon and Calchas involving a prophecy.

In yet another abrupt shift, we get a dramatic description of a storm sent by Zeus that stirs up the sea, destroys vegetation, and saps men's strength. West calls these lines "the finest passage of poetry yet known from the *Catalogue*" and suggests that they should be interpreted as "the first autumn" introducing a radical change in the world.[85] West argues that not only sailing and warfare but also the seasons were absent from the heroic period. Yet the *Catalogue* clearly attests to the presence of the first two,[86] and there is no reason to exclude the existence of seasonal change from the poem. It seems far simpler to link this description to the famous storm at Aulis that delayed the Greek expedition.[87]

Equally sudden is the transition to a lengthy description of a snake in spring that every third year gives birth to three young and avoids the path of men; but when winter comes on, it lies all coiled up. Zeus destroys the dread serpent with his bolts, but its spirit remains. In the spring, however, she – for it turns out that the serpent is female – returns to the light, and apparently gives birth to triplets in the following spring (129–39).[88] The cycle of births appears to occur three times (cf. line 162) and may parallel the nine sparrows devoured by the snake at Aulis as explicated by Calchas in the second book of the *Iliad*.[89] Both would appear to allude to the nine-year duration of the war at Troy before the city falls in the tenth. But in addition to presaging the course of the War, the omen of the serpent sloughing off its skin and giving birth can also be understood as an emblem of the cosmic *Zeitwende*, with the end of the old order and the inauguration of something new. Yet there is also an element of continuity: the serpent, with her new skin, herself survives. Zeus had blasted the snake with his thunderbolts, much as he had destroyed the heroes. But the *psyche* (139) that is left behind still has the power of generation, perhaps of a new race of men, the race of iron, who, according to the *Works and Days*, do not represent a new creation, but rather a measure of continuity, after the gods have distanced themselves from mankind. But only in the *Catalogue* does the twilight of the heroes signify a return to the *status quo ante*, ὡς τὸ πάρος περ. The

---

[85] West (1961) 133. Cf. Mayer (1996) 2–3. Nagy (1979) 220, n. 5, believes the passage is metaphoric: "men die much as leaves fall from trees."

[86] Fr. 205 M–W mentions that the Myrmidons invented sailing, and fr. 204.59 credits Idomeneus with sailing from Crete.

[87] Cf. Aeschylus, *Agamemnon* 192–204. West (1961) 120, n. 207, draws a parallel to the storms that delayed the Greeks at Aulis, but he still assumes the heroes have been removed to the Islands of the Blest (204.102–3).

[88] West (1985) 120 sees a parallel between the regeneration of the snake and the heroes.

[89] Cf. ευν, perhaps ἐννέα (?) at line 175. West notes that the openings of lines 176–77 seem to parallel *Works and Days* 90–91, but in the *Works and Days* the lines have nothing to do with the heroes or the Islands of the Blest.

Catalogue, then, concludes with Troy's destruction and the demise of the heroes, in accordance with Zeus's plans.

The preceding reconstruction has necessarily been highly speculative. If, however, it carries some persuasive force, then Calchas and his prophetic ability to interpret the gods' decrees bring both the heroic age and the *Catalogue* to a close. This possibility suggests some intriguing intersections between the *Catalogue* and the epic tradition, as well as the two Hesiodic compositions. Much in the manner of archaic ring composition, these lines of contact bring us back to the very beginning of our inquiry as we come to its conclusion.

Conclusion: Hesiod and Calchas at Aulis

Hesiod marks the beginning of his poetic career by his encounter with the Muses who, according to him, know "the things that are and those that will be and were before" (τά τ᾽ ἐόντα τά τ᾽ ἐσσόμενα πρό τ᾽ ἐόντα). In the *Theogony*, through the Muses' inspiration, he is enabled to sing "the things that will be and were before" (τ᾽ ἐσσόμενα πρό τ᾽ ἐόντα), which I have interpreted not as past and future, but as that which has been and will be, in other words, that which is eternal and divine. Accordingly, the *Theogony* recounts how the everlasting gods and the other eternal constituents of the cosmos came into being. The cosmogonic process ends with the inauguration of the permanent and stable order under the sovereignty of Zeus, an order embracing the radiant abodes of the Olympians as well as the shadowy realm of the dark forces in the nether world. The human sphere, while not completely excluded, is viewed obliquely from the perspective of the divine. In the *Works and Days*, on the other hand, Hesiod claims to recount "things as they are," *ta etetuma* (10), i.e. from the human perspective: the contingent nature of human life, its subjection to time and mortality, and the rules imposed by the eternal gods that regulate it. Each of these compositions on its own presents only a partial vision, but the study of both together makes manifest the whole, or Hesiod's cosmos, both the human and the divine.

The Muses are essential to the subject matter of the *Theogony*. Without their aid and intervention, Hesiod as a mere mortal cannot have access to knowledge of cosmic beginnings and the evolution of the divine order. But the *Works and Days* require no such authorization, since there Hesiod speaks from his own experience and knowledge of human life. Indeed, Hesiod presents himself as the *panaristos* who can think things through to the end on his own; and it is on this basis that he has both the right and the authority to instruct Perses.

The dual source of knowledge to which Hesiod lays claim resembles the assertion of Phemius, the Ithacan bard in Odysseus' palace:

αὐτοδίδακτος δ' εἰμί, θεὸς δέ μοι ἐν φρεσὶν οἴμας
παντοίας ἐνέφυσεν.

I am self-taught, and a god implanted in me
All sorts of songs. . . .   (*Od.* 22.347–48)

Despite the divine perspective of the *Theogony*, Hesiod nevertheless occasionally acknowledges that, although authorized by the Muses, his transmission of things divine remains limited by the inescapable fact that he is, after all, a human being rather than a god. This limitation emerges most forcefully in the Muses' mocking words to their disciple, which playfully insist on the incommensurability between divine and human knowledge. But there are other examples in the course of the poem: for instance, when Hesiod breaks off his enumeration of the rivers, "because it is difficult for a mortal man to tell the names of all of them" (369); or when, in the catalogue of monsters, he interjects a "they say" (φασι 306) when describing the horrendous mating of Echidna and Typhaon.[1]

The *Works and Days* subtly but appropriately inverts this pattern by including two sections where Hesiod claims access to knowledge that transcends his human experience: in the "Days" and, most importantly, in the passage on sailing. In the former, Hesiod sets out to describe the "days that are from Zeus" (765, 769), and notes that few mortals have knowledge of them or can name them correctly (814, 818, 820). In the discussion of seafaring, Hesiod openly declares his human ignorance of navigation. Since his experience of the sea is narrowly limited, he cannot speak *etetuma* about it; nevertheless, Hesiod asserts his super-human ability to enunciate "the mind of Zeus" (661) through the mediation of the Muses' teaching (cf. 484). Both poems, then, draw attention to Hesiod's mediating role. Thus, it is through the combination of his own talent, intelligence, and the Muses' gifts that Hesiod possesses knowledge of both the divine and the human, of τά τ' ἐόντα τά τ' ἐσσόμενα πρό τ' ἐόντα.

In the first book of the *Iliad,* these same words describe Calchas, the resident seer of the Greek expedition against Troy.

> . . . τοῖσι δ' ἀνέστη
> Κάλχας Θεστορίδης, οἰωνοπόλων ὄχ' ἄριστος,
> ὃς ᾔδη τά τ' ἐόντα τά τ' ἐσσόμενα πρό τ' ἐόντα.

> . . . among them arose
> Calchas, son of Thestor, by far the best of the interpreters of omens,
> Who knew the things that are and those that will be and were before.
>   (*Il.* 1.68–70)

---

[1] Cf. Stoddard (2000) 108–9.

If I have interpreted line 31 of the *Theogony* correctly, the same phrase here signifies that Calchas knows not the present, past, and future in a purely temporal sense, as it is usually understood, but that he has knowledge of matters both human and divine as well as their conjunctions and interrelations.[2] Such knowledge is fully appropriate to a seer, whose function it is to interpret and mediate divine intentions as they influence human affairs. Indeed, Calchas goes on to demonstrate precisely this skill in the first book of the *Iliad*: he knows that the plague devastating the Greek camp is due to Apollo's wrath, and he knows what provoked it. He explains to the Achaeans not the course of future events, but the cause of the plague that is devastating the army. The mantic art Calchas deploys in the first book of the *Iliad* exactly parallels his earlier revelation to the assembled Greeks at Aulis when he traced the cause of the storm to the wrath of Artemis and announced its terrible remedy: there, the sacrifice of Iphigeneia; here, the return of Chryseis. The Iliadic passage continues by citing an apparent proof of Calchas' prophetic knowledge:

καὶ νήεσσ' ἡγήσατ' Ἀχαιῶν Ἴλιον εἴσω
ἣν διὰ μαντοσύνην, τήν οἱ πόρε Φοῖβος Ἀπόλλων.

And it was he who led the ships of the Achaeans into Ilium
Through his prophetic skill, which Phoebus Apollo had granted him.

(*Il.* 1.71–72)

We can, of course, take this statement in a general sense to mean that Calchas' prophetic skill guided the Greeks during the expedition to Troy. But the text and the verb ἡγήσατ' suggest a more concrete activity. Indeed Proclus reports the tradition from the Epic Cycle that the Greeks did not succeed in finding Troy on their first try, but ended up in Mysia.[3] In *Iliad* 2, Calchas again appears in his prophetic role when Odysseus recalls the seer's interpretation of the sign given to the army at Aulis before its departure for Troy (*Il.* 2.299–330). It is that omen, and Calchas' interpretation of it, that I suggested brought the *Catalogue* and the heroic age to a close. Present at the mustering of the troops at Aulis, Calchas, through the prophetic powers granted by Apollo, may well have guided the Greek ships to their Trojan destination. At any rate, the seer must have accompanied the Greek host on their journey from Aulis to the site of Troy.

---

[2] Cf. *Hymn to Apollo* 132, where the new-born Apollo describes his prophetic power not in temporal terms but as mediating the intentions of Zeus to mankind. Cf. Miralles and Pòrtulas (1998) 16: "le poète et le devin peuvent être consacrés comme des mortels dont le regard intérieur . . . embrasse cette non-interruption temporelle entre l'avant, le maintenant et l'après, la seule qui peut donner aux hommes la perception de l'ordre divin du monde, la clé de la condition humaine."

[3] Proclus, *Chrestomathia* (p. 104, Allen). The *Catalogue* alludes to this incident in fr. 165 (M–W).

In declaring his ignorance of ships and sailing, Hesiod not only mentions Aulis, but also alludes to the great Trojan expedition.

δείξω δή τοι μέτρα πολυφλοίσβοιο θαλάσσης,
οὔτέ τι ναυτιλίης σεσοφισμένος οὔτέ τι νηῶν·
οὐ γάρ πώ ποτε νηὶ γ᾽ ἐπέπλων εὐρέα πόντον,
εἰ μὴ ἐς Εὔβοιαν ἐξ Αὐλίδος, ᾗ ποτ᾽ Ἀχαιοί
μείναντες χειμῶνα πολὺν σὺν λαὸν ἄγειραν
Ἑλλάδος ἐξ Ἱερῆς Τροίην ἐς καλλιγύναικα.

I shall show you the measures of the much-billowing sea,
Even though totally unskilled in sailing and ships;
For I never sailed in a ship on the broad sea at all –
Except to Euboea from Aulis, where once the Achaeans,
Waited out a stormy season and gathered a great host,
From holy Hellas to Troy of the fair women.   (648–53)

Hesiod went only as far as Aulis; he never made the heroic voyage to Troy. Nevertheless, through the gift of the Muses, his knowledge of the human and the divine rivals that of Calchas; indeed, he goes so far as to give lessons in navigation to Perses without any first-hand knowledge.

Now, according to Hesiod, the invention of seafaring is coeval with the heroic age. But whereas the goal of heroic sailing was *kleos*, in Hesiod's age of iron, it is *kerdos*, gain. Unlike that *mega nepios* Perses, however, Hesiod is impervious to the seduction of mere material profits; much like the heroes of old, he too undertakes a voyage by sea for victory and *kleos*.[4] Hesiod's expedition to Aulis was motivated by poetic *kleos*, for it was there that he won the tripod that he dedicated to the Muses of Helicon who had first initiated him in their art:

ἔνθα μέ φημι
ὕμνῳ νικήσαντα φέρειν τρίποδ᾽ ὠτώεντα.
τὸν μὲν ἐγὼ Μούσῃσ᾽ Ἑλικωνιάδεσσ᾽ ἀνέθηκα,
ἔνθά με τὸ πρῶτον λιγυρῆς ἐπέβησαν ἀοιδῆς.

There I declare that I
Carried off the eared tripod, after I was victorious in song.
And I dedicated it to the Heliconian Muses,
There where they first initiated me in shrill song.   (656–59)

Indeed, this passage provided the inspiration for the *Contest of Homer and Hesiod*.[5] Attributed to the fifth-century rhetorician, Alcidamas, the *Contest*

---

4 Precisely *not*, as he says, on the heroic-sounding εὐρέα πόντον (650).
5 On the *Contest*, see Hess (1960); and West (1967); and Heldmann (1982); and, most recently, Graziosi (2002).

pits Hesiod against Homer. Meeting in Aulis, the two poets proceed to Chalcis, where it is Hesiod who sets the rules for their debate, first posing questions and riddles, and then demanding that Homer improvise verses on the lines Hesiod set. The audience applauds Homer's skill and assigns the victory to him, much to Hesiod's annoyance; but King Paneides (All-knowing) intervenes and asks each of the contestants to offer their finest poetry. Homer presents a splendid passage describing the clash of Greeks and Trojans on the battlefield, while Hesiod recites the opening of his farmers' almanac. Again the crowd cheers for Homer, but the King awards the prize to Hesiod because his poetry celebrates farming and peace rather than war.

The *Contest* appears to be a vindication of Hesiod and an implied critique of heroic epic: Hesiod the poet of peace is contrasted with Homer the war poet. But this simple interpretation leaves several questions unanswered. Although Hesiod sets the agenda for the contest, he barely competes; for the most part, he sets the puzzles that Homer must solve.[6] Second, it is he who behaves like a bad sport by envying Homer's success. As to the substance of the contest, Hesiod is presented only as the poet of the *Works and Days*, while Homer cites mainly from the *Iliad*. While this strategy serves to sharpen the contrast between the two poets, it does neither of them justice. Finally, the award of the prize to Hesiod is based not on aesthetic but moral considerations – that peace is to be preferred to war; the outcome is both contrary to expectation and yet foreordained:[7] after all, Hesiod's victory trophy was displayed at the Muses' sanctuary at Helicon. Nevertheless, despite its problematic character, the *Contest* points to what may be considered a genuine Hesiodic challenge to Homer.

Another contest may offer a more Hesiodic version of that challenge. A competition between Calchas and another seer, Mopsos, was narrated in the *Melampodia*, a poem attributed to Hesiod (fr. 278 M–W).[8] The contest took place in Gryneion, where there was an important sanctuary of Apollo. It described how, on his way back from Troy, Calchas was defeated by the prophet Mopsos when he could not answer a riddle; after his defeat, Calchas died of chagrin. Intriguingly enough, in some of the *Vitae* of Homer, of

---

[6] Graziosi (2002) argues that both poets demonstrate their skill and wisdom and that "the two sides are evenly balanced" (71). While I believe that this assessment ultimately corresponds to Hesiod's judgment of Homer, I am not sure that it is in keeping with the spirit of the *Certamen*.

[7] The dynamics of the *Certamen* has many parallels to the contest of Aeschylus and Euripides in the *Frogs*. There too, Dionysus' judgment involves an unexpected reversal.

[8] See Löffler (1963) 48–49. The Hesiodic connection remained alive at least until Virgil, who in the Sixth Eclogue celebrates Gallus' poem on the origins of the Gryneian grove in the context of a Hesiodic *Dichterweihe*. Gryneion lies about 20 kilometers north of Kyme, on which see below.

which the *Certamen* forms a part, it is Homer who dies of frustration at being bested when he, likewise, fails to find a solution for a riddle.[9] Here, however, it is the figure of the seer Calchas with his knowledge of both the human things and the divine (τά τ᾽ ἐόντα τά τ᾽ ἐσσόμενα πρό τ᾽ ἐόντα) who appears as the representative of heroic poetry and the emblem of that challenge.

However that may be, in Hesiod's allusion to heroic epic and his comparison of his brief journey by ship to the Greek expedition against Troy, several recent critics have detected more than mere autobiographical detail: they have recognized a metaphor suggesting a polemic confrontation between two kinds of poetry, Hesiod's own and martial epic.[10] In linking his poetic victory with the grandest and most heroic expedition, Hesiod invites us to compare his poetry to that of Homeric epic. The *kleos* Hesiod won with his song can thus be equated with the immortal *kleos* of the Trojan expedition. But the confrontation between two kinds of poetry, Hesiod's own and martial epic goes beyond simple polemics. Hesiod's challenge, I suggest, arises not from his conviction that Homer lies or from some putative ambivalence toward the heroes and heroic epic. His assertion of superiority is both more profound and more comprehensive.

In this context, I would like to bring in another piece of what is usually assumed to be genuine autobiographical information.[11] In the same passage

---

[9] In Keaney and Lamberton (1996) 4, Homer is said to have died of ἀθυμία after not being able to solve the riddle posed by the fishermen. Cf. *Vita Herodotea*, 35.

[10] Cf. Nagy (1990) 78: "Perhaps, then, this passage reveals an intended differentiation of Hesiodic from Homeric poetry." Cf. Thalmann (1984) 152–53. Rosen (1990) pushes the metaphor and also limits Hesiod's poetry to the *Works and Days*, believing that "Hesiod contrasts his inability to compose . . . poetry on a Homeric scale with his qualifications for composing his poem on the 'earth,' *Works and Days*" (100). Rosen also thinks that the passage "implies that Hesiod's performance at the funeral games for Amphidamas resembled Homeric epos, but was, at best, a minor venture into the realm of heroic poetry" (101) and that Hesiodic poetry constitutes "a less ambitious genre" (104, n. 21). Rosen (1997) 486–87 detects an ambivalent attitude toward the heroes and heroic epic in the *Works and Days*; he also suggests that the *Theogony* should be considered a *prooimion* and thus belongs to the genre of heroic *epos* (481–82). I believe, however, that Hesiod's victory at Chalcis was occasioned by the performance of the *Theogony* to which he proudly "signed" his name. Walcot (1960) thinks that Hesiod is here "alluding to an epic recitation about the Greeks at Aulis, with which he won the victory." Both the *Certamen* and Dio's variant of it (where Homer seems to be the winner) also largely pit the *Iliad* against the *Works and Days*, as does Aristophanes in the *Frogs* 1033–36. Clearly, the contrast is more effective; the inclusion of the *Theogony* and the *Odyssey* would cloud the picture. Cf. Heldmann (1982) 42–44.

[11] Few scholars doubt the historicity of Hesiod's father. In fact, Cook (1989) 170–71 argues that Hesiod learned the craft of *aoide* from him. Nagy (1990) 73, who does not believe in a historical Hesiod, considers the father a symbol of reverse colonization. For Griffith (1983) 61, the "father is a negative paradigm of a man who unwisely looked to the sea for prosperity." Ironically, however, in the archaic period, Kyme was considered unusually wealthy.

on navigation, Hesiod mentions that his father migrated from Aeolian Kyme,

> οὐκ ἄφενος φεύγων οὐδὲ πλοῦτόν τε καὶ ὄλβον,
> ἀλλὰ κακὴν πενίην, τὴν Ζεὺς ἄνδρεσσι δίδωσιν·
> νάσσατο δ' ἄγχ' Ἑλικῶνος ὀιζυρῇ ἐνὶ κώμῃ,
> Ἄσκρῃ, χεῖμα κακῇ, θέρει ἀργαλέῃ, οὐδέ ποτ' ἐσθλῇ.

> Not to escape wealth or riches and prosperity,
> But wretched poverty, which Zeus gives to men;
> And he settled near Helicon, in a miserable village,
> Ascra, foul in winter, vile in summer, at no time any good.

> (637–40)

Whether true or false, Hesiod's assertion of his Kymean origins has suggestive affinities to traditions that assign this same homeland to Homer.[12] To be sure, all notices of Homer's birthplace are substantially later than Hesiod, but that does not preclude a possibly ancient tradition associating Homer with Kyme. Indeed the so-called *Herodotean Life* recounts how Homer was conceived in Kyme (2) to which he later returned impoverished. There he requested public support from the Council, but when he was turned down, he cursed the Kymeans and left for δῆμον ἐς ἀλλοδαπῶν ἰέναι ὀλίγον περ ἐόντα ("to go to a foreign people, even if they were of no account," 11–15). The emigration of Hesiod's "father" to Ascra bears a striking similarity to Homer's self-exile, but the two apparently went their separate ways.

Hesiod's supposedly autobiographical reference may then contain a metaphorical rather than a literal significance, suggesting a common origin for both poets, but also differentiating their poetic paths and careers. At any rate, as he tells us, Hesiod did not make the heroic journey to Troy, but his father, whether real or fictive, crossed the seas to miserable Ascra, so that his son might encounter the Muses at the foot of Helicon. Hesiod thus suggests that heroic epic is no match for his own poetry, not, however, as often maintained, because of Homer's falsehoods. Rather, Hesiodic poetry comprehends the divine and human cosmos, spatially, from the Olympian heights to the depth of Tartarus, and temporally, from its first beginnings to the present. In opposition to Homer, Hesiod would claim that his vision is by no means a rejection of the heroic tradition (which indeed it subsumes), but that it is far more universal and complete. His dual vision comprehends

---

[12] In Keaney and Lamberton (1996), Ephorus, from Kyme himself, claims that Homer came from there too and that Hesiod was Homer's uncle (2). But the tradition must be older, since the Sophist Hippias also ascribed Homer's birthplace to Kyme (*FGrH* 6.13).

both the divine and the human cosmos and unites the traditions of theogonic poetry with those of "wisdom" literature, the divine world of Being and the ephemeral human world of Becoming. The gulf Hesiod detects and illuminates between the divine and human perspective points forward to the philosophical endeavors of Empedocles, Parmenides, and Heraclitus. By constructing his *Theogony* and his *Works and Days* as complementary visions of the cosmos, Hesiod reveals his ambition to encompass the whole that embraces the harsh realities of human life as well as the lovely songs of the Muses that make it bearable.

Bibliography

Abramowicz, S. (1940–46) "Quaestiuncula hesiodea (De monstrorum stemmate in *Theogonia*)," *Eos* 41: 166–72.

Aly, W. (1913a) "Hesiodos von Askra," in Heitsch: 50–99.

(1913b) "Die literarische Überlieferung des Prometheusmythos," in Heitsch: 327–41.

Amory, A. (1966) "The Gates of Horn and Ivory," *YClS*: 20: 1–57.

Arrighetti, G. (1975) "Esiodo fra epica e lyrica," in *Esiodo: Letture Critiche*, ed. G. Arrighetti. Milan: 5–34.

(1993) "Notte e i suoi figli: tecnica catalogica ed uso dell' aggettivazione in Esiodo (*Th.* 211–225)," in *Tradizione e innovazione nella cultura greca da Omero all'età ellenistica. Scritti in onore di B. Gentili* 1, ed. R. Pretagostini. Rome: 101–14.

(1996) "Hésiode et les Muses: Le Don de la vérité et la conquête de la parole," in *Métier*: 53–70. Italian version in *Athenaeum* 80 (1992) 45–63.

(1998) (ed.) *Esiodo Opere*. Turin.

Arthur, M. (1982) "Cultural Strategies in Hesiod's *Theogony*: Law, Family, Society," *Arethusa* 15: 62–82.

(1983) "The Dream of a World without Women: Poetics and the Circles of Order in the *Theogony* Proem," *Arethusa* 16: 97–116.

Athanassakis, A. N. (trans.) (1983) *Hesiod: Theogony, Works and Days, Shield*. Baltimore.

(1992a) (ed.) *Essays on Hesiod* 1. *Ramus* 21.1.

(1992b) (ed.) *Essays on Hesiod* 11. *Ramus* 21.2.

Austin, J. L. (1975) *How To Do Things With Words*. Cambridge, Mass.

Bakker, E. (1997) "Storytelling in the Future," in *Written Voices, Spoken Signs: Tradition, Performance, and the Epic Text*, eds. E. Bakker and A. Kahane. Cambridge, Mass.: 11–36.

(1999a) "Homeric OYTOΣ and the Poetics of Deixis," *CP* 94: 1–19.

(1999b) "Pointing to the Past: Verbal Augment and Temporal Deixis in Homer," in *Euphrosyne: Studies in Ancient Epic and its Legacy in Honor of Dimitris N. Maronitis*, eds. J. N. Kazazis and A. Rengakos. Stuttgart.

(2002) "Polyphemos," *Colby Quarterly* 38: 135–50.

Ballabriga, A. (1986) *Le Soleil et le Tartare: L'Image mythique du monde en Grèce archaïque*. Paris.

(1990) "Le Dernier adversaire de Zeus: Le Mythe de Typhon dans l'épopée grecque archaïque," *RHR* 207: 3–30.

(1998) "L'Invention du mythe des races en Grèce archaïque," *RHR* 215: 307–39.

Bamberger, B. (1842) "Über des Hesiodus mythus von den ältesten Menschengeschlechtern," reprinted in Heitsch: 439–49.

Becker, A. S. (1993) "Sculpture and Language in Early Greek Ekphrasis: Lessing's *Laocoon*, Burke's *Enquiry*, and the Hesiodic Description of Pandora," *Arethusa* 26: 277–93.

Benardete, S. (1967) "Hesiod's *Works and Days*: A First Reading," ΑΓΩΝ 1: 150–74.

(2000) "The Crisis in First Philosophy," in *The Argument of the Action: Essays on Greek Poetry and Philosophy.* Chicago: 3–14.

Benveniste, E. (1969) *Le Vocabulaire des institutions indo-européennes* (2 vols.). Paris.

Bernabé, A. (1987) (ed.) *Poetarum epicorum graecorum. Testimonia et fragmenta.* Leipzig.

Bettini, M. (1993) (ed.) *Maschile/Femminile: Genere e ruoli nelle culture antiche.* Rome.

Beye, C. (1972) "The Rhythm of Hesiod's *Works and Days*," *HSCPh* 76: 23–43.

Bianchi, U. (1963) "Razza aurea, mito delle cinque razze ed Elisio," *SMSR* 34: 143–210.

Blaise, F. (1992) "L'Épisode de Typhée dans la *Théogonie* d'Hésiode (v. 820–885): La Stabilisation du monde," *REG* 105: 349–70.

Blaise, F. and Rousseau, P. (1996) "La Guerre (*Théogonie*, v. 617–720)," in *Métier*: 213–33.

Blaise, F., Judet de La Combe, P., and Rousseau, P. (1996) (eds.) *Le Métier du mythe: Lectures d'Hésiode.* Lille. (= *Métier*)

Blumenberg, H. (1985) *Work on Myth*, trans. R. M. Wallace. Cambridge, Mass.

Blümer, W. (2001) *Interpretation archaischer Dichtung: Die mythologischen Partien der Erga Hesiods* (2 vols.). Münster.

Blusch, J. (1970) *Formen und Inhalt Hesiods individuellen Denkens.* Bonn.

Boedeker, D. (1983) "Hecate: A Transfunctional Goddess in the *Theogony*?," *TAPhA* 113: 79–93.

Bollack, J. (1971) "Mythische Deutung und Deutung des Mythos," in *Terror und Spiel: Probleme der Mythenrezeption,* ed. M. Fuhrmann. Munich: 111–18.

Bona Quaglia, L. (1973) *Gli "Erga" di Esiodo.* Turin.

Bonnafé, A. (1983) "Le Rossignol et la justice en pleurs (Hésiode 'Travaux' 203–212)," *Bulletin de l'Association Guillaume Budé*: 260–64.

(1984) *Poésie, nature et sacré: Homère, Hésiode et le sentiment grec de la nature.* Lyon.

(1985) *Eris et Eros: Mariages divins et mythe de succession chez Hésiode.* Lyon.

Bradley, E. (1966) "The Relevance of the Proemium to the Design and Meaning of Hesiod's *Theogony*," *SO* 41: 29–47.

Brague, R. (1990) "Le Récit du commencement. Une aporie de la raison grecque," in *La naissance de la raison en Grèce. Actes du Congrès de Nice Mai 1987*, ed. J.-F. Mattéi. Paris: 23–31.

Braswell, B. K. (1981) "*Odyssey* 8.166–77 and *Theogony* 79–93," *CQ* 31: 237–39.

Bravo, B. (1985) "*Les Travaux et les Jours* et la cité," *Annali della Scuola Normale di Pisa*, classe di lettere e filosofia, ser. 3, 15, 3: 705–65.

Brillante, C. (1994) "Poeti e re nel proemio della *Teogonia* Esiodeo," *Prometheus* 20: 14–26.

Broccia, G. (1954) "*Kryptein bion*: Lavoro e vita nel mito esiodeo di Pandora," *PP* 9: 118–36.

(1958) "Pandora, il *pithos* e la Elpis," *PP* 13: 296–309.

Brown, A. S. (1997) "Aphrodite and the Pandora Complex," *CQ* 47: 26–47.

(1998) "From the Golden Age to the Isles of the Blest," *Mnemosyne* 51: 385–410.

Brown, L. T. (1987) "Ο κυνικισμός στὸν Ησίοδον," ΑΡΦ 3: 11–15.

(1994) *The Dog in Ancient Life*. London.

Brown, N. O. (1953) (ed.) *Hesiod: Theogony*. Indianapolis.

Brugmann, K. (1904/5) "Ἑκών und seine griechischen Verwandten," *Indogermanische Forschungen* 17: 1–11.

Büchner, K. (1968) "Das Proömium der Theogonie des Hesiod," in *Studien zur römischen Literatur* vii. Wiesbaden: 9–42.

Burgess, J. (2001) *The Tradition of the Trojan War and the Epic Cycle*. Baltimore.

Burkert, W. (1985) *Greek Religion*. Cambridge, Mass.

Bussanich, J. (1983) "A Theoretical Interpretation of Hesiod's Chaos," *CP* 78: 212–19.

Calabrese de Feo, M. R. (1995) "La Duplice fisionomia di Pandora in Esiodo," in *Poesia Greca*, ed. G. Arrighetti (Ricerche di Filologia Classica 4). Pisa: 101–21.

Calame, C. (1995a) *The Craft of Poetic Speech in Ancient Greece*, trans. J. Orion. Ithaca. (French edition 1986)

(1995b) "Variations énonciatives, relations avec les dieux et fonctions poétiques dans les *Hymnes Homériques*," *MH* 52: 2–19.

(1996) "Le Proème des *Travaux* d'Hésiode: Prélude à une poésie d'action," in *Métier*: 169–89.

Carrière, J.-C. (1986) "Les Démons, les héros et les rois dans la cité de fer: Les Ambiguités de la justice dans la mythe hésiodique des races et la naissance de la cité," in *Les Grandes figures religieuses. Fonctionnement pratique et symbolique dans l'Antiquité*. Paris: 193–261.

Casabona, J. (1966) *Recherches sur le vocabulaire des sacrifices en grec*. Aix-en-Provence.

Casanova, A. (1979) *La Famiglia di Pandora: Analisi filologica dei miti di Pandora e Promiteo nella tradizione esiodeo*. Florence.

Cerutti, M. V. (1998) "Mito di distruzione, Mito di fundazione; Hes. Fr 204, 95–103 M.–W.," *Aevum Antiquum* 11: 127–78.

Chantraine, P. (1968–80) *Dictionnaire étymologique de la langue grecque* (2 vols.). Paris.

Clark, M. (2001) "Was Telemachus Rude to his Mother? *Odyssey* 1.356–59," *CPh* 96: 335–54.

Classen, C. J. (1996) "ΑΡΧΗ in its Earlier Use," in *Studies in Memory of A. Wasserstein*, eds. J. Price and D. J. Wasserstein, vol. 1. Jerusalem: 20–24.

Claus, D. (1977) "Defining Moral Terms in the *Works and Days*," *TAPhA* 108: 73–84.

Clay, D. (1992) "The World of Hesiod," in *Essays on Hesiod* ii, ed. A. Athanassakis. *Ramus* 21: 131–55.

Clay, J. S. (1984) "The Hecate of the *Theogony*," *GRBS* 25: 27–38.

(1988) "What the Muses Sang: *Theogony* 1–115," *GRBS* 29: 323–33.

(1989) *The Politics of Olympus*. Princeton.

(1993a) "The Generation of Monsters in Hesiod," *CP* 88: 105–16.

(1993b) "The Education of Perses: From 'Mega Nepios' to 'Dion Genos' and Back," *MD* 31: 23–33.

(1996) "The New Simonides and Homer's *Hemitheoi*," *Arethusa* 29: 243–45.

(1999a) "The Whip and Will of Zeus," *Literary Imagination* 1: 40–60.

(1999b) "*Iliad* 24.649 and the Semantics of ΚΕΡΤΟΜΕΩ," *CQ* 49: 618–21.

Cole, T. (1983) "Archaic Truth," *QUCC* 13: 7–28.

Combellack, F. M. (1948) "Speakers and Scepters in Homer," *CJ* 43: 209–17.

Cook, R. M. (1989) "Hesiod's Father," *JHS* 109: 170–77.

Crubellier, M. (1996) "Le mythe comme discours: Le Récit des cinq races humaines dans *Les Travaux et les Jours*," in *Métier*: 431–63.

Daudet, A. (1972) "ΧΑΛΚΩΙ ΕΡΓΑΖΟΝΤΟ," *Recherches de Philologie et de Linguistique* 3: 199–25.

Davies, D. R. (1992) "Genealogy and Catalogue: Thematic Relevance and Narrative Elaboration in Homer and Hesiod," PhD dissertation, University of Michigan.

Davies, M. (1991) (ed.) *Poetarum Melicorum Fragmenta* 1. Oxford.

(1995) "Agamemnon's apology and the unity of the *Iliad*," *CQ* 45: 1–8.

Davis, S. (1979) "Perlocutions," *Linguistics and Philosophy* 3: 225–43.

De Heer, C. (1969) ΜΑΚΑΡ – ΕΥΔΑΙΜΟΝ – ΟΛΒΙΟΣ – ΕΥΤΥΧΗΣ: *A Study of the Semantic Field Denoting Happiness in Ancient Greek to the End of the Fifth Century* BC. Amsterdam.

Deichgräber, K. (1951–52) "Etymologisches zu Ζεύς, Διός, Δία, Δίκη (Hesiod 'Erga' 248–266)," *Zeitschrift für vergleichende Sprachforschung* 70: 19–28.

(1965) "Die Musen, Nereiden, und Okeaninen in Hesiods Theogonie," *Akademie der Wissenschaften und der Literatur in Mainz* 4. Wiesbaden: 175–207.

Detienne, M. (1967) *Les Maîtres de vérité dans la Grèce archaïque*. Paris.

(1972) *Les Jardins d'Adonis*. Paris.

Detienne, M. and Vernant, J.-P. (1974) *Les ruses de l'intelligence: La mètis des Grecs*. Paris.

Dickie, M. (1973) "*Dike* as a Moral Term in Homer and Hesiod," *CPh* 73: 91–101.

Diels, H. and Kranz, W. (1934) (eds.) *Die Fragmente der Vorsokratiker* (5th edn.). Berlin.

Derossi, G. (1975) "L'Inno ad Ecate di Baccilide (fr. 1.B Sn.) e la 'figura' arcaica della dea," *Quaderni Triestini per il lessico della lirica corale greca* 2: 16–26.

Di Gregorio, L. (1975) (ed.) *Scholia vetera in Hesiodi Theogoniam*. Milan.

Diller, H. (1946) "Hesiod und die Anfänge der griechischen Philosophie," reprinted in Heitsch: 688–707.

Dräger, P. (1997) *Untersuchungen zu den Frauenkatalogen Hesiods*. Stuttgart.

Duban, J. M. (1980) "Poets and Kings in the *Theogony* Invocation," *QUCC* 33: 7–21.

Duchemin, J. (1974) *Prométhée: Histoire du mythe, de ses origines orientales à ses incarnations modernes*. Paris.

Douglas, M. (1966) *Purity and Danger*. London.

Edmunds, S. T. (1990) *Homeric Nepios*. New York.

Edwards, G. P. (1971) *The Language of Hesiod in its Traditional Context*. Oxford.

Erler, M. (1987) Das Recht als Segenbringerin für die Polis," *SIFC* 3 ser. 5: 5–36.

Evelyn-White, H. G. (1936) (ed.) *Hesiod, the Homeric Hymns and Homerica*. Cambridge, Mass.

Falkner, T. (1989) "Slouching towards Boeotia: Age and Age-Grading in the Hesiodic Myth of the Five Ages," *CA* 8: 42–60.

Ferrari. G. (1988) "Hesiod's mimetic Muses and the strategies of deconstruction," in *Post-Structuralist Classics*, ed. A. Benjamin. London: 45–78.

Fick, A. (1887) *Hesiods Gedichte*. Göttingen.

(1894) *Die griechischen Personennamen* (2nd edn.). Göttingen.

Flach, H. (1873) *Die Hesiodische Theogonie*. Berlin.

Fontenrose, J. (1974) "Work, Justice, and Hesiod's Five Ages," *CPh* 69: 1–16.

Ford, A. (1992) *Homer: The Poetry of the Past*. Ithaca.

Fowler, R. L. (1998) "Genealogical Thinking, Hesiod's *Catalogue*, and the Creation of the Hellenes," *PCPhS* 44: 1–19.

Fränkel, H. (1962) *Dichtung und Philosophie des frühen Griechentums*. Munich.

Friedländer, P. (1914) "Das Proömium von Hesiods Theogonie," reprinted in Heitsch: 277–94.

(1931) Review of F. Jacoby, *Hesiodi Carmina Pars I: Theogonia* (Berlin 1930), reprinted in Heitsch: 100–30.

Fritz, K. von. (1956) "Das Proömium der hesiodische Theogonie," reprinted in Heitsch: 295–315.

(1947) "Pandora, Prometheus, and the Myth of the Ages," *Review of Religion* 11: 227–60.

Fuss, W. (1910) *Versuch einer Analyse von Hesiods* ΕΡΓΑ ΚΑΙ ΗΜΕΡΑI (1. Theil). Borna–Leipzig.

Gagarin, M. (1973) "*Dike* in the *Works and Days*," *CPh* 68: 81–94.

(1974) "Hesiod's Dispute with Perses," *TAPhA* 104: 103–11.

(1990) "The Ambiguity of Eris in the Works and Days," in *Cabinet of the Muses. Essays on Classical and Comparative Literature in Honor of T. G. Rosenmeyer*, eds. M. Griffith and D. J. Mastronarde. Atlanta: 173–83.

Gatz, B. (1967) *Weltalter, goldene Zeit und sinnverwandte Vorstellungen*. Spudasmata 16. Hildesheim.

Genette, G. (1982) *Palimpsestes*. Paris.

Gerhard, E. (1853) (ed.) *Hesiodi Carmina*. Berlin.

Goettling, C. (1843) (ed.) *Hesiodi carmina*. Gotha.

Goldschmidt, V. (1950) "Théologia," *REG* 63: 20–41.

Goodwin, W. (1889) *Syntax of the Moods and Tenses of the Greek Verb*. London.

Graziosi, B. (2002) "Competition in Wisdom," in *Homer, Tragedy and Beyond: Essays in Honour of P. E. Easterling*, eds. F. Budelman and P. Michelakis. Cambridge: 54–74.

Green, P. (1984) "*Works and Days* 1–285: Hesiod's Invisible Audience," in *Mnemai: Classical Studies in Memory of Karl K. Hulley*, ed. H. D. Evjen. Chico, California: 21–39.

Griffin, J. (1980) *Homer on Life and Death*. Oxford.

Griffith, M. (1983) "Personality in Hesiod," *CA* 2: 37–65.

Groningen, B. A. van (1957) "Hésiode et Perses," *Med. Kon. Neder. Akad. Wetenschappen, Afd. Letterkunde*, NR 20, 6: 153–66.

  (1958) *La Composition Littéraire archaïque grecque, Med. Ned. Ak. Afd. Letterk.* NS 65, 2. Amsterdam.

Gruppe, O. (1841) *Ueber die Theogonie des Hesiod*. Berlin.

Guarducci, M. (1926) "Leggende dell'antica Grecia relative all'origine dell'umanità e analoghe tradizioni di altri paesi," *Atti della Reale Accademia Nazionale dei Lincei: Memorie delle classe di scienze morali, storiche e filologiche*: 2, 323: 379–459.

Hamilton, R. (1989) *The Architecture of Hesiodic Poetry*. Baltimore.

Harrell, S. E. (1991) "Apollo's Fraternal Threats: Language of Succession and Domination in the *Homeric Hymn to Hermes*," *GRBS* 32: 307–29.

Heath, M. (1985) "Hesiod's Didactic Poetry," *CQ* 35: 245–63.

Heiliger, K. (1983) "Der Freierkatalog der Helena im hesiodeischen Frauenkatalog 1," *MH* 40: 19–34.

Heitsch, E. (1963) "Das Prometheus-Gedicht bei Hesiod," reprinted in Heitsch: 424–35.

  (1966a) (ed.) *Hesiod*. Darmstadt. (= Heitsch)

  (1966b.) "Das Wissen des Xenophanes," *RhM* 109: 193–235.

Heldmann, K. (1982) *Die Niederlage Homers im Dichterwettstreit mit Hesiod*. Hypomnemata 75. Göttingen.

Henderson, J. (1987) *Aristophanes Lysistrata*. Oxford.

Hermann, G. (1827) "De mythologia Graecorum antiquissima dissertatio," *Opuscula* 2. Leipzig: 167–94.

  (1839) "De Apolline et Diana pars posterior," *Opuscula* 7. Leipzig: 299–314.

Hess, K. (1960) *Der Agon zwischen Homer und Hesiod, seine Entstehung und kulturgeschichliche Stellung*. Meisenheim.

Heubeck, A. (1955) "Mythologische Vorstellungen des alten Orients im archaischen Griechentum," reprinted in Heitsch: 545–70.

  (1980) "Πρόφασις und kein Ende (zu Thuc. 1.23)," *Glotta* 2–4: 222–36.

Hölscher, U. (1968) *Anfängliche Fragen: Studien zur frühen griechischen Philosophie*. Göttingen.

Hoffmann, H. (1971) "Hesiod Theogonie V. 35," *Gymnasium* 78: 90–97.

Hofinger, M. (1969) "L'Eve grecque et le mythe de Pandore," in *Mélanges de linguistique, de philologie, et de méthodologie de l'enseignement des langues anciennes, offerts à M. René Fohalle à l'occasion de son soixante-dixième anniversaire.* Gembloux: 205–17.

Hubbard, T. K. (1996) "Hesiod's Fable of the Hawk and the Nightingale," *GRBS* 36: 161–71.

Jacoby, F. (1930) (ed.) *Hesiodi Carmina: Pars 1: Theogonia.* Berlin.

Janko, R. (1981) "The Structure of the Homeric Hymns: A Study in Genre," *Hermes* 109: 9–24.

(1982) *Homer, Hesiod and the Hymns: Diachronic development in Epic diction.* Cambridge.

Johnston, S. I. (1989) *Hekate Soteira: A Study of Hekate's Roles in the Chaldean Oracles and Related Literature.* Atlanta.

Jones, N. F. (1984) "Work 'In Season' in the Works and Days," *CJ* 79: 307–23.

Jouan, F. (1966) *Euripide et les légendes des chants cypriens.* Paris.

Judet de la Combe, P. (1993) "L'Autobiographie comme mode d'universalisation. Hésiode et Hélicon," in *La Componente Autobiografica nella Poesia Greca e Latina fra Realtà e Artificio Letterario: Atti del Convegno Pisa 16–17 maggio 1991*, eds. G. Arrighetti and F. Montanari. Pisa: 25–39.

(1996) "La Dernière ruse: 'Pandore' dans la *Théogonie*," in *Métier*: 262–99.

Judet de la Combe, P. and Lernould, A. (1996) "Sur la Pandore des *Travaux*. Esquisses," in *Métier*: 301–13.

Kahn, C. H. (1973) *The Verb 'Be' in Ancient Greek.* Dordrecht.

Kakrides, J. Th. (1972) "Probleme der griechischen Heldensage," *Poetica* 5: 152–63.

Kambylis, A. (1965) *Die Dichterweihe und ihre Symbolik: Untersuchungen zu Hesiodos, Kallimachos, Properz und Ennius.* Heidelberg.

Kassel, R. (1973) "Kritische und exegetische Kleinigkeiten IV," *RhM* 116: 97–112.

Keaney, J. J. and Lamberton, R. (1996) (eds.) [Plutarch] *Essay on the Life and Poetry of Homer.* Atlanta.

Kerschensteiner, J. (1944) "Zum Aufbau und Gedankenführung von Hesiods *Erga*," *Hermes* 79: 149–91.

Kirchhoff, A. (1889) *Hesiodos' Mahnlieder an Perses.* Berlin.

Kirk, G. S. (1960) "The Structure and Aim of the *Theogony*," in *Hésiode et son influence.* Entretiens Hardt 7. Vandoeuvres.

Klaussen, R. H. (1835) "Ueber Hesiodus Gedicht auf die Musen," *RhM* NS 3: 439–69.

Knox, B. M. W. (1982) "Work and Justice in Archaic Greece," *Thought* 57: 317–31.

Koenen, L. (1994) "Cyclic Destruction in Hesiod and the *Catalogue of Women*," *TAPhA* 124: 1–34.

Kohl, W. (1970) "Der Opferbetrug des Prometheus (Zu Hesiod, Theog. 538–540)," *Glotta* 48: 1–36.

Krafft, F. (1963) *Vergleichende Untersuchungen zu Homer und Hesiod.* Göttingen.

Kraus. M. (1987) *Name und Sache: Ein problem in frühgriechischen Denken.* Amsterdam.

Kraus, T. (1960) *Hekate.* Heidelberg.

Krischer, T. (1965) "ΕΤΥΜΟΣ und ΑΛΗΘΗΣ," *Philologus* 109: 161–73.

(1971) *Formale Konventionen der homerischen Epik.* Zetemata 56. Munich.

Kristeva, J. (1969) *Semiôtikè*. Paris.

Laks, A. (1996) "Le Double du roi: Remarques sur les antécédents hésiodiques du philosophe-roi," in *Métier*: 83–89.

Lamberton, R. (1988) *Hesiod*. New Haven.

Lardinois, A. (1998) "How the Days Fit the Works in Hesiod's *Works and Days*," *AJPh* 117: 319–36.

Latacz, J. (1971) "Noch einmal zum Opferbetrug des Prometheus," *Glotta* 49: 27–34.

Latimer, J. F. (1930) "Perses versus Hesiod," *TAPhA* 61: 70–79.

Latte, K. (1946a) "Der Rechtsgedanke im archaischen Griechentum," *A&A* 2: 63–73. (= *Kleine Schriften* [Munich 1968] 233–51)

(1946b) "Hesiods Dichterweihe," *A&A* 2: 152–63. (= *Kleine Schriften* [Munich 1968] 60–75).

Lauriola, R. (1995) "Il ΓΕΝΟΣ di Iapeto: Considerazioni sull' ordinamento genealogico della *Teogonia* esiodea," in *Poesia Greca. Recerche di Filologia Classica* 4, ed. G. Arrighetti. Pisa: 73–100.

Leclerc, M.-C. (1992) "L'Epervier et le rossignol d'Hésiode: Une fable à double sens," *REG* 105: 37–44.

(1993) *La Parole chez Hésiode: A la recherche de l'harmonie perdue*. Paris.

(1994) "Facettes du temps dans Les *Travaux et Les Jours* d'Hésiode," *RPh* 68: 147–63.

(1998) "Le partage des lots. Récit et paradigme dans la *Théogonie* d'Hésiode," *Pallas* 48: 89–104.

Ledbetter, G. (2003) *Poetics Before Plato*. Princeton.

Leinecks, V. (1984) "Ἐλπίς in Hesiod, *Works and Days* 96," *Philologus* 128: 1–8.

Lemke, D. (1968) "Sprachliche und strukturelle Beobachtungen zum Ungeheuer Katalog in der *Theogonie* Hesiods," *Glotta* 46: 47–53.

Lendle, O. (1957) *Die "Pandorasage" bei Hesiod: Textkritische und motivgeschichtliche Untersuchungen*. Würzburg.

Lenz, A. (1975) "Hesiods Prozesse," in *Dialogos für Harald Patzer zum 65 Geburtstag*. Wiesbaden: 23–33.

(1980) *Das Proöm des frühen griechischen Epos*. Bonn.

Lévêque, P. (1988) "Pandora ou la terrifiante féminité," *Kernos* 1: 49–62.

Levet, J. P. (1976) *Le Vrai et le faux dans la pensée grecque archaïque*. Paris.

Livrea, E. (1966) "Il proemio degli Erga considerato attraverso i vv. 9–10," *Helikon* 6: 442–75.

(1967) "Applicazione della 'Begriffsspaltung' negli *Erga*," *Helikon* 7: 81–100.

Lobel, E. (1956) (ed.) *Oxyrhynchus Papyri* 23. London.

Löffler, I. (1963) *Die Melampodie: Versuch einer Rekonstruktion des Inhalts*. Meisenheim.

Lonsdale, S. H. (1989) "Hesiod's Hawk and Nightingale (*Op*. 202–12): Fable or Omen?" *Hermes* 117: 403–12.

Loraux, L. (1978) "Sur la race des femmes et quelques-unes de ses tribus," *Arethusa* 11: 43–87.

Loraux, N. (1996) *Né de la terre: Mythe et politique à Athènes*. Paris.

Luginbühl, M. (1992) *Menschenschöpfungsmythen. Ein Vergleich zwischen Griechenland und dem Alten Orient*. Bern.

Luther, W. (1935) *"Wahrheit" und "Lüge" im ältesten Griechentum*. Borna–Leipzig.

Maehler, H. (1963) *Die Auffassung des Dichterberufs im frühen Griechentum bis zur Zeit Pindars*. Göttingen.

Malkin, I. (1998) *The Returns of Odysseus: Colonization and Ethnicity*. Berkeley.

Mancini, M. (1986) "Semantica di ῥητός e ἄρρητος nel prologo agli Ἔργα di Esiodo," *AION* 8: 175–91.

Marconi, M. (1952) "Il Mito di Gaia nella teogonia esiodea," *Acme* 5: 561–72.

Marg, W. (ed.) (1970) *Hesiod: Sämtliche Gedichte*. Zurich.

Marquardt, P. A. (1981) "A Portrait of Hecate," *AJPh* 102: 243–60.

Marsilio, M. S. (2000) *Farming and Poetry in Hesiod's Works and Days*. Lanham, Maryland.

Martin, R. (1942–43) "The Golden Age and the ΚΥΚΛΟΣ ΓΕΝΕΣΕΩΝ (Cyclical Theory) in Greek and Latin Literature," *GR* 12: 62–71.

Martin, R. P. (1984) "Hesiod, Odysseus and the Instruction of Princes," *TAPhA* 114: 29–48.

(1989) *The Language of Heroes: Speech and Performance in the Iliad*. Ithaca.

Martinazzoli, F. (1946) "Lo sdoppiamento di alcuni concetti morali in Esiodo e la ἐλπίς," *SIFC* 21: 11–22.

Masaracchia, A. (1961) "L'Unità delle *Opere* esiodee e il loro rapporto con la *Teogonia*," *Helikon* 1: 217–44.

Massa Positano, L. (1971) "Il proemio degli Erga," in *Studi filologici e storici in onore di Vittorio De Falco*. Naples: 27–56.

Matthiessen, K. (1977) "Das Zeitalter der Heroen bei Hesiod (Werke und Tage 156–173)," *Philologus* 121: 176–88.

Mayer, K. (1996) "Helen and the ΔΙΟΣ ΒΟΥΛΗ," *AJPh* 117: 1–15.

Mazon, P. (1914) *Hésiode: Les Travaux et les Jours*. Paris.

(1928) (ed.) *Hésiode*. Paris.

McLaughlin, J. D. (1981) "Who is Hesiod's Pandora?" *Maia* 33: 17–18.

Méautis, G. (1939) "Le Prologue à la *Théogonie* d'Hésiode," *REG* 52: 573–83.

Meier-Brügger, M. (1990) "Zu Hesiods Namen," *Glotta* 68: 62–67.

Merkelbach, R. and West, M. L. (1967) (eds.) *Fragmenta Hesiodea*. Oxford.

(1968) "Les Papyrus d'Hésiode et la géographie mythologique de la Grèce," *Chronique d'Egypte* 43: 133–55, reprinted in *Hestia und Erigone: Vorträge und Aufsätze*, eds. W. Blümel, B. Kramer, J. Kramer, and C. E. Römer. Stuttgart 1996: 67–86.

Meyer, A. (1887) *De Compositione Theogoniae hesiodeae*. Berlin.

Meyer, E. (1910) "Hesiods Erga und das Gedicht von den fünf Menschengeschlechtern," reprinted in Heitsch: 471–522.

Mezzadri, B. (1988) "Structure du mythe des races d'Hésiode," *L'Homme* 28: 51–57.

(1989) "La Double Eris initiale," *Métis* 4: 51–60.

Mikalson, J. (1972) "Prothyma," *AJPh* 93: 577–83.

Miller, M. H. (1977) "La Logique implicite de la cosmogonie d'Hésiode," *RMM* 82: 433–56.

Millett, P. (1984) "Hesiod and his World," *PCPhP* 210: 84–115.

Minton, W. (1970) "The Proem-Hymn of Hesiod's *Theogony*," *TAPhA* 101: 357–77.

Miralles, C. (1991) "Hesíodo, *Erga* 42–105. La invención de la mujer y la tinaja," in *Estudios actuales sobre textos griegos*, ed. J. A. López Férez. Madrid: 33–45.

(1993) "Le Spose di Zeus e l'ordine del mondo nella 'Teogonia' di Esiodo," in *Maschile/Femminile: Genere e ruoli nelle culture antiche*, ed. M. Bettini. Rome: 17–44.

Miralles, C. and Pòrtulas, J. (1998) "L'image du poète en Grèce archaïque," in *Figures de l'intellectuel en Grèce ancienne*, eds. N. Loraux and C. Miralles. Paris: 15–63.

Mondi, R. (1984) "The Ascension of Zeus and the Composition of Hesiod's *Theogony*," *GRBS* 25: 325–44.

(1989) "ΧΑΟΣ and the Hesiodic Cosmogony," *HSCPh* 92: 1–41.

Most, G. W. (1993) "Hesiod and the Textualization of Personal Temporality," in *La Componente autobiografica nella poesia greca e latina fra realtà e artificio letterario: Atti del Convegno Pisa, 16–17 maggio 1991*, eds. G. Arrighetti and F. Montanari. Pisa: 73–92.

(1997) "Hesiod's Myth of the Five (or Three or Four) Races," *PCPhS* 43: 104–27.

Moussy, C. (1969) *Recherches sur* ΤΡΕΦΩ *et les verbes grecs signifiant "nourrir."* Paris.

Mueller, L. (1954) "Wort und Begriff 'mythos' im klassischen Griechisch," PhD dissertation, University of Hamburg.

Muellner, L. (1996) *The Anger of Achilles: Mênis in Greek Epic*. Ithaca.

Muetzell, W. J. K. (1833) *De Emendatione Theogoniae Hesiodeae*. Leipzig.

Murad, E.W. (1998) "Words for Words," MA thesis, University of Virginia.

Muth, R. (1951) "Zu Hesiod *Op.* 1–10," *AAHG* 4: 185–89.

Naddaf, G. (1986) "Hésiode, précurseur des cosmogonies grecques de type 'evolutioniste'," *RHR* 23: 339–64.

Nagler, M. (1992) "Discourse and Conflict in Hesiod: Eris and the Erides," *Ramus* 21: 79–96. (= *Essays on Hesiod* 1, ed. A. Athanassakis).

Nagy, G. (1979) *The Best of the Achaeans*. Baltimore.

(1989) "The Pan-hellenization of the 'Days' in the *Works and Days*," in *Daidalikon. Studies in Memory of Raymond V. Schroder, SJ*, ed. R. F. Sutton Jr. Wauconda, Illinois: 273–77.

(1990) *Greek Mythology and Poetics*. Ithaca.

(1996) "Autorité et auteur dans la *Théogonie* hésiodique," in *Métier*: 41–52.

Neitzel, H. (1975) *Homer-Rezeption bei Hesiod: Interpretation ausgewählte Passagen*. Bonn.

(1976) "Pandora und das Faß: Zur Interpretation von Hesiod, *Erga* 42–105," *Hermes* 104: 387–419.

(1977) "Zum zeitlichen Verhältnis von Theogonie (80–93) und Odyssee (8, 166–177)," *Philologus* 121: 24–44.

(1980) "Hesiod und die lügenden Musen," *Hermes* 108: 387–401.

Nelson, S. A. (1997–98) "The Justice of Zeus in Hesiod's Fable of the Hawk and the Nightingale," *CJ* 92: 235–47.

(1998) *God and the Land: The Metaphysics of Farming in Hesiod and Vergil.* Oxford.

Neschke, A. (1996) "*Dikè*. La Philosophie poétique du droit dans le 'mythe des races' d'Hésiode," in *Métier*: 465–78.

Nietzsche, F. (1960) *Zur Genealogie der Moral*, in *Friedrich Nietzsche: Werke in drei Bänden*, ed. Karl Schlechta (2nd edn.). Munich: 2.763–900.

Nilsson, M. P. (1969) *Geschichte der griechischen Religion* (3rd edn., 2 vols.). Munich.

Northrup, M. (1983) "Where Did the *Theogony* End?" *SO* 58: 7–13.

O'Bryhim, S. (1996) "A New Interpretation of Hesiod *Theogony* 35," *Hermes* 124: 131–38.

(1997) "Hesiod and the Cretan Cave," *RM* 140: 95–96.

Østerud, S. (1976) "The Individuality of Hesiod," *Hermes* 104: 13–29.

Otto, W. F. (1952.) "Hesiodea," in *Varia Variorum: Festgabe für Karl Reinhardt*. Cologne: 49–57.

Paley, F. A. (1961) (ed.) *The Epics of Hesiod with an English Commentary*. London.

Pellizer, E. (1975) "Per l'unità dei 'Giorni'," in *Studi triestini di antichità in onore di L. A. Stella*. Trieste: 169–82.

Pertusi, A. (ed.) (1955) *Scholia Vetera in Hesiodi Opera et Dies*. Milan.

Perysinakis, I. (1986) "Hesiod's Treatment of Wealth," *Métis* 1: 97–119.

Pfister, F. (1928) "Die Hekate-Episode in Hesiods Theogonie," *Philologus* 84: 1–9.

Philippson, P. (1936) "Genealogie als mythische Form," *SO* Suppl. 7, reprinted in Heitsch: 651–87.

Philips, F. C. (1973) "Narrative Compression and the Myths of Prometheus in Hesiod," *CJ* 68: 289–305.

Podbielski, H. (1986) "Le Chaos et les confins de l'univers dans la *Théogonie* d'Hésiode," *EC* 54: 253–263.

(1994) "Der Dichter und die Musen im Prooimion der Hesiodeischen [sic] Theogonie," *Eos* 82: 173–88.

Pötscher, W. (1994) "Die Zuteilung der Portionen in Mekone," *Philologus* 138: 159–74.

Pratt, L. (1993) *Lying and Poetry from Homer to Pindar: Falsehood and Deception in Archaic Greek Poetics*. Ann Arbor.

Preller, L. (1852). "Die Vorstellungen der alten, besonders der Griechen, von dem ursprunge und den ältesten schicksalen des menschlichen geschlechts," *Philologus* 7:

Preller, L. and Robert, C. (1887) *Griechische Mythologie* (4th edn.). Berlin.

Prellwitz, W. (1929) "Participia praesentia activi in der Zusammensetzung," *Glotta* 17: 144–47.

Price, T. H. (1978) *Kourotrophos*. Leiden.

Prier, R. A. (1974) "Archaic Structuralism and Dynamics in Hesiod's *Theogony*," *Apeiron* 8: 1–12.

(1989) *Thauma idesthai: The Phenomenology of Sight and Appearance in Ancient Greek*. Tallahassee.

Pucci, P. (1977) *Hesiod and the Language of Poetry*. Baltimore.

(1996) "Auteur et destinataires dans les *Travaux* d'Hésiode," in *Métier*: 191–210.

Puelma, M. (1972) "Sänger und König: Zum Verständnis von Hesiods Tierfabel," *MH* 29: 86–109.

(1989) "Der Dichter und die Wahrheit in der griechischen Poetik," *MH* 46: 65–100.

Pullyn, S. (1997) *Prayer in Greek Religion*. Oxford.

Raaflaub, K. (1993) "Homer to Solon: The Rise of the Greek Polis, the Written Sources," in *The Ancient Greek City-State*, ed. M. Hansen. Copenhagen: 41–105.

Race, W. H. (1992) "How Greek Poems Begin," *YClS* 29: 13–38.

Ramnoux, C. (1986) *La Nuit et les enfants de la Nuit* (2nd edn.). Paris.

(1987) "Les Femmes de Zeus: Hésiode, *Théogonie*, vers 885 à 955," in *Poikilia: Études offertes à Jean-Pierre Vernant*. Paris: 155–64.

Rawlings, H. (1975) *A Semantic Study of Prophasis to 400 BC. Hermes* Suppl. 33. Wiesbaden.

Redfield, J. (1993) "The Sexes in Hesiod," *Annals of Scholarship* 10: 31–61.

Reinhardt, K. (1960) "Prometheus," in *Tradition und Geist: Gesammelte Essays zur Dichtung*, ed. C. Becker. Göttingen: 190–226.

1961. *Die Ilias und Ihr Dichter*. Göttingen.

Reitzenstein, R. (1924) "Altgriechische Theologie und ihre Quellen," reprinted in Heitsch: 523–44.

Richir, M. (1995) *La Naissance des dieux*. Paris.

Riedinger, J.-C. (1992) "Structure et signification du 'Calendrier du Paysan' d'Hésiode (*Travaux* vv. 383–617)," *RPh* 66: 121–41.

Robert, C. (1905) "Zu Hesiods Theogonie," reprinted in Heitsch: 154–74.

Rohde, E. (1898) *Psyche: Seelencult und Unsterblichkeits Glaube der Griechen*, 2nd edn. Freiburg.

Rosen, R. (1990) "Poetry and Sailing in Hesiod's *Works and Days*," *CA* 9: 99–113.

(1997) "Homer and Hesiod," in *A New Companion to Homer*, eds. I. Morris and B. Powell. Leiden: 463–88.

Rosenmeyer, T. G. (1957) "Hesiod and Historiography (*Erga* 106–201)," *Hermes* 85: 257–85.

Roth, C. P. (1976) "The Kings and Muses in Hesiod's Theogony," *TAPhA* 106: 331–38.

Roth, R. (1860) "Der Mythus von den fünf Menschengeschlechtern und die indische Lehre von den vier Weltaltern," reprinted in Heitsch: 450–70.

Rotondaro, S. (1997). "Il Tempo, Zeus, la Memoria e l'Uomo nella *Teogonia* di Esiodo," *AAN* 108: 55–63.

Rousseau, P. (1996) "Instruire Persès: Notes sur l'ouverture des *Travaux* d'Hésiode," in *Métier*: 93–167.

(1993) "Un Héritage disputé," in *La Componente autobiografica nella poesia greca e latina fra realtà e artificio letterario: Atti del Convegno Pisa, 16–17 maggio 1991*, eds. G. Arrighetti and F. Montanari. Pisa: 41–72.

Rudhardt, J. (1981a) "Les Mythes grecs relatifs à l'instauration du sacrifice: Les rôles corrélatifs de Prométhée et de son fils Deucalion," in *Du Mythe, de la religion grecque et de la compréhension d'autrui.* Cahiers Vilfredo Pareto. Revue européenne des sciences sociales 19: 209–26.

(1981b) "Le Mythe hésiodique des races et celui de Prométhée: Recherche de structures et des significations," in *Du Mythe, de la religion grecque et de la compréhension d'autrui.* Cahiers Vilfredo Pareto. Revue européenne des sciences sociales 19: 245–81.

(1986) *Le Rôle d'Eros et d'Aphrodite dans les cosmogonies grecques.* Paris.

(1993) "À propos de l'Hécate hésiodique," *MH* 50: 204–21

(1996) "Le Préambule de la *Théogonie*," in *Métier:* 25–39.

Russo, J. (1992) *A Commentary on Homer's Odyssey*, vol. 3. Oxford.

Rutherford, I. (2000) "Formulas, Voice, and Death in *Ehoie*-Poetry," in *Matrices of Genre: Authors, Canons, and Society*, eds. M. Depew and D. Obbink. Cambridge, Mass.: 81–96.

Rzach, A. (1902) (ed.) *Hesiodi carmina.* Leipzig.

(1912) "Hesiodos," in *RE* 8.1: 1164–239.

Saïd, S. (1977) "Les Combats de Zeus et le problème des interpolations dans la Théogonie d'Hésiode," *REG* 90: 183–210.

(1979) "Les Crimes des prétendants, la maison d'Ulysse et les festins de l'Odyssée," *Etudes de Literature Anciennes.* Paris: 9–49.

Samuel, A. E. (1966) "The Days of 'Hesiod's' Month," *TAPhA* 97: 421–29.

Schadewaldt, W. (1926) *Monolog und Selbstgespräch. Untersuchungen zur Formgeschichte der Griechischen Tragödie.* Neue Philologische Untersuchungen 2. Berlin.

Schiesaro, A. (1996) "Aratus' Myth of Dike," *MD* 37: 9–26.

Schlesier, R. (1982) "Les Muses dans le prologue de la 'Théogonie' d'Hésiode," *RHR* 199: 131–67.

Schmid, W. and Stählin, O. (1929) *Geschichte der griechischen Literatur.* Munich.

Schmidt, J.-U. (1985) "Die Ehen des Zeus: Zu Hesiods Weltdeutung durch seine 'Theogonie'," *Wort und Dienst* 18: 73–92.

(1986) *Adressat und Paraineseform: Zur Intention von Hesiods 'Werken und Tagen.'* Hypomnemata 86. Göttingen.

(1988a, 1989) "Die Aufrichtung des Zeusherrschaft als Modell – Überlegungen zur Theogonie des Hesiod," *WJH* 14: 39–68 and 15: 17–37.

(1988b) "Die Einheit des Prometheus-Mythos in der 'Theogonie' des Hesiod," *Hermes* 116: 129–56.

Schmitt, A. (1975) "Zum Prooimion des hesiodischen Frauenkatalogs," *WJA*: 19–31.

Schmoll, E. A. (1994) "Hesiod's *Theogony*: Oak and Stone Again," *Scholia* 3: 46–52.

Schoele, A. (1980) "ΜΑΚΑΡΕΣ ΘΝΗΤΟΙ bei Hesiod," *Acta Antiqua Academiae Scientiarum Hungaricae* 8: 255–63.

Schoemann, G. F. (1857a) "De nymphis Meliis Gigantibus et Erinysin," *Opuscula academica*, vol. 2. Berlin: 125–46.

(1857b) "De Phorcyne eiusque familia," *Opuscula academica*, vol. 2. Berlin: 176–214.

(1857c) "De Hecate Hesiodea," *Opuscula academica*, vol. 2. Berlin: 215–49.

(1868) (ed.) *Die Hesiodische Theogonie.* Berlin.

Schubart, W. and von Wilamowitz-Moellendorff, U. (1907) *Berliner Klassikertexte* v, 1. Berlin.
Schwabl, H. (1963) "Aufbau und Struktur des Prooimions der hesiodischen Theogonie," *Hermes* 91: 385–415.
  (1969) "Aufbau und Genealogie des hesiodichen Ungeheuerkatalogs," *Glotta* 47: 174–84.
  (1970) "Hesiod," *RE* Suppl. 12: 434–86.
Schwartz, J. (1960) *Pseudo-Hesiodeia: Recherches sur la composition, la diffusion et la disparition ancienne d'œuvres attribuées à Hésiode.* Leiden.
Schwenn, F. (1934) *Die Theogonie des Hesiodos.* Heidelberg.
Schwyzer, E. (1950) *Griechische Grammatik* (2 vols.). Munich.
Scodel, R. (1982) "The Achaean Wall and the Myth of Destruction," *HSCPh* 86: 33–50.
Searle, J. R. and Vanderveken, D. (1985) *Foundations of Illocutionary Logic.* Cambridge.
Sellschopp, I. (1934) *Stilistische Untersuchungen zu Hesiod.* Hamburg.
Sharrock, A. (2000) "Intratextuality: Texts, Parts, and (W)holes in Theory," in *Intratextuality: Greek and Roman Textual Relations*, eds. A. Sharrock and H. Morales. Oxford.
Siegmann, E. (1969) "χίμαιρα, Hesiod *Theog.* 319," *Hermes* 96: 755–57.
Sihvola, J. (1989) *Decay, Progress, the Good Life? Hesiod and Protagoras on the Development of Culture.* Helsinki.
Sinclair, T. A. (1932) (ed.) *Hesiod: Works and Days.* London.
Slatkin, L. M. (1986) "Genre and Generation," *Métis* 1: 259–68.
  (1991) *The Power of Thetis: Allusion and Interpretation in the Iliad.* Berkeley.
Smith, P. (1980) "History and Individual in Hesiod's Myth of the Five Races," *CW* 74: 145–63.
Snell, B. (1975) *Die Entdeckung des Geistes* (4th edn.). Göttingen.
Solmsen, F. (1949) *Hesiod and Aeschylus.* Ithaca.
  (1954) "The 'Gift' of Speech in Homer and Hesiod," *TAPhA* 85: 1–15.
  (1963) "The 'Days' of the *Works and Days*," *TAPhA* 94: 293–320.
  (1970) (ed.) *Hesiodi Theogonia, Opera et Dies, Scutum.* Oxford.
Solomon, J. (1985) "In defense of Hesiod's 'schlechtestem Hexameter'," *Hermes* 113: 21–30.
Sorel, R. (1980) "L'Inconsistance ontologique des hommes et des dieux chez Hésiode," *Revue Philosophique* 4: 401–12.
  (1982) "Finalité et origine des hommes chez Hésiode," *RMM* 87: 24–30.
Stein, E. (1990) *Autorbewußtsein in der frühen griechischen Literatur.* Scripta Oralia 17. Tübingen.
Stiewe, K. (1962) "Die Entstehungszeit der hesiodischen Frauenkataloge 1," *Philologus* 106: 292–99.
  (1963) "Die Entstehungszeit der hesiodischen Frauenkataloge 2," *Philologus* 107: 1–29.
Stoddard, K. (2000) "The Narrative Voice in the *Theogony* of Hesiod," PhD dissertation, University of Virginia. Charlottesville.

Stokes, M. (1962) "Hesiodic and Milesian Cosmogonies – 1," *Phronesis* 7:1–37.

Stroh, W. (1976) "Hesiods lügende Musen," in *Studien zum antiken Epos*, eds. H. Görgemanns and E. A. Schmidt. Meisenheim: 85–112.

Svenbro, J. (1976) *La Parole et le marbre*. Lund.

Tandy, D. and Neale, W. (1996) *Hesiod's Works and Days*. Berkeley.

Thalmann, W. (1984) *Conventions of Form and Thought in Early Greek Epic Poetry*. Baltimore.

Theraios, D. K. (1974) "Logos bei Hesiod," *Hermes* 102: 136–42.

Treu, M. (1957) "Das Proömium der hesiodischen Frauenkataloge," *RM* 100: 169–86.

Verdenius, W. J. (1962) "Aufbau und Absicht der Erga," in *Hésiode et son influence*. Entretiens Hardt 7. Vandoeuvres: 111–59.

  (1971) "Hesiod, *Theogony* 507–616: Some Comments on a Commentary," *Mnemosyne* 24: 1–10.

  (1972) "Notes on the Proem of Hesiod's *Theogony*," *Mnemosyne* 25: 225–60.

  (1985) *A Commentary on Hesiod, 'Works and Days' vv. 1–382. Mnemosyne* Suppl. 86. Leiden.

Vernant, J.-P. (1965a) "Le Mythe hésiodique des races," in *Mythe et pensée chez les Grecs* 1. Paris: 13–79.

  (1965b) "Hestia-Hermès: Sur l'expression religieuse de l'espace et du mouvement chez les Grecs," in *Mythe et pensée chez les Grecs* 1. Paris: 124–70.

  (1974) "Le Mythe prométhéen chez Hésiode," in *Mythe et société en Grèce ancienne*. Paris: 178–94.

  (1979) "À la table des hommes: Mythe de fondation du sacrifice chez Hésiode," in *La Cuisine du sacrifice en pays grec*, eds. M. Detienne and J.-P. Vernant. Paris: 37–132.

  (1985) "Méthode structurale et mythe des races," in *Histoire et Structure: À la mémoire de Victor Goldschmidt*, eds. J. Brunschwig, C. Imbert, and A. Roger. Paris: 43–60.

  (1986) "Corps des dieux 'Corps obscur, corps éclatant'," in *Corps des dieux*, eds. C. Malamoud and J.-P. Vernant. Le Temps de la Réflexion 7: 19–45.

  (1991a) "Death in the Eyes," in *Mortals and Immortals: Collected Essays*, ed. F. Zeitlin. Princeton: 111–38.

  (1991b) "Greek Cosmogonic Myths," in *Mythologies*, ed. Yves Bonnefoy, and translation compiled under the direction of W. Doniger. Chicago: 1. 366–75.

Vian, F. (1952) *La Guerre des Géants: Le Mythe avant l'époque hellénistique*. Paris.

Vidal-Naquet, P. (1991) "Valeurs religieuses et mythiques de la terre et du sacrifice dans l'*Odyssée*," in *Le Chasseur noir* (3rd edn.). Paris: 39–68.

Voigt, E.-M. (1984–) (ed.) *Lexikon des frühgriechischen Epos*. Göttingen.

Von der Mühll, P. (1970) "Hesiods helikonische Musen," *MH* 27: 195–97.

Wackernagel, J. (1981) *Vorlesungen über Syntax mit besonderer Berücksichtung von Griechisch, Lateinisch und Deutsch* (3rd edn.). Basel.

Wade-Gery, H. T. (1949) "Hesiod," *Phoenix* 3: 81–93.

Wakker, G. (1990) "Die Ankündigung des Weltaltermythos (Hes. *Op.* 106–108)," *Glotta* 68: 86–90.

Walcot, P. (1957) "The Problem of the Proemium of Hesiod's *Theogony*," *SO* 33: 37–47.

    (1958) "Hesiod's Hymns to the Muses, Aphrodite, Styx and Hecate," *SO* 34: 5–14.

    (1960) "Allusion in Hesiod" *REG* 73: 36–39.

    (1963) "Hesiod and the Law," *SO* 38: 5–21.

Walsh, G. B. (1984) *The Uses of Enchantment: Early Greek Views of the Nature and Function of Poetry*. Chapel Hill.

Wees, H. van. (1992) *Status Warriors: War, Violence and Society in Homer and History*. Amsterdam.

Wehrli, F. (1956) "Hesiods Prometheus (Theogonie V. 507–616)," reprinted in Heitsch: 411–18.

Welcker, F. G. (1865) *Die Hesiodische Theogonie*. Elberfeld.

West, M. L. (1961) "Hesiodea," *CQ* 11: 130–45.

    (1966) (ed.) *Hesiod: Theogony*. Oxford.

    (1967) "The Contest of Homer and Hesiod," *CQ* 17: 433–50.

    (1978) (ed.) *Hesiod: Works & Days*. Oxford.

    (1985) *The Hesiodic Catalogue of Women: Its Nature, Structure, and Origins*. Oxford.

    (1997) *The East Face of Helicon: West Asiatic Elements in Greek Poetry and Myth*. Oxford.

Wilamowitz-Moellendorff, U. von. (1905) "Lesefrüchte 92," *Hermes* 40: 116–24. (= *Kleine Schriften* 4. Berlin (1962): 169–77).

    (1916) *Die Ilias und Homer*. Berlin.

    (1928) (ed.) *Hesiods Erga*. Berlin.

    (1931) *Der Glaube der Hellenen* (2 vols.). Berlin.

    (1959) *Euripides Herakles* (2nd edn., 3 vols.). Darmstadt.

Wirshbo, E. (1982) "The Mekone Scene in the *Theogony*: Prometheus as Prankster," *GRBS* 23: 101–10.

Wismann, H. (1996) "Propositions pour une lecture d'Hésiode," in *Métier*: 15–24.

Wissowa, G. et al. (1894–) (eds.) *Paulys Realencyclopädie der classischen Altertumswissenschaft*. Stuttgart.

Worms, F. (1953) "Der Typhoeus-Kampf in Hesiods Theogonie," *Hermes* 81: 29–44.

Zanker, G. (1986) "The *Works and Days*: Hesiod's Beggar's Opera?" *BICS* 33: 26–36.

Zeitlin, F. (1996) "Signifying Difference: The Case of Hesiod's Pandora," in *Playing the Other: Gender and Society in Classical Greek Literature*. Chicago: 53–86.

Zimmermann, R. C. (1932) "Zum Proömium des hesiodischen Theogonie," *Philologus* 87: 421–29.

Indexes

SUBJECT INDEX

INDEX LOCORUM

Printed in the United States
151787LV00006B/164/P

9 780521 117685